TURNING CLOUDS INSIDE OUT:

A COUNTRY WOMAN'S LIFE IN THE TWENTIETH CENTURY

A Biography

by Catherine R. Ashton

Catherine R. Ashton

The National Library of Canada has catalogued this publication as follows:

Ashton, Catherine R., 1940-
Turning clouds inside out : a country woman's life in the twentieth century / Catherine R. Ashton.

Main entry under title: Turning Clouds Inside Out: A Country Woman's Life in the Twentieth Century

1. Beach, Margaret Isabella, 1900-2000.
2. Teachers--Ontario--Biography.
3. Farmers' spouses--Ontario--Biography.
4. Ontario--Biography. I. Title.

FC27.B375 2006 920.72'09713 C2006-902809-5

Includes bibliographical references.

ISBN 0-9780577-0-8

Published in Orillia, Ontario, Canada

Available in Canada by mail:
Catherine R. Ashton
3799 Fairgrounds Road
R. R. 2, Orillia, ON
L3V 6H2

or by e-mail: cashton@sympatico.ca

Cover by J.B.Emberson
Printed in Canada by Rose Printing, Orillia, Ontario

CONTENTS

ACKNOWLEDGEMENTS

Sometimes I think I was born to create this book. Throughout my life, as I listened to my mother's stories and conversations, I absorbed a deep sense of her values. During the last dozen years of her life, she devoted many hours to taping with me her stories and experiences. The letters, clippings, notebooks, date books and other memorabilia she had kept provided invaluable details after her death. Everything fell into place. There was no turning back.

Out of their deep respect for my mother, many who knew her well and others who knew her less well or not at all provided invaluable assistance. Family members include my brother and sister-in-law, Bev and Norma Beach, my nephew Edward Beach, nieces Joanne Burnett and Marilyn Burch, and my son James, all of whom participated in interviews, provided materials, and answered questions that arose during the writing. Bev and Norma also graciously hosted me for research sessions in the Uxbridge community. To my cousins Winnifred Wallace and Kathleen Jones, a special thank-you for supplying photos, information, conversations, and wildly enthusiastic support.

For interviews on tape or by phone I am grateful to Laura (Beach) Ashton, Lily Hope, Florence (Harrison) Kemp, Evelyn (Beach) Rae (dec.), Barbara Spinney, and Grace (Beach) Thompson (dec.). For the information in their letters, my thanks to Dave Beach (dec.), Shirley Chapman, Florence (McFadyen) Francis, Cheryl Haines, Karen Owens, Frances Shelley Wees (dec.), and Timothy John Wees.

I am very grateful to my aunts, Annie Laurie Wallace and Jessie (Wallace) Stanley, and my great-uncle, Andrew McFadyen, for the genealogy work they did many years ago on the Wallace and McFadyen families. Individuals who helped with other research include Helen Alsop, president of the Beaverton-Thorah-Eldon Historical Society, who provided the 1895 map of Thorah Township; Allan McGillivray, curator at the Uxbridge Historical Centre, who provided Uxbridge Township maps and genealogical information about the Beach and Rusnell families; Loreen Rice Lucas, who shared her experiences in the world of self-publishing; and John Steen, who shared his genealogy software, "My Brother's Keeper".

Finally, I am deeply grateful to my wise and honest friend, Rosemary Golding, for her advice on two early drafts of *Turning Clouds Inside Out* as well as for her constant moral support and encouragement; to my daughter-in-law, Crystal Dolliver, for the final critique; and to my husband, Vern, for always being there for me. Without their input, this book would be a lesser work.

Catherine R. Ashton
September 2006

PROLOGUE

"The Wisdom of Folly"
by Ellen Thornycroft Fowler
1860-1929

A merry heart goes all the day,
Your sad tires in a mile-a.
-Shakespeare—A Winter's Tale.

The cynics say that every rose
Is guarded by a thorn which grows
To spoil our posies;
But I no pleasure therefore lack;
I keep my hands behind my back
When smelling roses.

Though outwardly a gloomy shroud
The inner half of every cloud
Is bright and shining;
I therefore turn my clouds about,
And always wear them inside out
To show the lining.

My modus operandi this—
To take no heed of what's amiss;
And not a bad one;
Because, as Shakespeare used to say,
A merry heart goes twice the way
That tires a sad one.

published by Albert Whitman & Company in A Book of Living Poems, third edition, (1937) compiled by William R. Bowlin

(author credit, stated in the third edition, was traced to Mr. A. L. Felkin)

==

My mother, Margaret Isabella Wallace, was born on Sunday September 16, 1900. That old saying—"But the child that is born on the Sabbath day/Is fair and wise and good and gay"—suited her well.

The face she turned to the world was usually sunny. She liked jokes (including playing them on others), a good visit, and a good party. She had a way of making a bad situation better, of renewing hope in a despairing soul. But she was neither naïve nor shallow. Her deep spiritual, emotional and mental intelligences knew and understood the dark side. She had her own way of dealing with it.

This method was brilliantly revealed in a bit of conversation near the conclusion of her ninetieth birthday party Open House. Isabel, the "significant other" of a grand niece of Isabel's, the niece herself, and I stood in a cluster. "Significant other" made a dark and gloomy comment to which I replied, "Every cloud has a silver lining, you know." He typically responded, "Every silver lining has a cloud." Then Isabel chipped in. "Yes, I find I've spent a good deal of my life turning clouds inside out." That's when I recognized the theme of this biography: 'Turning clouds inside out'—a perfect description of my mother's life and times.

Verses quoted at the beginning of each chapter, taken from Isabel's lifetime collection in books and clippings, reflect one of the methods she used to turn her clouds inside out. Unless otherwise stated, personal quotes within the text are hers, taken from the seventeen tapes we recorded together from 1989 to 1999. Words that may be unfamiliar to the twenty-first century reader are explained in the Glossary. Appendix material supplements some of the subjects discussed in the chapters. Appendixes A, B, M and P, which list relevant descendants, are intended to be a guide for reader clarification. They do not attempt to represent a complete genealogy of the Wallace, McFadyen, Beach, and Rusnell families.

The twentieth century through which my mother lived had a generous share of clouds, as all centuries do. And she had her share of clouds, as all people do. This book tells the story of one 'ordinary' yet extraordinary country woman who lived a life of vigour, enthusiasm and determination in central and southern Ontario, Canada, within the span of that twentieth century.

Catherine R. Ashton
September 2006

CHAPTER ONE: I Should Have Died Three Times

Isabella sat on the edge of her seat, long brown ringlets bouncing, dark brown eyes shining with excitement and wonder. She watched the fields and villages fly past the window at a remarkable speed. Her father's horses had never run that fast, pulling the family's buggy or sleigh. She listened to the man walking down the aisle call out, "Newspaper, get your newspaper here" and "Chocolates, oranges, chocolates, bananas…" Isabella didn't need a newspaper. Those treats, however, which she usually had only at Christmas or at a summer garden party, were tempting.

But she didn't have any money—and her older brothers and sisters kept dozing off. The night before, they'd been at a wedding reception for an uncle on the McFadyen side of her family. While she was tucked in bed, they'd danced for hours, just as Highland Scottish people loved to do. Getting up early to catch the train had been hard for them. They had all boarded the train at eight o'clock in a village near their home. They were going to visit a family of cousins on the Wallace side for part of the Christmas holiday. Her brothers and sisters managed to stay awake until they changed trains in another village. There, they boarded the Toronto train that would stop at the town where her cousins lived. Then her siblings dozed off again. Suddenly little Isabella felt the weight of responsibility. Her excitement gave way to worry. If they were asleep, she wouldn't know when the train had reached the station where they needed to get off. What would she do?

Her young brow furrowed with wrinkles, she nudged her siblings awake. To keep her from interrupting their rest, they decided to buy something from the man going up and down the aisle. Her face relaxed a little as she thought over the offer. She was wearing a new dress that her oldest sister, Annie, had made her for Christmas. She didn't dare take an orange. She imagined the juice squirting all over her and her new dress. Chocolates weren't a good idea. How would she clean her fingers? What if she got chocolate on her dress? She made the practical choice and asked for a banana.

Isabella was six years old. She'd never been this far away from home, or traveled in this way. As she slowly ate the banana, she thought about why she was on this big train just like ones she'd sometimes heard thundering through the country near her parents' farm. Her mother said this trip was a reward for being such a good patient. Earlier that month, when Isabella was doing her usual little job of carrying wood from the woodshed to the woodbox in the farmhouse kitchen, she had detoured around her mother, who was working at the woodstove. Then Isabella stumbled and fell over a wooden box in the middle of the floor. The gash over her eye bled a lot. Her family lived seven and a half miles from their doctor. The closest hospital was in Toronto, many miles away. So her mother had treated the wound and life went on. Isabella wished she didn't have so many accidents.

The accident in the kitchen would not be her last. Over ninety years later, my mother, Isabel, said to me, a touch of wonderment in her voice, "I should have died three times". Then she described three travel accidents from her lifetime. These and other travel stories spanning the twentieth century, like the window on her first train ride, offer glimpses into the landscape; this time, the landscape of Margaret Isabella (Wallace) Beach—my mother. Despite her close calls, she embraced the transportation revolution of the twentieth century with the same curiosity and enthusiasm that she'd shown during her first train ride, when she was best known as Isabella.

Her first serious travel accident occurred almost five years later, in November 1911. That day, her brother Reid, who no longer attended school, had a dental appointment in Beaverton. So he gave the younger children a ride to school, which was three and a half miles from their home. He was driving a horse and buggy, the only form of transportation the family had, aside from a horse-drawn sleigh in the winter. A buggy, Mom explained, had only two seats. Since they were high, it was a cool place to ride. There was a 'buggy spread', but it didn't hold a candle to the buffalo robe that kept them warm in the sleigh. The spread was usually made from cotton or mixed fibres. A family often had several, each for a different occasion. Buggy equipment also included a rubber cover, held on by loops, to put over the spread and the dashboard during a rainstorm.

While Reid was on the way to Beaverton from the school, snow began to fall. Snow was still falling as he headed home at noon. Mom remembered the day quite well: "Oh, it was cold, bitter cold. And that old school—was it a cold school. Oh, the floors were cold—no basement under it, you know." Her feet were so cold that she was looking forward to lunchtime when she could warm them at the box stove. But Reid turned up to take all the Wallace children home. The storm was so bad he realized he'd only have to turn around and come back for them if he drove home alone. He loaded the three young Wallaces into the buggy. When they set out, Mom said, "Reid had the lines, and Minnie was sitting on his knee, and then Willie sat on the other part of the seat, and then I was on Willie's knee. When we were turning in the gate [at home], we turned a little too short, the back wheel hit a bump hidden with the snow, and I fell out of the buggy. And there I was—on the ground between the two wheels. Reid yelled 'Whoa!' and Dick [the driving horse] stopped 'on a dime' or I could very well have been killed…and it's a wonder I didn't have my neck broken anyway. Mother was lookin' out the kitchen window, and she was just flabbergasted that the buggy didn't go over me." When Isabella got inside the house, she was crying. Her mother, Kate, thought she was crying because of the accident. But, no. Isabella had very cold feet. And one of her big toes was frozen.

She had many more buggy rides over the next few years. Cars were a rare sight in the early 1900s, especially in the country. Into the twenties, they became more commonplace. Her father, William Wallace, bought his first car in 1925. Will had no intention of driving it, but made sure that each of his girls learned to drive so that they could chauffeur him. Isabel commented in our interview on her father's choice of vehicle: "And he wasn't going to go with no Model T side curtains. The car was a secondhand Overland sedan." Her cousin, Bruce Wallace, was selected to bring the Overland from Toronto to their Thorah Township farm. "Dad went down to Toronto, and then, of course, Dad thought Bruce knew all anybody needed to know about a car, and he was a good driver and all the rest of it. Well, so he was… Bruce was quite a mechanic-minded kid. And he and [my next youngest sister] Minnie started out from Toronto. So he let Minnie drive, so she'd be learning to drive on the way home. She was the first one [in the family] that drove that car. Anyway, Minnie was tellin' me how they got in the ditch, you see. What a time they had gettin' the thing home!"

Before long, cars featured in most of Isabel's travels. Prior to her marriage, her fiancé, Walter (who lived on a farm in Uxbridge Township, about forty-five miles south-west of the Wallace's Thorah Township home), had made sure he had a car to come and visit her. Isabel and he, both outgoing people, truly enjoyed their car and the mobility it gave them to socialize. After they were married in 1926, they usually went to the town of Uxbridge on Saturday night to shop. Often they included in their grocery order a jar of olives and a box of crackers, which they had consumed by the time they reached their farm seven miles out of town. I'm amazed that this ritual didn't cause an accident of some sort as they bumped along the unpaved road, Isabel handing Walter crackers and feeding him olives with her hatpin!

Instead, the second serious accident Mom experienced took place right in the town of Uxbridge. She and Walter had gone to a Saturday street dance that was part of the 1927 boys' and girls' home reunion. They planned to go to Isabel's parents' place on Sunday morning, so had to get up early, do the farm chores, and arrive in time for church service at St. Andrew's Presbyterian Church in Bolsover, where the Wallaces regularly attended. On their way home that Saturday night, in the west end of Uxbridge, "There was another car coming into town as we turned [left] off the street... I *knew* that man was going to run into us," Isabel declared. The driver was waving his arms and talking excitedly to the man in the passenger seat. Walter hadn't noticed the other car. "But he was driving, you see, and he wasn't looking at the other guy driving. He was looking at his own business. And I just clamped myself like this… You're not supposed to interfere with the driver, so they always taught us, because that's what causes an accident sometimes. So I wasn't sayin' a word. The driver of the other car never looked and went slam-bang into our old Model T on the driver's side. Walter couldn't get the door open. It buckled up the running board…and you couldn't open either door."

The impact threw Isabel out of the car. Luckily she fell on the ground, not on pavement. "But I was 'out' a little bit, you know, and Walter did the very worst thing he could have done. And here he was pickin' me up and goin' to carry me to the doctor's. And I said, 'Oh, let me down. I'm all right. I'm all right.' I 'came to' while he had me up. Anyhow, I managed to get myself back into the car, and we drove on home." Isabel experienced no serious repercussions from this accident because, she thought, "I was young and my flesh was healthy. But I'm telling you, it could've been really very serious." Next morning, they were late getting to the Wallace farm because Walter had to straighten the running board after he did the chores. They were the only family members who hadn't attended the 11 a.m. service at which her father was made an elder of the church. Her dad said something like, 'Well the rest of them all managed to get here'. Isabel calmly replied, "'Well you're just kinda' lucky that you weren't comin' to my funeral instead of me comin' to your ceremony'. And so then, of course, they all stood still until they'd heard the story, and they knew then that they were very lucky indeed," she concluded. She and Walter visited her parents and many other relatives and friends often over the years, all within the province of Ontario, usually by car.

In Canada's Centennial year, 1967, they went with me, my husband Vern, and our two and a half-year-old son, James, to Expo '67 in Montreal. That July, driving our well loaded station wagon and pulling a tent trailer, we joined hundreds of tourists headed for Montreal. On the way, we found convenient campsites in Ontario. In Quebec, we had to camp about ten miles north of Montreal, then take a shuttle bus to the Expo site. Our trailer had two double beds that pulled out at each side. With five of us, it was a little crowded, but nobody complained. My parents were used to using an outdoor toilet and managing without running water, even though they'd never gone camping together. Operating the farm on their own through some hard times, they'd had little time or money for such holidays. Since Mom and Dad were genuinely at home in the outdoors and highly sociable, the camp setting suited them well. This trip, there were no accidents.

The third time she felt she should have died occurred in the spring of 1968. Isabel's sister Chris had persuaded her to go to Vancouver, British Columbia, to attend a wedding and have a good holiday. On the return trip, their niece Kathleen was driving a car to Castlegar for a leasing company. At Castlegar, they were to pick up another car for the rest of the trip east. As they approached the town, from a distance they observed the largest tire fire in Canada up to then. It had melted telephone and hydro wires for miles, burned for weeks, and been treated with every available fire retardant, mostly administered from aircraft. Their excitement had just begun. From Castlegar they took the suggested shorter route, which included thirty miles of gravel road. These conditions didn't bother the country-raised trio from Ontario. They followed this road to catch a small car ferry. After a short river crossing, they drove into rain. "Having no knowledge of the approaching elevation of the Monashee mountains," Kathleen told me much later in a letter, "with this big eight cylinder car-of- the-times, I came around a curve maybe a little too fast for driving conditions." By this time the rain had changed to snow. "We slipped into the mountain on the right side. There was enough momentum to push us to the left, sideways twenty feet down the cliff. The left wheels rested against two stumps. There we hung, afraid to move."

Isabel looked at the incident in this way: "I never can understand how [we survived]—well, I know how, because like the sparrow and the robin…" and she quoted this verse:

Said the robin to the sparrow, 'I'd really like to know
Why those human beings rush about and worry so.'
Said the sparrow to the robin, 'Friend, could it be
That they have no loving Heavenly Father
Like looks after you and me?'

"So that's the only reason because really the three of us could've been down at the bottom of those hills up there in B.C. in '68." Mom's spiritual strength told her that she, Chris, and Kathleen were personally cared for by their God. She used the accident details to prove her point. "There we were, sliding down on that snow, sliding down and sliding down. And Kathleen and I were in the front. She was driving. She had her seat belt on, and I had mine on and we were kinda' leanin' this way, you know, as much as you could, not to let the [car] go." Chris, who was in the back seat, wasn't wearing her seat belt, so she slid right against the side of the car. Suddenly the car stopped.

While they were trying to figure out what to do, a pickup truck appeared on the road above them. The young man driving it had seen the tracks, so stopped and came down the bank. "Of course we weren't the first people went down there," Mom told me. "In fact, they told us the next day, that there was a car went down there with four people in it, and they never got it up. It was too far down." The young man decided to take his family home, then come back to get the three of them up the slope. So,"we just sat carefully—never breathed, hardly". Soon he was back. Isabel continued, "Kathleen says, 'You take these old aunts first and get them out'. Oh, Kathleen was so scared something'd happen to us… What'd it matter about us? She was more important in the world than we were, really. But anyway, he took us up, one by one." He didn't use a rope or any other assistance, because the car hadn't gone down far. They just climbed carefully up the steep rock-covered bank.

The man took them to a motel that wasn't yet open for business, run by a woman named Margaret. She welcomed them warmly, providing everything they needed. Naturally, they all were shaken by the experience. Mom described her own response: "I guess I looked like nothing on earth. Of course that's the worst of me, anyway. That's the way I was when I was a kid. People would think I was gonna' be dead the next day. I guess [Margaret] thought I was gonna' faint or something or another, so she poured me a little brandy… I just sipped a little of it, and then I put it over. And I did a thing I shouldn't have done, but of course it was really in a sense Chrissie's fault. Chrissie says, 'Oh if you don't want it, put it down the sink'. And I went and put [Margaret's] brandy down her sink. And I don't think she was too happy about it. But I says, 'Oh I'm all right now. I feel all right'." Since Margaret had no motel beds yet, she gave her bed to Chrissie and Isabel; Kathleen and Margaret slept on a pullout couch in the living room.

As the three rescued women were eating breakfast next morning, the road maintenance crew came to clear the road of snow. Not missing a cue, Isabel took note of the situation: "And one of those men—that was, I think, his third year on that particular route, for looking after the roads, you see—he says, 'Ever since they put me on this road, I've been tellin' them that's a dangerous corner and they should have better signage on it'. And that's what Kathleen had already said. She'd said, 'I watch so carefully, every time there's anything like that', because she was used to the fact that they'd put special signs up for the truckers." Mom went on, "Just goes to show you. I'd like to talk to this man Harris [premier of Ontario at the time of telling me the story in 1997] and tell him, 'Look, when you're ninety years old, you'll know a few things more than you know now. And this is something that you don't know. And I'm gonna tell you. The powers that be wouldn't listen to this man [in B.C.]. So if the people that sat with their feet on the desk and in their swinging chair, enjoyin' their soft comfort had listened to that man, we might not have been over the side of the bank, you see." And with that my mother (as she would often say about her commentaries on current affairs) got off her soapbox. A tow-truck operator got the car up to the road. "And that was the second Sunday in May. That's where we spent Mother's Day that year. But anyhow, we were very very thankful."

My mother really should have died four times. That same spring (Isabel's grandson Ed told me in our interview) she'd decided to buy a 1968 blue Ford Fairlane, which was equipped the same as a Mustang. And that, he said, "…is the one she rolled over in the gateway of the go-kart track—and came out with a scratch on her little finger." She wasn't wearing her seat belt, a circumstance that Ed believed saved her. If she had been wearing it, he said, she would have been upside down on her head, likely with a broken neck. Instead, she came to rest in the back seat, on the roof. Ed went on: "And they put that car back together and she drove it until one front corner rotted out of it, which would be well into the '80s. She drove all over the place [although not in Toronto] but to such places on the outskirts as Lemonville and Markham…" A few times she drove it to visit our family in Orillia. She also did enumeration work for federal elections, driving up and down the country roads of Uxbridge Township. She was in her early eighties when she did her last enumeration.

As other modern methods of travel became available, Mom tried a few, just for fun. After her experience in British Columbia, I guess she figured she had nothing to lose. That summer of 1968, she rode with Ed on his motorcycle from the farm to his home just down the road. That was the only motorcycle ride she had. She was almost sixty-eight years old. She hadn't even been a bicycle rider in her youth. Her joyrides included a snowmobile, too, Ed told me. "She'd ride on it going back and forth to [my parents'] house. I've taken her down there, I think, on Christmas Day." When she was in her seventies, he also took her to visit a close neighbour. One vehicle she didn't ride was the ATV, which was purchased in 1983 and which was actually a one-person vehicle. Possibly the fact that she was eighty-two years old had some bearing on the decision—though not necessarily.

These transportation adventures in my mother's long and richly lived life provide a cameo of how she lived it. She was well grounded in reality, practical and responsible. Yet she had a tremendous sense of fun, a thirst for knowledge and adventure, a willingness to change and try new things far exceeding that of the average person. When she officially became a senior citizen and started collecting a government pension, she physically appeared and mentally functioned perhaps fifteen years younger than her contemporaries. She engaged with life, even when it dealt her terrific blows. Her deep faith, practised in personal devotions, regular church attendance, and community involvement, helped her dissipate many clouds of discouragement.

Although one can never know for certain what moulds a person's character, little Isabella's Scots pioneer roots, farm upbringing, and close family life certainly made a substantial contribution to hers.

Wallace Family Portrait
circa 1908

Back Row (left to right): Duncan George, Viola Catherine, Annie Laurie, John Reid.
Front Row (left to right): William (Will), Minnie Elsie, Margaret Isabella, William (Willy) Alexander, Christena (Chrissie) May, Catherine (Kate) Anne, Jessie Agnes.

CHAPTER TWO: True Pioneers

Sunday Morning

If I could turn life's pages back and from its golden store
Could take some precious moments and make them mine once more
I would not ask for wealth or fame, nor far-flung fields to roam,
But just for Sunday morning on the old farm home.

Those were days of toil and hardship, care that could not be denied,
But the Sabbath brought a respite—worldly tasks were laid aside.
House all shining, quiet, peaceful, mother's face so dear, so blest,
Father's voice in prayer uplifted, "Lord we thank Thee for Thy rest".

Clean white cloth upon the table, silver gleaming, china gay,
With a place laid for the preacher should he honour us today;
On the spare bed little garments, dainty ruffles, snowy white,
All that mother love could compass to make Sunday a delight.

And the old horse with the carriage, faithful friend for many a year,
Gladly do I pay a tribute to a memory still dear.
Well he knows it's Sunday morning; hear him whinny "Don't be late"
As impatiently he watches for our coming at the gate.

No stained windows, no grand organ, made that little church so fair.
Plain the people were and humble, but 'twas love that brought them there.
And the awe and holy quiet, emblem of the heavenly grace,
God was near and very precious as we met Him in His place.

I cannot have that little bit of Heaven on earth today;
I cannot be a child again, so free from care, so gay.
But when life's week of toil is o'er and I to rest have come,
It will be Sunday morning in the old farm home.

Mabel Tackabury

"Oh they were pioneers, you know," my mother Isabel often told me, a touch of pride in her voice. "My parents were true pioneers and so were Grandma and Grandpa Wallace." That set of grandparents, George Wallace and Catherine (McBain) Wallace, was married in Toronto (known at the time as Muddy York) on March 17, 1863. On their honeymoon, according to family lore, they walked north to what is now Ravenshoe, just a little below the southern shore of Lake Simcoe, where they took up residence in a small tin building.

When they moved to Concession 10 of Thorah Township in the mid-1870s, they couldn't get all the way up the concession from what is now number 12 highway to their farm. "They had to go up the Portage Road and come across somebody else's property to put their feet on their own land," Mom explained. "And there was a place at the back end near the line fence, where [other settlers] had built their house and barn. They were doing that sort of thing when they opened up first, you know. And those buildings were put there permanently, the house and all. They had that long lane to go in and then…you practically backed out of the barn into the line fence."

George Wallace was a farmer, but like many he supplemented his income in the winter by working in Muskoka logging camps. George stayed at the camp most of the winter. Occasionally he'd come home for the weekend. Monday morning, he got up at 3 or 4 a.m. to drive his team of horses to the camp. Being a teamster, he didn't do the heaviest work; the job had a certain prestige about it. In his absence, Grandma Wallace looked after the livestock. "She was a tough old girl," Mom told me. Just what a pioneer woman needed to be. Appendix A shows the Wallace direct line descendants, starting with Isabel's great-grandfather John Wallace.

By coincidence, when Isabel's father William (Will) and his family, the Wallaces, were moving into Thorah Township, in 1874 or 1875, her mother Catherine (Kate) and her family, the McFadyens, were moving in Eldon Township, closer to Thorah.

Isabel's maternal grandparents, Duncan McFadyen and Christena (MacLean) McFadyen, were married by Rev. John McTavish at the Woodville manse on April 3, 1862. Their first home was at Hartley, where Catherine Anne and Gilbert were born in 1863 and 1864, just one year, seven months and eighteen days apart. Other children were born at Balsam Lake, Glenarm, Eldon Station and (the last six of the twelve) Bolsover. This last home was on the double town line between Victoria County and Ontario County and between Eldon Township and Thorah Township. The McFadyen direct line of descendants, starting with Isabel's great-grandfather Donald McFadyen, is in Appendix B.

Soon after the McFadyens moved to this last farm with its log house, they added a kitchen and a second storey, then bricked the whole structure. During the construction, Catherine Anne (Kate) suffered an accident that left a permanent mark. Mom often told this story about my grandmother, as a precautionary tale: "Mother was down in the basement [that had been dug for the new house]. Uncle Gilbert (Mother was supposed to be around twelve years old and Gilbert would be around eleven or so) was havin' a great time. You see, the floor was being laid and you know how they put the joists to lay the boards on. And he was hoppin' and skippin' and jumpin' around up above…and he says to Mother, 'Look, see what I can do'. And he had a pair of scissors in his hand and he was lettin' them fall down and then he'd run around and go down and pick them up and then come back and let them fall again. And Mother looks up, and the scissors hit her in the eye. But it didn't damage the ball, you see. But it spoiled the sight… And I don't know the particulars, 'cause the gory part of it was never told to me. I wasn't anxious to hear it anyway. I don't like that sort of thing." My mother was not destined for a career in medicine. Her talents lay elsewhere.

When her mother, Kate, was old enough, because "She was the oldest of the family, and in those days girls worked out, a hired girl, really…", she worked for the Bruce family, who lived on the Centre Road, now called Highway 12, at the intersection of the eighth concession. (See 1895 map of Thorah Township). On the south-east corner of the fifth concession and the Argyle Road sat the Old Stone Church, built in 1840, the first church in the area. On Sundays, "The people from Brechin walked down to it for service, because there was no church in Brechin. They used to carry their shoes in the summer and walk in their bare feet, because they had to get their shoes made by a shoemaker." I calculated the distance on today's Highway 12 and was astounded to learn that some of these church-goers walked a round trip of almost thirty miles. After the church service, "The Bruce place was the halfway house where people would go to have a meal oftentimes". The family needed extra help. Kate had told Isabel they'd bake a dozen or more loaves of bread on Saturday to prepare for Sunday. The Bruce family's generosity was remarkable. "The Bruce's gave the people food, no charge. They were quite community-minded." The people who stopped in for a meal had little or no money to pay for it. They were pioneers, just like Kate's parents.

The Bruces "...were quite well off, and had a lot of land". They paid Kate good wages, more than many other girls earned. Later, Kate often spoke to her and Will's family about her experiences there. "They were out in the world more than Mother or than any of the MacFadyens," and helped Kate to expand her horizons. Isabel and her siblings were ultimately the beneficiaries of this informal education. The Bruces had encouraged Kate to get a glass eye but she hadn't saved much for it. Her pay often was needed at home. She learned many of the household skills, however, such as cooking, cleaning and sewing—skills a married woman required to run a household efficiently throughout the year. Eventually "Dad was getting anxious to get married, but Mother didn't want to get married until she got the glass eye because she wouldn't be having work then. She'd be at home paying off a mortgage instead of paying for a glass eye." So William Wallace got the glass eye as his wedding gift to Kate McFadyen. He told his daughter Chris, after Kate had died in 1937, 'Well, I guess the most unusual wedding gift was the one that I gave your mother'. He wanted her to have the eye for their wedding photo, taken following the marriage ceremony in the manse of St. Andrew's Presbyterian Church in Orillia on September 18, 1888.

Always a keen observer, Isabel had noticed that, "It never looked like a glass eye. I had a teacher at school, and he had very staring bright blue eyes that just stood out. And he had one that was a glass eye. And you could tell it every time, it was so dead, you know. But Mother's seemed to have life—it moved, or it wouldn't have worn like [it did]." After a few years, the glass eye no longer fit. Once when Kate was washing clothes, her eye fell into the rinse water tub. It was time to get a new glass eye.

So what was pioneer life like for Will and Kate, this newly married couple in the late 1800s in central Ontario? With all our amenities and technology, we twenty-first century Canadians can hardly imagine. My mother didn't have to imagine. She knew.

"[My parents] had to build a house. The farm had no buildings on it when they went there in 1888 except what my mother called a shantyman's shanty." Their house was modeled on Will's parents' home, located approximately two miles west of their farm. East of Will and Kate's, "There was a roadway, left for a road, but it wasn't *built* for a road, built up and ditched and everything. It was sand or earth all the time...to go to the townline east, to my [McFadyen] grandmother's house [in Eldon Township]".

Before he was married and when his and Kate's older children were young, Will went to the logging camps in the winter with his father. As far as my mother knew, he didn't take a team of horses, as he was a young man and would be doing harder work. Probably this work helped pay for the farm. The camp experience affected his views on life, too. Isabel's first cousin Gilberta (McFadyen) Nicholls had once remarked on how 'stiff' Will was about things such as playing cards. "But I understood," Mom told me, "and I think anyone that wanted to use their head could understand. Dad went off to the bush to work when he was a young man, in the wintertime, and to earn money, and the people would sleep in bunks and had another place where the kitchen was and you ate, and they played cards and gambling. Gambling and cards went together for Dad, especially euchre cards." By payday some of those men owed all their pay in gambling debts. Isabel, however, knew a person could play a lot of card games and not gamble. "He had to find that out before he died," she said of her dad. "He wouldn't have euchre cards in his house, but he'd have Lost Heir. But you could cheat in Lost Heir just the same as you could with the other. It didn't make sense, so he finally could see for himself that he may as well give up, that it was how you used them [that mattered]."

By 1888, Will had increased his livestock holdings of cattle, pigs and hens. In the summer he grew potatoes, turnips, hay, and grain. When Isabel arrived in 1900, number seven out of nine children, her father was a full-fledged farmer. The family still had very little money to purchase goods, however, because "you had to get land and more land all the time". So they 'made do'. For example, the hammock slung between two trees at their home "… wasn't a canvas hammock like lots of people were buying at that time and putting up". The McFadyen grandparents had one of those. Her family's hammock was made from a hollowed out barrel padded with old quilts and held together with heavy wire. My mom's pride in this ingenuity and ability to provide for the family stayed with her. She practised similar skills and passed them on to her own family.

Kate did purchase many regular household items from Sandy Bouey, who traveled the countryside with horses and a light wagon, selling goods from his store in Argyle. "He used to come to our place," Isabel recalled, "but he didn't go any farther because he didn't have a licence to come into our township. He used to slip down there because Mother had a large family and bought quite a few [things]—yardage and print to make aprons and dresses for us kids." He sold canned groceries, too. The Native people (called Indians at the time) also visited homes to sell their handmade articles. These were generally practical items with a specific purpose. "When they came to our place on the farm, it was when I was quite young, before I went to school. Mother got these baskets from the Indians that had made them, and they called them buggy baskets because they were made just the depth of the 'trunk' of the buggy." There was a cover over this area, with a spring on it. People filled the basket with eggs to take to market, or with sandwiches for the church picnics. Another of these Native-made items my grandmother had purchased, now part of my heritage collection, was a knitting basket woven from elm strips, some of them dyed blue.

Mom often said that her mother possessed a terrific amount of common sense, which included an innate sense of the psychology of human behaviour. When an illness, accident or injury happened to any of her brood of nine, Kate usually looked after it. As this incident illustrates, there was often no choice. The year was 1907. "We went to the barn to play—Minnie and Willie and I. The men weren't around. The older boys, Duncan and Reid, were probably in the bush cutting wood for the next winter, to keep the place warm. Dad was in Beaverton to the nomination meeting for the councillors and reeve…the last Monday in the old year (that was the rule at that time) and then the first Monday in the new year, you went to vote." He'd gone with the driving horse. "So we three kids were alone up in the barn part, and Willy got fooling with the straw-cutting [machine]. It had a crank on it that you could crank and manually cut the straw if you were just doing a little bit, but it also had a metal pulley where you put a belt on it and attached it to a belt on a treadmill. Grandpa Wallace had a horse that was good on the treadmill, and he'd tread…and keep it turning to cut a lot of straw."

Willy decided to get some straw, to show Minnie and Isabella how the straw-cutting machine worked. He'd seen the men operating it with the horse. Willy, who was just shy of nine years old, demonstrated this way, Mom told me: "He'd go around to the other side where the crank was, and crank it and get it going real fast and then he'd jump around and he'd put his hand on this pulley wheel that was going round and round… And he says to me, 'You can't do that'. And I says, 'Well, I can'." He performed this action two or three times, but he wouldn't take his hand off the machine. Isabel thought he wasn't giving her a chance. She saw other wheels coming together in the box of the machine. Being too young to realize they were cogwheels that came together to operate the knife, she stuck her hand in the box. The mechanism pulled her hand in.

She was wearing a mitten, which may have helped—or may have made things worse. Typically, she held no rancour towards Willy. "My brother had great presence of mind for a young lad… He jumped around there and stopped that crank and then turned it back and I could pull my mitt out and my hand." She saw that the knife had cut the end off the little finger of her right hand. The situation facing Kate was dreadful. Beaverton was the closest community with a doctor. The Wallaces had no telephone. Nobody could take Isabel to the doctor's office seven and a half miles away to tend the injury because Will was in Beaverton with the driving horse. Although they had another farm horse, the family owned just one cutter. Most families had just one driving outfit for each of winter and summer. It would be dark when Will got home. Treatment couldn't wait. "Mother, bless her heart, how she stood it, I don't know. I wasn't standing it too well. She looks at me and she says, 'Do you think you need a drink?' So she got me a drink. She thought I was going to keel over, and no wonder. All the blood was agoin' every old where." Isabel held her hand over a pail while Kate looked for something to bind up the finger and something to put on it. Isabel couldn't remember what was applied—possibly turpentine and Vaseline.

Ten or fifteen years later, a doctor who had served in the First World War, Dr. Dowsley, bought the Beaverton practice of the retiring Dr. Grant. Soon after, a man working in the butcher shop caught his hand in the meat slicer. Dr. Dowsley was close by, so the man ran down to his office. "This doctor claimed that if you were healthy and had good healthy blood, you should just wrap a wound up in its own blood. That's what they had to do in the war. That's what he did for the butcher." And that's pretty well what Kate did for Isabel. She had the finger bandaged up long before Will got home. Meanwhile, Isabel was instructed to lie on a couch in the kitchen and rest her arm on a chair. Kate didn't undo the bandage for two or three days. She told Will that the finger looked good, but she'd like to have the doctor check it. He agreed, and off they went to see Dr. Grant in Beaverton, who declared, 'You made a wonderful job, Mrs. Wallace. There's not a thing the matter'. He advised Will and Kate to put a shingle or something else light and straight inside the bandage, then gradually keep pushing it back, so the finger would be straightened out. The nail grew back, but from the second knuckle on, this baby finger was crooked, possibly because of the splint.

When she was almost eight, Isabel again tested her mother's medical skills. She was playing in the yard near the woodshed when she stepped on a board. The nail in it penetrated her bare foot. "We went barefoot as soon as we could hide our shoes," she chuckled as she told the story. Of course the foot bled. Somehow she got the board off and herself into the house. Kate's procedure for this mishap was as follows: "Mother just took the wash basin and put hot water in it, just as hot as you could stand without scalding me, and dashed my foot in and out of it. I don't know if she put turpentine in that water or if she put salt in that water. I know she put something in it. And then she bound it up with turpentine. Turpentine was the thing that was supposed to save that foot. I'm not sure which foot it was, to tell you the truth." The pioneer mother had wrought another of her little miracles.

Getting an education for their children was another great challenge for Will and Kate. When their oldest, Annie, was ready for school, she had to trudge three and a half miles to Egypt School on the corner of the ninth concession and the Centre Road. Not one child in their family who'd gone to Egypt School passed the entrance class (which is today's grade eight), my mother told me. She described the difficult situation: "Annie was very young, and, really, she should've gone back and tried it a second time. But with so many children enrolled and one teacher, they'd be glad to be rid of her. Duncan was in the entrance class, but he just lived for the horses." He never really tried the entrance exams, but stayed home to help Will. Reid and Viola had both tried the entrance exams and not succeeded. By that time, Kate needed Viola to help at home with the younger children, so she and Will didn't push her to return to school. Isabel knew Viola was a good student with a good memory. So she really should have passed. The Wallace children nearly always failed spelling. My mother thought this was because Kate "had the Gaelic, and she made mistakes in spelling. She wrote to me one time when I was in high school, and she starts her letter off, 'Dear Ishbl'." Her mother was no help to the children in that subject.

Will recognized how difficult success would be for his children because they had to walk three and a half miles and often missed school. When she was older, Isabel learned that her dad had been so concerned about the school situation that "he had made up his mind he was going to sell that place and go where he could send his kids to school and educate them, and he wasn't going to put up with it". But then he talked to other neighbourhood parents about the situation. They formed a group to lobby the area school inspector for another school to serve the newer settlers. "Dad and John Windatt were the leaders, but they had plenty behind them in the community." An old man who lived near Beaverton provided one obstacle. Every time the group tried to initiate plans for a new school, that man said if the school section was broken up their taxes would rise, and that his school section would also lose the government grant for each student who attended the new school. Most of this activity went on while Isabel was living at her Aunt Tene's and attending Argyle School, which she could walk to comfortably. She regretted that she had missed many discussions about the new school. After nearly five years of work by Will and the group, everything was arranged. In 1911, construction of the Beaver School got underway—a stone's throw west of the Wallace farm.

The year 1911 was exceptionally busy for Kate and Will. With their growing family of nine, they had decided to expand their house. They hired the contractor who was working on the school. Everyone got a good deal. In addition, the Canadian Pacific Railway had started to build a railway stub line from Peterborough to Port McNichol right through the farm, to move western grain from the boats to the grain mills in Peterborough. Will and Kate did well by the CPR's decision. They were paid for the land used for the rail line. Since there were no sleeping quarters at the farm for the workers, the CPR renovated a caboose car with an upstairs window and bunks for sleeping. It was parked in the pasture between the Wallace's barn and the road. These workers got their meals at the Wallace farm, all paid for by the CPR—and all very helpful income for a family expanding its home. The railway men came into the summer kitchen just to wash themselves and to eat. As soon as they'd finished eating, they went back to work, to the caboose, or to relax outdoors. "Once they had a bit of track put down, they came back and came back and came back because they liked it so well. It was all so easily looked after, and they were getting good meals…with Mother and Chrissie and Viola workin' their hearts out—and their shoe leather," Mom commented.

She couldn't remember how her family had managed when the old part of the house was torn apart inside. Only two partitions, one upstairs and one downstairs, were untouched. The renovations even included a bathroom, which had been converted from a small bedroom. It had no toilet or running water because there was no power to move the water. Their house didn't have an attic to put pipes in, either. Her Uncle John Wallace, who had learned plumbing, and her Uncle George Wallace worked on the bathroom. They installed a large water tank on the floor of the bathroom. Water ran into the tank from the eavestrough, which had collected it from the metal shingles on the new part of the house. They laid the hot water tank down with heavy planks under each end so that the water would run into the footed bathtub. The water was heated from the wood stove in the 'winter kitchen' below. The bathroom also had a washstand with a basin on it, but no tap. "We got [the water] into the bathtub. That was the important thing. You could do your feet and every part of you in the bathtub. And that was wonderful. And that bathroom was so cosy and warm with the water heater and the pipes around. It was the warmest room in the house." Clearly, she enjoyed this taste of luxury.

With regard to the rest of the house, she said, "What was commonly called the pantry was turned into what I called 'a workshop', where you did your work… It was more of a kitchen. The cupboards were in there and the sink." The pipe to the sink came from the cistern in the cellar. A pump took the water out of the cistern. The pipes, located just above the floor by the baseboard, went into the wood-burning part of the woodstove to heat the water. So that stove, which they'd bought new, couldn't be moved. The stove from the original 'winter kitchen' was moved into the 'summer kitchen' to use for baking, especially in the summer. A wood furnace was installed, too. Isabel described it as "…just like the steam engine on a threshing machine. A big door opened, and you put in this big log". In later years, they burned old ties off the railroad, some received free, some purchased from the railway company when new ones were installed during the summer. Wood also came from the bush on the farm. For its time, the Wallace home was quite advanced. Having grown up in a house without central heating or running water, I can fully appreciate the pleasure these amenities brought. What fills me with admiration is that Mom didn't complain about the lack of such amenities in her marriage home, either in her telling of this story or, to my knowledge, at any other time.

As an adult, Isabel, whom I picture as a bright and lively child with intelligence shining in her dark brown eyes, had many detailed recollections from 1911, even though she didn't return to her parents' home from Aunt Tene's until that August. "I still get a kick out of it, you know, because when you live through it, you have all the little side lines to enjoy, if you know what I mean." Some of the carpenters slept in the boys' room in the house. Willy slept on the floor in the hall, where Kate had made a 'shakedown' with the feather tick. There was a curtain—"[Mother] always kept a curtain across there because she'd have boxes of things, you know, you'd have to store. When you've got a family like that, your winter things were put in boxes for the summer and your summer things were put in boxes for the winter. And the boxes were stored in this part of the hall that was back behind the staircase."

The contractor, Mr. Tom Morrow, had two sons, Tom and Robert (called Bobby). Bobby provided some good laughs at the expense of the mason, Mr. MacArthur, who was bricking the new school and the Wallace house. MacArthur was "kind of fond of his bottle. Of course, at that time, Brechin had a bad name for itself for the hotel there. Now and again, MacArthur kind of forgot to come to work, or wasn't fit in the early morning." One evening, MacArthur had been to Brechin. When he came in he "wasn't too steady on his feet. He came [into the summer kitchen] and he sat on the first chair right at the door". He got talking and asked Bobby, 'Where's your Dad?' Bobby's reply? 'Oh, he's out preachin' temperance'. Of course everybody laughed. Everybody included both the other workmen and the family. "And MacArthur didn't say another word." Since no form of alcohol was allowed in the Wallace home, this incident made a strong impression on ten-year-old Isabel.

Sister Annie, who worked in Toronto and came home weekends, thought the new house should be sound-proofed for their dad's bedroom. Isabel understood the request. She had seen that Annie had difficulty entertaining in their home, because Will went to bed early. Farm people had to. The horses needed time to eat in the morning before going to work on the land. One night when some "great singers, with good strong voices" were at the house, Annie played the pump organ for a hymn sing. You'd think the staunch Presbyterian Will would have been pleased. But the organ stood in the corner near the dining room. Will and Kate's bedroom was over the 'front room' next to the dining room. He'd been disturbed. "And Dad came downstairs and made some remarks. It wakened me because he spoke kind of loudly. There was kind of a 'scene'…and it wasn't that late. It might have been ten o'clock." Mom conceded that her father was strict about discipline, very strict regarding what his children should and shouldn't do, "but that was the times, that was the way it was". Perhaps this approach was connected to the Scots Presbyterian background, as well. Isabel later recognized that "It was hard on the older ones of the family. We younger ones didn't have that because he'd got over it. And, well, the world was turning and it was changing." She did, however, maintain some of that strictness in her family. When we were in school, my brother and I were not allowed to do homework on Sunday. We needed to be organized enough to have it done early in the weekend. By the time I'd reached grade ten, she relaxed this rule. I was a serious student. I think she realized that I needed my Friday or Saturday night social time just as much as I needed to get the homework done.

In September 1911, Isabel celebrated her eleventh birthday in the family's newly renovated home. How excited she must have been! She was almost over her health problems, which had been part of the reason for her going to live with her Aunt Tene (details in Chapter Three). She was now well enough to walk the seven miles a day round trip to Egypt School. Her parents didn't send their youngest, Jessie, however, because when she'd started in the spring the walk had made her legs ache. Older sister Chrissie didn't go to school that fall either. She was needed in the house to help feed the railway construction gang that was still eating and living at the farm. And at first Willie didn't attend because he was helping to finish outside work before freeze-up time. One of his jobs was to mix cement. Machinery to do the job didn't exist. In her mind's eye, Mom could see her next oldest sibling using a shovel to turn the materials over and over. At Christmas the family paused, gave thanks, and celebrated in their new dining room, which Annie had decorated. I like to think that they ate their special dinner at the new dining room table purchased from Eaton's catalogue, the same table that now accommodates most meals in my home.

William Wallace Home, circa 1912

Beaver School, Thorah Township

Everyone in the neighbourhood had hoped the Beaver School, as it was to be called, would be ready for fall, but "This was a new school section starting, so they had to work around a very slim bank account". Debentures (just like a mortgage on a person's land or house) were used to pay for the school. The debtor could pay just the interest until able to pay off the principal. When the school was ready in December, the school board had to find a teacher—a somewhat difficult task in that month. Finally they got Eva Luke, who taught school with a third class certificate, which she had earned by spending six months in a Model School after receiving her lower school certificate for two years of high school studies. Normal Schools awarded graduates a second class certificate. At Teacher's College, a person could get a first class certificate. A third class certificate had to be upgraded after five years of teaching, once the inspector had verified that the individual was sufficiently capable to be rehired. In adulthood, Isabel pronounced Eva Luke "a very good teacher. I remember quite well lots of things that I [learned] and that I think about when I look back. She was really a better teacher than Mae McGuiness, and we had her the next year—and she'd gone to high school and to Peterborough Normal School."

When Beaver School opened in January 1912, Chrissie was in the senior fourth (equal to today's grade eight). Willie, Isabel, Minnie and Jessie also attended. Every one of the thirty-two seats was full. Chrissie had just six months to study for her high school entrance exams. She didn't pass that June. Mom must have been quite disturbed by this situation. The exams weren't exceptionally difficult, she explained to me, but everyone had to go town to write them—in a strange town, in a strange school, with a stranger to supervise, and "a bunch of youngsters you knew only a few of, because they were brought in from all over the township". The pitch of her voice rose with emotion as she explained these circumstances. Perhaps recalling her own entrance exam experiences, she summarized: "It was such a strain that there was more to it than just the knowledge part of it."

The farm business continued to grow through this pioneering period. Will and Kate's place was accessed off Concession 10 of Thorah Township, but the farm itself was in Concession 9, the south half of Lot number 6. When the north half of Lot 6, Concession 10, came up for sale, Will bought it as a ranch. At times he used this property for crops. "They drew the grain (maybe had a kind of a bee and some of the neighbours, and I suppose an uncle or two) to the home barn so they would not have to move the threshing machine over there." The property included a log barn and what my mother described as "a cute little cottage". She didn't know what year this property was bought, but said "I remember the year it was paid for, and the reason I remember, it was the first time that my father left home overnight, and I was so concerned (but I wasn't saying anything) because Dad wasn't gonna' be home." She was young, probably six or seven. Will had sent the last payment. He was expecting his deed and other papers by return mail through a lawyer. When they didn't come, "He made up his mind that writing letters was no good. He was going to see that this thing went through right. So he was goin' on the train to that place…and I couldn't understand how we were gonna' get the night in without him. I was really scared, inside of me. Whatever would happen? And if anything did happen, who'd be looking after it or what would we do?" To me, this story demonstrates her admiration of him as leader of the family—an attitude that neither my mother's first cousin Florence (McFadyen) Francis nor I could understand. We had experienced Will as stern, inflexible, emotionally distant. My mother had instinctively known how much he loved and cared for her and the rest of his family.

Later, Isabel also realized that this incident demonstrated her parents' careful financial planning. "Mother and Dad were that way… You sort of knew you could handle a thing financially before you did it. And you wouldn't have thought they would've had the mortgage paid on our home farm too quickly, you see, because it was a really pioneer undertaking, in the beginning, but then as the two boys, Duncan and Reid, got old enough they could extend themselves in the amount of land they used... But then they were using Grandfather's farm 'cause Grandfather I never remember him farming at all. 'Grandfather isn't well enough to do the heavy work,' they'd say." Isabel seemed to make extra allowance for Grandpa Wallace when she said, "But of course, [Grandfather] kept the stables clean, and he had a horse and buggy and all that... And he did things around." For example, when a child got scarlet fever, measles or mumps, the whole family was quarantined. Grandfather Wallace was appointed by the township council to get the list of food the quarantined family needed, buy the groceries and deliver them to the home.

St. Andrew's Presbyterian Church in Bolsover played a significant part in my mother's family life. In retrospect, she approved of its approach: "We were brought up in the Presbyterian church, and the Presbyterian minister *was* a minister. He ministered to the people. He visited. In fact, I heard Mr. Burkholder [the minister who performed our wedding ceremony] say he had a book...where he put all the names down when he visited." With this method, he saw all members of his congregation within a certain period of time. All of the ministers visited their parishioners. One of those visits was unforgettable for my mother.

It was summer. The men were just coming in from the field for dinner. Kate had asked Isabel to drain the potatoes. The potato pot had a fancy lid on it; the handle clipped on to the lid and was supposed to hold it. There was a spout for draining. As Isabel drained the cooking water into a pail that held leftovers to feed the pigs, the potatoes bumped the lid off. Some fell into the pail, but there were still plenty left for the family's meal. Then somebody said, "There come the Lindsays, over the railway track." Mr. Lindsay had come to Bolsover as a student minister in 1914, the winter before the war started. Now all four of them—the parents and two boys, Douglas and Francis—were driving in the lane. Certainly the Lindsays, both university graduates, were welcome visitors. They "knew how to talk right—had lots of things to say, and what they said, they said properly". Mom was in contact with the parents until their deaths, and their children most of her life. She laughingly told me, "[The Lindsays] knew that at the Wallace's you just pushed over and put on another plate." Kate quickly solved the potato problem. She simply put some cold cooked potatoes into the pot with the hot ones. But the potato incident bothered Mom. "I felt so terrible and I never forgot it. And when I was keeping house for myself...I drained potatoes into a clean dish. I certainly learned that lesson." This story vividly demonstrates my mother's practical streak, learned through imitation augmented by keen intelligence. She kept up her way of draining potatoes as long as she still cooked them.

Many of the Wallace family's values no doubt came from their dedication to the Bolsover Presbyterian Church and its work. Although Will's financial motto was 'Look after the cents and the dollars'll look after themselves', my mother said, "Neither mother nor dad were tight." Or, as one of her cousins once observed, "Well, Uncle Will has his faults, but being stingy isn't one of them." This compliment would equally fit Kate, who often sent food or other items to either of the grandparents. Sometimes the Wallace grandparents would send down to their house for honey, if they didn't have any to make honey and lemon for Grandma Wallace's cough. "They didn't think anything of it. That's the way it was. Or [Mother would] visit a neighbour and take some little thing. They really believed in sharing."

Every Sunday, Isabel's family attended church and Sunday School. Sunday was considered the Biblical day of rest. "We didn't work unnecessarily on Sunday. But you had to have food, and the animals had to have food… But because we went to church in the morning, for our noon meal, we'd have the potatoes cooked ahead of time, and whatever vegetables, and Mother always had the baking done, for bread, and sometimes she made sugar buns, sometimes pies, puddings, and biscuits/scones." Often on the way home from church, two of the children would stay at Grandma McFadyen's for lunch, then walk home for supper. Once in a while, they stayed overnight. Or, if they were at home for the afternoon, they'd walk down the other direction to Grandma Wallace's to have supper with her, especially in the summer. After Sunday lunch, Kate and Will usually lay down for a rest. The men and the older children who were working needed this extra break. At other times, church families or neighbours came to visit. If no one else was around, the children "…often started preparing for the next week's Sunday School (learning a 'golden text') because we got a card for knowing the golden text, being present, for catechism (when we got older) and for [giving to the] collection. When we had enough of these smaller cards we got a larger one with a lovely picture on it and also a suitable Bible verse."

A favourite Sunday occupation for Isabel involved her oldest sister Annie who "…would take us younger kids and she'd read to us Sunday afternoon. And we had some storybooks not too bad, a lot better than the first school library I landed into when I started to teach." The family also subscribed to the *Farmer's Advocate* magazine, which included good stories, poems, and children's pages. The family had reading materials from Sunday School, too. The young children usually lay on the bed while Annie half sat up to read. For a while she read the Elsie books, but that didn't last long. "They were maybe too much one-sided to live long in a sense because it was almost like a Bible." Again, my mother's perceptive mind did its analysis. She recognized the impact of this Sunday reading ritual and other ways that her oldest sibling contributed. "Annie was really something for our family," she concluded. 'Really something' meant that Annie was a key cog in the family's functioning and financial success. If Mom had explained or said anything more to me, she would have cried, so deep was her love and gratitude towards Annie.

Then, "As we got older, our Sunday afternoons were spent out on the lawn [in the summer] when we had the house built and the lawn fixed up and everything." The children had a heavy quilt to put on the ground. They also had a bench made from a spool bed that Grandfather Wallace had bought at a sale and presented to the family for the new house. Or they might be on the verandah where they would read or chat. Many activities were forbidden. The Sabbath was to be a day of rest. "You were supposed to write letters on Sunday afternoon. When Annie was working in Toronto, we'd write to Annie, or the aunts." Sending postcards was popular too. Will mailed the letters and postcards in Gamebridge when he went (usually every two days) to pick up mail they'd received. Rural mail delivery began around 1916. The house got telephone service just after the First World War. By then, the Wallace family had passed the pioneer stage with honours.

So many of Mom's deepest values clearly stemmed from this pioneer upbringing: use common sense; don't spend what you don't have; rely on your own resources; use your ingenuity to provide what you want or need; work hard and you will succeed; share with others; nourish the spiritual side. I have no doubt that these solid values, learned in her pioneer family, contributed significantly to her ability to turn the challenging clouds of her own life inside out, and to her pride in the Scottish stock from which she'd come.

CHAPTER THREE: An Awful Lot of Fun!

No Idle Words

There are no idle words where children are.
Thoughts spoken in their hearing carry far,
Producing fruit for evil or for good
In our great future brotherhood.

The word dropped lightly from our thoughtless lips
Into the fertile child-mind seeps and drips
And intertwines with thoughts and feelings so
It may decide the course in which some soul may go.

So speak not thoughtlessly when they are by;
Your words fall not on sterile ears or dry.
Thoughts sown in plastic minds are carried far—
There are no idle words where children are.

Author unknown

When I began interviewing my mother for this biography, she asked, "Where would you like me to start?"

"At the beginning," I replied.

And so she did, again and again astounding me with her 'one in a million' powers of observation and memory for detail. Names, dates, comments, conversations: either they rolled off her tongue or she stopped to say, "Let me think a minute". If she couldn't retrieve the information she wanted, she persevered. Nine times out of ten, it came to her. Even in her ninety-ninth year, when we did our final tape recording together (although we had reached only 1928 in her life—albeit with a multitude of asides), she exhibited just a tiny slowing of the retrieval process, a measured gathering of her thoughts. She was remarkably blessed with her mental capacities.

She began her personal story by recounting what her oldest sister Annie had said about how Isabella had come into the world so suddenly. "[Annie] had gone to Sunday School and church with the rest of the family (my father had taken them) and my mother was home with the younger child. When they got home, Annie couldn't understand why she was shuffled off to Grandmother's house so quickly. And of course Mother had started in labour while they were at church. And so she always told me, and therefore I knew, that I was born on Sunday, September the sixteenth, 1900."

What would this seventh child be named? When Will was going to Beaverton about a month after Isabel's birth, Kate reminded him that the birth needed to be registered. Isabel's name turned out to be quite the puzzle. "My father didn't seem to know whether he'd registered me as Isabella Margaret or Margaret Isabella… But I had two aunts, one on each side of the house, called Margaret that I was to be called after, and then I had this Aunt Belle, we called her, and her name was Isabella. But when I was christened at church, I was supposed to have been christened and named, not Margaret Isabella, as my father thought he'd put it in Beaverton, but

Isabella Margaret... So it always seemed to be somewhat of a bugbear, and strange as it may seem, Aunt Belle was in the same mess with the Isabella and the way you spell it. When she died (You see, she didn't marry and she didn't have children nor a husband to leave her estate to and it was left to the nieces and nephews.) I got a letter like all the rest of them did. In the lawyer's language...she was Isabel, also known as Isabella, and also known as Bella, and also known as Belle. And so," Isabel concluded with typical self-deprecating humour, "when I die, I guess I'll be 'also known' as this, that, and the other."

By school age, she was generally called Isabella Margaret, or Isabella. The boy across the road, who started school at about the same time as she did, sometimes came over and announced, 'I and Isabella may have a ride with Poppa this morning to school'. Her sisters and brothers, especially Willy, would tease her about 'I and Isabella', "...and I wouldn't answer. Then they shortened the Isabella to Bella. Mother said that's how I got called Bella." Though the teasing must have been painful for her at the time, my mother chuckled as she told this story in later years, delightedly mimicking the little boy tone of 'grand announcement' as she said 'I and Isabella'. By the time I was part of her life, she was always called Isabel, a name that seemed a good fit.

Her six older brothers and sisters ensured that Isabel always had playmates and something to do. In 1902, on May 14, her sister Minnie Elsie was born. The youngest of the Wallace family, Jessie Agnes, arrived in August 1904. As Isabel approached school age, they became the most likely playmates, as well as her brother Willie, who was about a year and a half older than she was—and one of her best friends.

People of this century may wonder what children played with in the days before ToysRUs, computers and video games. The Wallace children had no problem keeping occupied. For example, "We had a playhouse that my father built really for Annie, down at the foot of the yard at the side of the house." A rail fence separated the yard from the rest of the land. There weren't any wire fences then. "He built [the playhouse] with the slabs (if anybody knows what a slab is) off the logs to make the lumber...when they were doing the logging and clearing the land." She must have spent many hours in this structure. She told me numerous details, a smile lighting her face in reflection of happy childhood memories: "The playhouse was made with a shanty roof. A shanty roof is high at the front and you walk in and then it slopes down... And we could walk in, as children, and stand up in the thing. We could stand up at the back where this fence was. And in between the rails were the windows. In the summertime the windows let the light in, and in the winter they let the snow in. Of course, we couldn't play in it in the winter. And then there was even a little part put on afterwards...just a place where you went in to lie down, just like a box turned upside down. And that was your bedroom. Mother would give us dishes and things, sometimes with cracks in them... Of course we had toy dishes given by some of our aunts at Christmastime, and Santa Claus would give us something like that." The children made cupboards with wooden boxes from grocery stores, simply by turning the box on end and putting shelves in it.

In the winter, before the Wallace house was expanded in 1911, Kate let the girls go to the barn to play with their dolls. Isabel's keen observation and memory provided another detailed picture, this one of the stable part of the barn where she and her sisters played. She took this occasion to praise her pioneer father, Will, for his practical intelligence, of which I think she inherited or absorbed an impressive amount. "My father was a great one. See, they'd built the new barn in 1903 and had the new stable and everything, and he'd made wide passageways, unlike some barns where you could hardly manage with the narrow passageways." The horses were housed at one side of this passageway, the 'fat cattle' on the other. The floor was cement. "The horse stable was the first one we went into through the walking-in door. And then there was another swing door thing you went through, and then there was the feed room. There were bins for the different grains: wheat and oats and rolled oats (for the old horses that didn't have very good teeth). And then the chop for the pigs." The arrangement for feeding horses also impressed her: "Any of the stables I've been in, the horses could get their heads into the passageways, but they couldn't at our place, because there was a door that you put up and a wooden button that you turned and held that door up. When you went to put the hay in or the grain in their feed box, you'd let that door down and put in the food for the horses." The cattle mangers on the other side were built in a similar way. "So we used to sweep that [area], and we'd set up housekeeping in that passageway. And we'd play out there by the hour sometimes."

When Isabel was older, another part of the barn contributed to hours of winter fun. The barn was set back from the road about two hundred and forty feet. This space provided pasture for the animals in summer. At the roadway was a log fence. "They never seemed to make them quite as high as a rail fence. They'd use cross-pieces at the end of the logs, and you'd lay the log on that. Three logs high was about as high as they made them, because they'd be heavy to lift, you know. You see, a log is wide, and an animal can't get over it." To provide the full picture of the setting, she went on: "You see, the barn was on a foundation, to make the stable, and the wall of the stable was stone in those days. So to get into the barn—we used to call it a bridge, some people called it a gangway—you started at the bottom and made it slope till it came up to the level of the barn floor." The gangway was used to take the hay, grain and threshing machine into the upper wooden part of the barn. Since there were no hills on the farm to slide down, the children carried pails of water to dump on the gangway. "So we'd get that bridge glare ice with carrying water, and the snow and everything…and then we'd start there with the handsleigh, and sometimes we'd go over the log fence, the snow would be that deep. Oh, that's when we used to have fun!"

Winter evenings, the family often played card games, including 'Lost Heir'. They also played 'Authors', which six people could play. Each participant represented a well-known author, such as Charles Dickens or William Shakespeare. "You know, it was quite an educational game. You would [have to] get all the books...the number of cards that would be by the same author." When you asked another player for a card, you had to have the name of the book, as well as the author's name. The object was to collect all of one author's cards. Of course, "…when you'd have about four [cards], somebody'd find out and take them all away from you". Tiddley-winks, a game often mocked when I was growing up, was another one the children played and thoroughly enjoyed. Though far less sophisticated than today's computer games, it appears to have achieved some of the same ends in childhood development: fine-tuned observation skills, strategizing, and strong eye-hand co-ordination. "And another game, oh we did play a lot, because the adults played with that, was crochinole." Sometimes the adults let the younger children put the wooden piece on the board. They also played checkers, but in such a large family a game that only two could play was less popular. The children sometimes played 'Giveaway' with the checkers. "You lined the checkers up across the top and down to a point. And you had to get your checkers on your opponents' side and he his checkers on your side. You'd jump, but you didn't pick them off." Isabel could beat Willy in 'Giveaway', but Willy always beat her in checkers probably, she concluded, because there was more strategy in checkers.

'Button, button, who has the button?' was a strong favourite with the children on a long winter evening. As many as six might play. They used the front room table, which was covered by a cotton cloth woven in a red and white pattern and fairly thick and heavy—ideal for the game. "And Mother didn't have to say, 'Now don't muss up the tablecloth'. It would always flatten out when we got through with it, anyway." To play this game, "You had a string the size of the table, and as many people play as can get around the table. You put a button on the string and tied it up so the string was a circle." The button could move on the string. Everyone's hands, the string, and the button were under the tablecloth, and players were supposed to pass the button on. "You'd wiggle around to fool them, as if you were giving it to this person, and after all you didn't even have it." Whoever was 'it' had to find the button, saying, 'Billy Billy Button, who's got the button?'" This game, she declared, was a lot of fun, too. Listening to her description of their good times together, I realized what a close family my mother grew up in. The Wallace children must have had their arguments, but I heard very little about them in any of her stories.

School is a major part of any child's life. In the early 1900s there was no kindergarten. Children started school at six, sometimes as late as eight, which was the legal starting age. Isabel experienced her first taste when she was five—earlier than most children did then. Her Uncle Andrew McFadyen, who was living at home and teaching at Bolsover School to put himself through university, decided to take her to his school one Friday. "And of course, often in those rural schools, Friday afternoon, after last recess time, you'd have a little 'friendship time'. Usually you'd have a spelling match or a geography competition. Now, that day, they were having a spelling bee. They'd choose up sides and choose a leader first. And the leader would choose who they'd have to be on their team. And everybody got up, no matter who you were." The teacher ensured that neither team had too many little ones. During the choosing process, Isabel started to cry. When Uncle Andrew asked why she was crying, she told him, 'Well, I don't know how to spell'. He said, 'Well, if you don't want to get up, then you can just stay in your seat and listen to the rest of them'." And she did.

Her older siblings attended Egypt School, situated at the corner of the ninth concession of Thorah Township and the Centre Road (now Highway 12). "We had three and a half miles to walk, but that was the way it was and so I was to go someday, to get acquainted with the school." That day was near the end of June. She'd be six in September, but because of the distance she wouldn't be attending in September. Her most vivid memory of that day had little to do with formal education. She needed to use the outhouse, which was behind the school. She went out the girls' door/entrance, turned right around the corner of the school and started to follow the boardwalk. Then she got into trouble. "You know, the sidewalks in town used to be board…and they were built with joists the width of the sidewalk, the two long pieces, and then slats of boards. There'd be holes in between. And they had a sidewalk like that at the school." Isabel stepped on a board with a rusty nail in it. The board and the nail hit her knee, which bled. "I cried. There I was, that was my accident at Egypt School. That's the next accident I had. I was prone to accidents for a while there. It just seemed awful. I stayed all day, though…"

The next spring, after Easter, she began attending Egypt School on a regular basis. Mr Beggs, her teacher, was instructing ninety children in one room! "He was really a wonderful person. Somebody should have a plaque somewhere for some of these people that went beyond the line of duty, as it were." The desks were built to seat two children on a bench, with a desk behind. The bench and the desk were one unit. To accommodate all those children, Mr. Beggs put three on each bench. My mother remembered just where she sat, and with whom. Being small, she was wedged in between Flo McDougall and Lily Johnson who were in 'fifth class', which was the first part of high school. "It was quite a thing for me to watch them, with the red ink and the black ink and all the figuring that they'd be doing in the bookkeeping business. I didn't know much, and didn't do much writing. Usually there were about three classes in the primary, because they'd start at different times, and there'd be two in the first class, which had the 'first book' for reading. And then in the 'second book' there'd be junior and senior; 'third book', junior and senior; and 'fourth book', junior and senior." These divisions are equivalent to today's eight elementary school grades.

One fall day, Isabel walked in to school and got an unforgettable surprise: "…and here were these four great big men—three of them just filled the doorway, each one, when they walked through—coming to school! These were boys that had been out on the farm, and now everything was done, maybe a little bit of ploughing to do, but nothing else. Harvesting was all looked after, and that sort of thing." It was Phil and Nichol McDougall, brothers to Flo, one of Lily Johnson's brothers, and Billy Robinson. She had no trouble remembering Billy because he loved to tell the little children wild stories. "He says to me, (We'd be standing around the box stove, you know, keepin' warm) 'Now, you see that fly up there? You know, I can walk on the ceiling, just like that fly'. It puzzled me. I know I never answered him. But I looked at that ceiling. And I looked a long time. And I was picturing this great man walking upside down on that ceiling." After telling me this story, she laughed heartily at her youthful naiveté, concluding with, "Well that was my second episode, as it were…"

When last recess arrived, the primary children went home, unless they had to wait to walk with their older brothers and sisters. That was the case for Isabel. But she didn't mind. "I got a seat to sit in. I'd turn around—and I wasn't supposed to turn around—and the teacher would make me stand up in the aisle. I kind of liked that, because I could look out the window. The windows were high, you see, so you couldn't see anything if you were sitting in the seats." She'd look out the window on what is now Highway 12. Even then, it was "…kind of a busy road, and it was entertaining for me". I can well imagine those bright brown eyes absorbing the new environment and experiences into her curious mind.

When winter came, the daily school routine lost some of its appeal. Snow and cold winds created brutal walking conditions. "I guess it was one of the first snowstorms. I know it was a terribly bad storm and I think it was before Christmas holidays. We were going down the road. Of course my (Wallace) grandparents lived down the road about half a mile, and we had to go past their place to go to school. Viola, I remember, was hanging onto my hand, and the snow was deep enough, it was coming up to my thighs. By this time there'd been storms one on top of the other, and they didn't have ploughs like now, to be 'chasing it somewhere else'. Viola turns to Chrissie and says, 'We'll never get to school with this child. We'll have to leave her at grandmother's.' When we got down to grandmother's, I had to go in and stay 'til four o'clock." Isabel's biggest concern was the honey sandwiches that Kate had packed for her. She insisted that they stay with her. Having told the story, she went on to muse: "It was quite a problem in those days, to know what to make sandwiches out of. But you had your mother's good homemade bread, no additives." Kate used potato and potato water, sometimes mashing the potatoes right into the water they were cooked in—plus wheat flour, salt and yeast. There was no peanut butter in a jar. Occasionally they had cans of salmon, but that was too expensive in a family with five lunches to 'put up'. They often had roast beef, chicken, ham, and other meats from their own animals. Sometimes Kate spread homemade jams, raspberry or apple jelly or chili sauce on the bread over the butter. The Wallace children also had homemade cookies and apples—Tomlin Sweets and Russets and what they called a Sweet Crab—in their lunches.

Like the lunches, perhaps, the days offered little respite from the routine. "That's all you did was walk three and a half miles in the morning, and then you had to sit in school or be around in school, and then when it was over at four o'clock, you walked three and a half miles home. By that time it was suppertime, or nearly suppertime." In the fall and part of the winter, it was dark by the time they got home. Once the children had had supper at six o'clock and done a few little chores, it was bedtime. Some of the older children stayed up later to help milk the cows; they also milked one or two in the morning. Everyone had to be up before daylight to get ready for school. Isabel's and Minnie's long hair had to be combed and braided. They all left for school just before eight. "Mother would always have the clock between five and ten minutes fast. 'Now the clock will soon be striking'…and nobody said anything about whether it was fast or slow or anything. You went by the clock striking." She told me about these circumstances with little complaint. It's just the way things were.

But this routine began to take its toll on Isabel. "About the second year I was in school, it seemed that I'd be sick and in the morning I'd say, 'I can't go to school. I'm too sick'. But you couldn't see what was sick about me. I wasn't throwing up." Kate and Will took her to Dr. Grant, who decided her kidneys were the problem. He prescribed medicine for her kidneys, but her condition kept getting "a little worse and a little worse". The fall she was ten, she missed several days of school. Kate was concerned because at Isabel's age school was getting more important. Finally, Dr. Grant said, 'I can't do any more for this girl, as long as she has to walk three and a half miles to school'. So in January 1910, she "was bundled off" to Aunt Tene's place on the third concession in Eldon Township. Aunt Tene had married Jack McEachern the summer before. The school was only about a mile away from the McEachern farm, just south of the community of Argyle. When I asked Mom what it was like to be away from her family at that age, she said, "It was kind of hard. I was pretty lonely sometimes, but Uncle Jack was quite a good one to fraternize with, as you might say. He'd talk to you and take an interest in you, sort of. Some men wouldn't have done it the same as he did, but he kind of liked children, or appeared to."

She began to improve and attended school regularly. By spring of 1911, she did little jobs when she came home from school. On March thirty-first, when she had fed the hens and gathered the eggs, she looked up towards the house from the barn and saw Old Darky, the black horse that Aunt Belle and others from Grandma McFadyen's house drove. "And I said, 'Oh, there's Darky'. And I ran to the house with the eggs. When I got there, Aunt Belle was there, and Aunt Tene and Aunt Belle were crying their hearts out. Grandfather had died—my first experience of a family death. He was twelve years older than Grandmother…" At the time, embalming wasn't done in the rural areas. There were no funeral homes; his body wasn't taken to the church, but rested in the parlour of the McFadyen home. The funeral was delayed a bit while daughter Mary traveled from Omaha, Nebraska. Isabel went to the funeral with her Aunt Tene, who now had one young child, Farquar. She took care of him and the other young grandchildren upstairs over the kitchen at the back while all the adults attended the service in the front part of Grandma McFadyen's house. The days that followed must have been difficult for the young and thoughtful Isabel. She told me that being away from home was "…a sad part of it. I wasn't at home during that time with my own family for the grieving period, like you might have been." As a farm girl, she had experienced the deaths of animals. Her inquiring, growing mind was surely full of questions and concerns about the death of a human being who was close to her heart.

Isabel stayed at her Aunt Tene's until the middle of August. She spoke with some regret about this timing, though the arrangement was undoubtedly an advantage to Kate. "That was the year that so much went on and I always felt kind of badly that I wasn't at home all the time…I missed all that." The railway went through, the house was renovated, and the new Beaver School was built, almost across the road from her family's farm. "Of course, Aunt Tene and I went down there sometimes. She had a horse she could drive. I didn't know at the time, but Aunt Tene was pregnant for the next child, Duncan, and she may not have been feeling too well and didn't bother. And then Mother'd have to see that I had clothes for school. And we thought that we'd maybe be going to the [new] school, but we didn't."

That fall of 1911, with their older siblings still helping out at home, Isabel and Minnie went on their own to Egypt School. They loved going barefoot, especially Isabel. She realized in later years that she wasn't comfortable in shoes because of her feet, the "shape they were [in]", the way they were when she was born. She went on to recount some of her youthful adventures. One morning, Kate said she and Minnie needed to wear their shoes because it was cold. So they did. But when they got down past their Grandma Wallace's place, they took off their shoes and stockings, hid them among the cedar trees, and went to school barefoot. "But you know, by that time the sun had been up and it was warm enough and it didn't matter." On the way home they picked up the shoes and carried them—no problem with that on the return trip.

At threshing time, she and Minnie hurried home to see the steam engine and the threshing machine at work. They devised a game, running to one farm, then walking to the next one. They got home in an hour—before five o'clock. But the man operating the steam engine wasn't happy to see them. He'd say, 'If you don't get back there to the house, I'll just open this door [to the firebox of the steam engine] and put you in here with these logs'. "At first we didn't believe him. Finally, we got a little bit scared maybe he would. So then we'd hike for the house." Inside they found at least one consolation. In the sideboard where the dishes were kept was "…plenty of buttermilk bread or bannock, and you could eat to your heart's content at that when you came home from school if you were hungry, but you couldn't have [Mother's] yeast bread because it took too long to make it, and she might not have enough to make toast for breakfast." Almost twenty-four hours was required to make the twelve-loaf batch of yeast bread (two pans of six loaves each). "But Mother never refused us something to eat when we came home from school."

At school during recess and lunchtime they often played 'Collie in the Hole'. One child was designated as Collie. "We'd throw [the ball] against the school wall and then Collie was a dog. First he had to catch the ball. Then he'd chase all the children all around the school. The one that he caught would have to be Collie, and do the chasing." Sometimes the girls took their dolls to school and played 'house' in the leaves. Spring and fall, the gypsies appeared in the area, providing a new source of entertainment. "They'd have like a covered wagon, and they'd have a bed in there and everything, and they'd have a team of horses drawing it. They always had plenty of horses. Every spring they'd camp between…the Centre Road and Lake Simcoe." Of course the gypsies had children with them. Once there was a new-born in the caravan with its mother. "You know, we were afraid of [the gypsies]—we little kids." One time, Isabel and another little girl hid in the stooks in the grain field, next to the school. They were afraid the gypsies would steal them and carry them away, as that's what many older people claimed. "I was really frightened of them, really and truly I was," she confessed, adding, "I can't have been any more afraid of them than that other girl, though." As an adult, she knew that the negative images of the gypsies were unfair, commenting, "They were very nice people." She realized the two farmers living in that space "never bothered their heads about them at all", although the gypsies weren't above picking up a stray hen.

A second situation bothered her just as much as the gypsies. "They'd been telling us at school about some old tramp that was going along and he'd sleep under the culvert at the corner." She was afraid to go over that bridge alone, in case the tramp was there again, so suggested to the girl walking home with her that they go into a field and then come out on the road and avoid the bridge. When they got over to the corner of the tenth concession, she saw Grandpa Wallace coming with the horse and buggy from Gamebridge. The girls got to the corner first. "And when we came out on the road, he stopped and offered us a ride. He wondered what we were doing in there, and I said, 'Well we thought we'd just take a shortcut'." She didn't want to tell him they were scared of the tramp. "In my own mind…I had no idea that I was taking a 'longcut'. I never forgot that, because it was such a stupid thing, in a way. It shows, in as far as I was concerned, 'Well I had an answer ready', but at the same time, it was a queer answer." And she laughed heartily at her young foolishness.

Despite the challenges, Isabel did learn while at Egypt School. She had some problems with arithmetic, but she could add "like the mischief". Children who did well took "the head of the class". In those days, that's how the teacher got the children to work. But, she laughingly said, you could be at the foot before the day was over. When she first attended, Mr. Beggs asked the little children to count to one hundred. Some couldn't count at all. She and a boy named Reg could both count to ten; so they took turns being at the head of the class. "I know from them teasing me at home…that Reg wasn't going to get ahead of me. I was going to keep up with him." And what she learned stayed with her. "Even yet," she said in the mid-1990s, "in my adding, I use my tens and things. Nowadays they don't know how to teach them. When we were enumerating [in the 1970s] for the mini-census, one woman had her son's calculator." The census-takers all had to report to a place in Whitby. While the other woman used her calculator to add up the columns, Isabel was adding in her head. She was way ahead of the other woman—"thanks to George Beggs", my mother concluded.

Mr. Beggs sometimes came with his family to visit the Wallaces. They looked after Stella (who was not yet going to school) after Mrs. Beggs died in the Christmas holidays while the Beggs family was visiting in Thunder Bay. Mr. Beggs had to come back to teach in the new year. "What was he going to do with his little girl? And he came to Mother and Dad, of all places, and us so squeezed up, if we could take her—because that was before we built the new house, you know. What could they do but take her? And then he would come there for weekends." He and Stella did this until the summer holidays, giving him time to think about his situation. He made arrangements for Stella to go with a childless couple who lived on a farm near Lindsay. Later, Mr. Beggs got a school in that area.

By Christmas 1911, both the house and the new school were completed. The teacher that was hired, Eva Luke, needed somewhere to board. "Well, you know Mother and Dad. If a person didn't have a bed to sleep in or a table to sit up to, to eat, 'Well come in. There's room in our house'." So Eva was invited to live at the Wallace house, with the ultimate result that "We boarded the teacher for years then. It was really close by." The teacher in the Wallace home just became a part of the family. Miss Luke didn't show any favouritism: "The only advantage was that her mind was among us and was at the table when the conversation was on. Our place was always like that, from away back." I recall many similar lively dinner table discussions when we visited my mother's siblings and in our own home during my growing up years. Everyone relished the democratic exchange of views on topics ranging from farming to politics. While I didn't often express an opinion, my contributions were respectfully heard and considered. Such openness and generosity characterized my mother in an even broader way throughout her life.

Summer holidays in 1912 were "much the same as all farm holidays", the children busy helping with chores such as picking strawberries and wild raspberries. "But the big difference was the regular CPR trains" on the recently completed track. Mom and her siblings loved to count the loaded boxcars and to see the passenger trains once in the morning and again in the afternoon. When the train was heading back north from delivering grain to Peterborough, they'd count about a hundred empty boxcars. She recalled how the ground shook when the train went past and how "The train men waved [to us]. It seemed that they knew about those men who lived here and felt a part of the family [when the track was laid]."

In September 1912, Willy was in the entrance class (Senior Fourth) when Chris had to attend the second time. Chrissie passed this time and was ready to go to high school in Orillia. Isabel was in the Junior Fourth that year. "I can remember being in the bathroom washing my hands and combing my hair and the quarter to nine bell rings, and I'm down to school in time. What a treat." She now had 'little chores to do' before leaving for school. "But oh the little chores to do was a happy situation beside walking to school three and a half miles on a gravel road. That was an awful experience, in a sense, but you had it to do, and you did it. And we had an awful lot of fun doing it sometimes, you know." Perhaps it was this gruelling experience that set my mother's life-long pattern of making the best out of an unpleasant situation, of turning the clouds inside out. I do know that this attitude had a great influence on my behaviour and thinking. For example, I walked a mile and a quarter to elementary school and to catch my high school bus. I hated to miss school, so set out even when the weather was nasty, with the result that I received a perfect attendance award four out of five high school years.

As she grew older, Isabel had more house and/or farm chores to complete. Chrissie looked after the front of the house upstairs—cleaned the bedrooms, used the dust mop on the floors, and shook the rugs out on the balcony. "And I had the back upstairs," Isabel said, "which was the boys' room with two beds in it for three boys, and the bathroom and the square hallway as you went up. It had an oilcloth (linoleum) on the floor. The front part was hardwood floors, but the back part was the old floors from the original home…" She also became responsible for milking one cow. Because Willy had numerous chores to do after school, he usually persuaded her and Minnie to help "…especially in the winter when the skating was on because there was a lovely pond across from the school and …we just jumped the fence and went skating on the pond." They timed their skate by listening for the passenger train to go through at twenty minutes to five. Then the three of them raced home to do the chores. The first job was to take the chains off the cattle and let them out to water. The pumphouse was connected at the horse stable; she and Minnie took turns pumping. While the cattle were outside drinking, Willy cleaned out the stables and put down the straw bedding for them. "And Minnie and I looked after the turnips to pulp. One would put them in and the other would turn the pulper. And it would be quite a chore sometimes. And then we sliced some of them, and if you sliced them it was a little harder." When they got tired, they changed jobs. Sometimes the girls forked the straw, but not the hay because it was heavy and hard to get down from the haymow.

Weekend jobs included filling the woodboxes. A sheet metal box stove heated the front part of the house, while the kitchen cookstove did double duty. With her siblings, Isabel spent many hours working on firewood. The only saw available was a crosscut saw that required one man on each end, to cut the wood into appropriate lengths for the stove. The men and older boys did that sawing, then split the big blocks into smaller logs. She sometimes helped with the tree limbs, which were cut with a smaller saw. Willy used the saw and split the log; she gathered up the pieces. This activity kept them busy on many Saturdays during the winter. "No wonder," she philosophized in her nineties, "I tell the story about the man that had the lawyer that said there weren't enough woodboxes any more, when down in the city of Toronto he had so many of these boys that were getting into trouble that didn't have any woodboxes to fill, to keep them busy." Because Mom worked this story into many conversations, it often comes to mind now when newscasts and newspapers report shootings and robberies committed by young people in our cities and towns. Although I balked at the tasks (including filling the woodbox) she assigned me as an adolescent, I'm grateful to have learned the sense of pleasure and accomplishment that a completed physical task brings.

Asked about details of her school work in elementary school, Mom said, "When my older brothers and sisters were going to school, they didn't have too many textbooks that were very much good, but they always had readers and pictures. The first ones we had, I can picture so clearly... I have that bunch, right there." And she pointed to her bookcase. Her sister Annie had gathered the collection. The pictures in these books were old-fashioned. "I can see the little girls with frills on their pinnies and on the bottoms of their dresses there's a ruffle, and hats with ruffles…and the boys with knee breeches and stockings comin' up over their knees or sometimes down lower." The smaller first books were more like today's paperbacks, but made with linen cloth. Those for later study were hard cover. These books were so pivotal that "We called it books, instead of classes". So a neighbour might ask, 'What book are you in at school?' whereas now a child is asked what grade she is in. "That's about all that you had, that reader book, and then the teacher had to find all the rest—and it wasn't easy. And that's how they got started with the 'helps' that were wonderful for the teacher, and the students too, as time went on." Lessons for a month, produced in newsletter format by The Educational Book Company, cost about six cents. The parents, mostly farmers and other labourers, had little spare money. Fortunately, the provincial government, not the school section, paid the publisher. "That would have been better," she commented in one of her contemporary asides. "If they still did something like that, there wouldn't be so much waste." She recalled her own teaching experience in 1958 when "It grieved me beyond words" to witness the waste of materials such as drawing paper.

In her school days, classroom supplies were simple. "The teacher had to do an awful lot of blackboard work, and you had a slate to write on, and a slate pencil. The slates, of course, you rubbed them off…and you brought from home a clean cloth to wipe your slate and wash it, and you had a bottle with water in it." Some of the boys didn't bother with the water. They just spat on the slate. But they still dried it with the cloth. For arithmetic and spelling practice, the older children used a 'scribbler' (later called a notebook) made with newsprint and written on with a lead pencil. The curriculum was basically the three R's. The pupils' multi-purpose textbooks served as a speller and the source of poetry memory work assignments. Again Mom took the opportunity to express her opinion, formed through decades of experience with the Ontario education system: "It's an awful pity when they shoved memory work under the carpet for little kids, juniors especially, in the elementary school, because that was great training, and you got to appreciate. Sometimes, when you'd be walking to school and meet other children, you'd ask, 'Did you learn your memory work last night? Can you say that piece?' Two or three of the children would then put it together. And that was good for this 'top story' [the mind] and good for learning good literature, as far as that goes, because there were some good literature pieces in the readers."

Teachers often arranged their curriculum so that all the children in one family could use the same textbook, including for geography, her favourite subject. "I wish I had [a map from then]. I often wish I had one when I'm thinking about how Canada has changed and the boundaries, you know. And I can remember the first geography that I paid any attention to… when Manitoba was just a little square like that. And then the next book, the first book that I ever owned, it was up to the Bay and straight across from there and down. The territories were an awful size then—more territories than province in most of them. And Ontario," she went on. "There wasn't north Ontario and south Ontario when I was in school and when I first had geography." She and her classmates had to memorize the names of all the Ontario counties and county towns, make a map and put them on it. She felt she missed a great deal in science, because they studied mostly agricultural science. For example, she learned about breeds of chickens, cattle and horses. Another disappointment to her was "We had next to no art. Oh, it was terrible. But we could buy a book that had the paper in it, and you could tear it out if you made a mistake…and throw it away. And you used watercolours, and you did have crayons a bit, of course." Basically, the older grades used watercolours, while the younger ones had crayons.

Certain family experiences during these elementary school years became indelibly etched in my mother's brain and heart. One such event took place in the spring of 1913. Willy was ill in bed for several weeks. He had had pain in his abdomen. Dr. Grant eventually decided Willy had peritonitis, "a very serious thing in those days". The doctor gave a prescription. "Whatever Dr. Grant gave him, (and this wasn't the first or the second day that he was there)…my mother was sitting there…and Dr. Grant came down those steps from the bedroom and he says, 'Well, Mrs. Wallace, I've done all I can do for your boy. There's a power greater than mine that'll have to do the rest'. Wasn't that a wonderful thing for him to say? And an attitude? How many people nowadays would give credit where credit is due, you might say? But that's exactly what he said, and I was there and heard him—and it was in my head *forever*." Speaking these words into my tape recorder, Mom's voice broke as she re-experienced the overwhelming emotion of that moment— undoubtedly one of the most significant experiences of her life. "And mother was sitting there knitting everyday socks. If you missed a stitch, it wasn't a problem, because she was working on the leg of it. She was there just a-makin' her stitches count." Then Dr. Grant started walking back and forth between the kitchen and the dining room to the sitting room—"I don't know how many times. I didn't count it." Finally, he stopped and took out his watch.

Even in the intensity of the wait—or perhaps because of it—Isabel noticed the details. "For me, it was a marvelous watch. He just pressed the stem and the cover flew open, and there was his time. Of course he had a vest on, and he had a chain. The watch was in one pocket and the end of the chain was in the other pocket, and it went through the buttonhole. He looked at it, and he closed it up, put it back in his pocket, and started to walk again, not quite so long, and upstairs he went. When he came down a few minutes after, he says, 'Well, Mrs. Wallace, your boy's going to get better'. That's all as true as the fact that I'm sitting in this chair." She didn't know what this last thing was that Dr. Grant had tried, only that it worked. The miracle of Willy's recovery, the miracle of God at work in the Wallace household, made a deep permanent impression. "It was really something marvelous for a kid to take through life in my head. Is it any wonder that I was ready to join the church when I was fifteen, when I was home from high school for Thanksgiving?" And is it any wonder that a rock-strong faith in God remained an integral part of her entire life? The detail and intensity of her telling this story made me understand her faith as nothing else could have.

Because of Willy's brush with death, Isabel caught up to him at school. She passed from the Junior Fourth to the Senior Fourth, with Mae McInnis as the teacher—"the poorest teacher I ever had". That didn't stop her. She had decided she was going to pass. She did have her own hurdle to overcome. In the spring of 1914, before the Easter holidays, mumps broke out at the Beaver School. Four Wallace children went there and the teacher still boarded with the Wallaces. Kate was convinced that Willy had the mumps. She decided to take him to the doctor to make sure, before the children went back to school after the holiday. "And the doctor said, 'Oh I think it's just his glands. I don't think it's the mumps'. And so they came home happy and everything, and I hadn't got them yet, but you see I was in for my share almost the same time as Willy was."

After seeing the doctor, Willy went back to school. To help explain what happened to Willy, Isabel described the school's window arrangement: "That school had all the windows to the left, you see, so the light shone and wouldn't make shadows for you to write. The old schools had windows on both sides and there were shadows on both sides." Beaver School also had two windows at the back, in the west, possibly for air circulation. One of the first days after Easter holidays, the boys had been playing football. Still no one knew that Willy's swollen glands meant he had the mumps. After recess, in his seat near the back of the classroom, he enjoyed the open back window because he was so hot—probably the worst thing he could have done. "And then the mumps 'went down on him'." Again Willy was in bed, was seen by the doctor, and missed school.

Isabel didn't miss much school with the mumps. But the disease left her with a permanent weakness. "You see, that ear and that side of my face was affected by the mumps. And my ear was hurting so." She was in bed crying one night, trying desperately not to disturb the others, when suddenly she saw her mother at the foot of the bed: 'What's the matter?' 'My ear hurts; it's awful'. Kate acted quickly. "She went downstairs and got a little bag that she used to buy salt in for the table, put salt in it and heated it in the oven and brought it up and put it under my face. Salt kept the heat like a hot-water bottle, as it were. There weren't any hot-water bottles then, [I don't think]; I never saw them anyway. And I went to sleep. So, I got over it like that and there was nothing ever done about it." That ear was always prone to infection, as were Mom's sinuses. In my memory, she always bundled up in a scarf or a hat on a cold and/or windy day. By the time she was ninety she had very little hearing in that ear.

In June 1914, at age thirteen, Isabel tried the entrance exams. She gained the distinction of being the youngest in her family to pass the entrance. Willy also tried in 1914 and he too passed. He had turned fifteen on January 24. She believed he would have passed the entrance in 1913, except for his illness, because he always got good marks. Besides, at the Beaver School, conditions were much better than they'd been at Egypt School. "We weren't so crowded, and we got taught. And we had an opportunity to really take in the geography and the history, and how to do the arithmetic, and the teacher had time to see where we were having problems." In the Wallace family tradition, they celebrated the successful completion of these entrance exams with a trip to Toronto. Kate and Will took Isabel and Willy to their Uncle George's for a few days. They didn't stay over a weekend, because Kate wanted to be home by Saturday to make sure things were ready for the weekend, particularly for Sunday. Even though some of her family was with her, Isabel got homesick. "Oh I did wish to get home. It was awful stupid, you know. But it didn't last too overly long." Possibly she missed the fresh air and openness of the countryside—aspects of the rural life that she always enjoyed.

While in Toronto, the family went to the Canadian National Exhibition and the Ontario Legislature. In the legislature, Isabel "… was going to sit in the chair that my representative would be sitting in when the legislature was on. And Willie, just like a boy would do—and sometimes girls, but boys were always up to tricks like this—he pulls the chair back and I went 'kersouse' on the floor, and my back scraped down the chair as I went down." As planned, she stayed that night with her Aunt Margaret and Aunt Minnie at their boarding house. And she wet the bed. "That's what upset the apple cart. My system in that area was all skew-gee a little bit because of the bump. Oh I'll never forget that. I felt so terrible. I wouldn't have felt so badly if it'd been at Uncle George's because after all they had kids and understood that sort of thing." This incident prompted Dr. Grant to recommend she not go to high school that year. Chrissie was going to high school in Orillia, and her parents were paying her board. Isabel thought later that perhaps Will and Kate hadn't figured out if they could afford to board two girls in Orillia. Since she wouldn't be fourteen until mid-September, her parents also thought she was a little young to send away from home. Perhaps this decision was a relief to her, too. Because of her bladder problems, she never felt confident.

That summer she took piano lessons, as she'd done in previous years. Viola and Minnie were taking lessons too. The three of them drove to Beaverton and back with their horse named Old Frank. Kate seemed to think Isabel was doing well, because she spent time on the lesson, as well as playing other pieces. "And I was interested enough to find other [things]. And we had books there; there was one book in particular that had 'Old Black Joe' and 'Home Sweet Home'—these things that are almost like a hymn. And our hymns that we had from Sunday School, I'd be tryin' to play these, you know, and workin' on them, maybe with one hand. And so Mother thought I was practising. Well, I was, really. And then I'd do some of that, and then I'd go back to my lesson for a while… But I always got along quite well. And for years I had the music book with the lines and the scales." Although her own piano always graced the living room at my birth home, I can't remember ever hearing Mom play it. She did send me for lessons, possibly thinking I could take up the musical torch. I was a disappointment in that department. I practised infrequently and finally stopped taking lessons mid-way through grade six conservatory piano.

On August 4, 1914, the First World War officially began. The Wallace family kept up with news through the train. A newspaper was thrown off the train as it went by, each day except Sunday. With the new teacher, Miss Bertha Switzer, boarding there, the table talk was fascinating. During one of those meals, when Will had asked Miss Switzer how she liked teaching (because that was her first school), she said she'd be very interested in teaching high school subjects. "And Dad says, 'Well, there's a girl there. You can teach her the high school subjects'." Bertha liked this idea, so Isabel went back to Beaver School just before Christmas. Mom said this experience did three important things for her: "[Miss Switzer] taught me algebra…new to me if I went to high school and she taught me Latin. I might have taken a little bit of French. And she taught me bookkeeping, too." Isabel didn't need bookkeeping for Normal School, which she planned to attend, but it was a subject she could use. Her final mark would be part of the total for the departmental exams that were set in Toronto. I wonder when she suspected that Miss Switzer would one day be her sister-in-law. Her oldest brother, Duncan, married Bertha Switzer on December 23, 1916.

Isabel's advanced education ended abruptly. She told me this story: A boy named Grant Miller had been at school just a few months. Two of his sisters also attended. One day when the children were going home from school, the boys were in one group and the girls in another. The boys, who were a little bit ahead of the girls, ran when they heard the train coming. One of the boys said, "Let's beat the train!" They all got over the track safely, but little Grant looked back and saw his two sisters. He ran back and got caught by the train. "Oh my, that was terrible. And Viola stood in the summer kitchen door and was looking out and saw it happen." Naturally the school was closed for the next day, which was close to Easter. Since Miss Switzer had quite a distance to go home for vacation, the trustees closed the school until after Easter. The day of that accident was the last one Isabel set foot in Beaver School as a student.

At the same time, "War news in the spring of 1915 was progressively alarming". Isabel was fortunate to find other occupations at the farm and in the community. Willy had decided to make maple syrup. He'd already tapped the trees and hung new buckets to collect the sap. She and Willy walked from home on the railway track, then followed the trail used to get wood from the bush. They partially boiled the sap outside in a big iron kettle, then carried the sap to the summer kitchen, where they could boil it down to syrup without creating steam in the main house. Sometimes they went sucker fishing in the canal, or even in the ditch at her grandparent Wallace's corner—an enjoyable outdoor experience, inexpensive entertainment, and food for the large family.

Probably augmented by increased concern and conversations about the war, a June garden party at Bolsover became another pivotal event in my mother's life. The programme included a man reciting a patriotic piece. At the end of every verse, he said "with pride and joy", Isabel thought, "For I was born in Canada beneath the British flag". Hearing this several times made a strong impression. "I never forgot that. It just got under my skin." Near the end of her nearly one hundred years of life, during which she'd been an ardent Canadian patriot, she expressed regret that young people now do not have that strong, almost cellular, loyalty to Canada.

Reflecting on all these activities and experiences, Isabel acknowledged that the extra time at home had been good: "I was learning a lot and growing and developing a stronger body, too." She was ready for high school.

A gentle touch from teen-aged Isabel holds the family dog for this photo in which she models her best dress, made by sister Annie.

CHAPTER FOUR: Begin to Roam

Home
It isn't till you've gone from it
You really miss your home;
You never know how sweet it is
Till you begin to roam.
You miss the comfort that it held,
The old familiar things
That grow more precious every day
And pull at your heartstrings.
You miss the friendly arguments
The laughter and the fun,
The gathering round the radio
Each night when work is done.
The Sunday worship in the church,
The way you bowed in prayer—
How reverently you listened then,
You knew that God was there.
And though your steps may lead you on
To strange lands far away,
There's always a deep yearning to
Return again some day.
Though fortune, fame, be yours in store,
Beneath the sky's blue dome,
You'll never find the happiness
That once you knew at home.

Howard Sheldon Ernst

In August 1915, when Isabel was ready to attend the Orillia Collegiate Institute (OCI), her mother went to Orillia to find a boarding place for her. Chrissie had been boarding with the Glover family but hadn't received the usual certificate after her second year at OCI, so didn't expect to go back. Mrs. McBain, whose husband was a distant relative on the Wallace side and who lived on Mary Street, agreed to take Isabel as a boarder. Before long, Chrissie joined her. The OCI principal, Pick Lily, had her go into third year after all. "But then they did queer things when the war was on," Mom observed. She reasoned it out this way: "Because…many of the older boys had enlisted and there weren't as many of the younger ones coming along, they didn't have a very big group to put into the third year and the fourth year, so they put them both together. And the junior years, you see, the likes of me, it was getting more and more of them that were finding a way of getting to high school…"

"That winter," Mom said, "there were soldiers all over Orillia." Among them was Willy, who had decided to enlist after his seventeenth birthday in January 1916. He was in the 76th Battalion under Captain McKinley, who had been sent from England to recruit and organize this battalion. Albert Glover, the youngest boy of his family, was also in the 76th Battalion. Two of his brothers had already died in the war. Mr. Glover was quite perturbed that Albert had joined.

If he got killed, then all the Glover boys would be gone. Mrs. Glover often had Albert come home for a meal "...and so when Willy joined in February, Mrs. Glover says, 'You know, you girls should be boarding here, and then Willy could come with Albert and we could all be together'." In early March, Chris and Isabel went to live with the Glover family. The 76th Battalion left in April on a train loaded with high-spirited young men, waving to the huge crowd of Orillians at the station to see them off. Isabel was there with her family to say goodbye to Willy. Over eighty years later, in a newspaper article published in the Orillia *Packet & Times* on November 9, 1996, Isabel described Willy this way: "He really had a wonderful, quick way of thinking...of getting things through his mind." This quality and his physical fitness as a young farm boy perhaps led to his job when he went overseas: a message runner on the front. "He looked older," Isabel had stated. "You could never tell that he was [seventeen]. He was tall for his age too. You should have seen the send-off," she told the *Packet & Times* reporter, describing the people packed shoulder to shoulder beside the railway track (Size, 3).

On October 1, 1916, Willy wrote this letter from the front to his sisters Chrissie and Viola:

Dear Viola and Chrissie, Received both your letters and parcel and as time is very precious here I will have to write a double header letter in return.

The parcel was in jake condition not a thing crushed or spoiled. The only fault was it went too quick.

I got a parcel from the Orillia Red Cross girls last time out of the trenches and this time my share of what the money bought that the Orillia people have sent to Capt. Mert Plunkett so that's what it is to belong to a town like Orillia.

By the way, I met Mert the other night at the Y.M.C.A. He and his younger brother put on a concert with the assistance of the audience and he certainly knows how to entertain the boys.

I suppose the Canadian papers will be full of the great work that the Canadians have been doing here and I don't think that they can exaggerate it much for it was certainly wonderful work and a lot of inconvenience and privation. In one case a number of us spent three days without anything to eat or drink. Something that never happened to the Canadians before and not likely to again and the good work is continuing.

And now about writing letters you may think that I am not writing enough but it is impossible to write more. In 24 days we spent 18 in the trenches and five on the march so that just left one day and that's the day I wrote to Jessie so if you get a field post card don't be surprised we can send them almost anytime.

Well girls. I guess I had better finish for this time. These are not much letters but wait till I go home then you will get the news of the great war. Christmas you know.

Your loving brother Willie

Isabel, just a year and a half younger than Willy and his faithful playmate and workmate when they were growing up, kept that letter her entire life. Two weeks before the letter from Willy arrived at their home, her family at the farm received a telegram informing them of Willy's death. A week after writing the letter, he had died almost instantly from a chest wound in the Battle of Somme. Kate and Will had just arrived home from a holiday in the West, but it was Duncan who phoned Isabel and Chris in Orillia to tell them. Since the long Thanksgiving weekend was over, she did not get home from high school until Christmas. What a terribly difficult time. Unable to be home with her family, her heartache must have been unbearable.

Mom spoke little of her emotions at any time, but in later years did tell her niece Kathleen that good friends were a help that fall. She also revealed that she got "help from my previous decision"—her embracing of the Christian faith in the act of confirmation on Thanksgiving Sunday, 1915—and spoke of her "spiritual growth" in the faith during her mourning time. This response to her family's tragedy no doubt fed into her increasing ability to turn the clouds of life inside out and find a brighter outlook within. Still, some of the cloud remained throughout her life. How they came into her possession I do not know, but I know that she loved Willy so much that she needed to keep the two letters of condolence that her father had received. Private Tom C. Kennard thoughtfully wrote on October thirty-first a letter (Appendix C) describing the details he knew of Willy's death. Its merciful speed must have been some consolation to her and the rest of the family. Will also received a touching letter from Captain McKinley (Appendix D), who had been promoted to Major. He spoke about Willy's enthusiasm for service and his bravery. Mom read his letter over the phone to the *Packet & Times* reporter in 1996. "Beach still gets choked up with emotion reading the letter…" (Size, 3) he wrote. Little wonder. With the death of Willy, she had lost one of her best friends.

Isabel and Chris had left the Glover's home in June 1916, Isabel to go home for the holiday, Chris because she had finished her high school education. Albert Glover had also gone with the 76th Battalion in April and that, Isabel believed, led to Mr. Glover's stroke in 1917. Because he couldn't talk and was in a wheelchair, Mrs. Glover needed help. Chris and Viola were both home with Kate, so Chris went to Orillia to help Mrs. Glover. Isabel wasn't sure whether Chris was paid for this; she thought possibly not, considering the generosity of her parents. This arrangement, however, turned out to be a short one. Chris' friend, Olive Jackson, was working on munitions, so Chris took a job in one of the munitions factories. Many of Orillia's factories had been converted for this purpose. Brian Bethune clearly identified the importance of the munitions and other war-related factories when he wrote in a 2004 *Maclean's* article: "The Imperial Munitions Board became Canada's largest business, with 250,000 workers, 40,000 of them women, producing shells, aircraft and ships" (48). That summer, Chris began boarding with Mr. and Mrs. Kilbank, who lived across the street from her friend Olive's family. Isabel had boarded with the Christmans that school year. Because Mrs. Christman's first baby, Lorne, arrived in August, Isabel needed another place. When she returned to Orillia in September 1917, she joined Chris at the Kilbank home. Chris continued working on munitions while Isabel attended OCI.

What did Isabel do, besides attend class and study? She described a party with some young people her age that Lillian Grant had invited her to. "I'd be seventeen. And we'd just have a little party: imagine (now they'd snort at you) spin the pie plate on its edge and musical chairs, and things like that. They didn't give prizes and that sort of thing. If a person didn't succeed, he/she'd have to get up and ask a riddle, or perform some entertainment." She also socialized through her church, St. Andrew's Presbyterian. "The group that met from ten to eleven, the Christian Endeavour, was a mixed group." They gathered in the new education wing where they had a meeting, as Young People's groups did then, followed by contests such as scrambled words. They all learned how to lead a prayer and to read scripture from the Bible in public. Someone delivered a religious message, too. These activities no doubt made a significant contribution to the spiritual growth that Mom said she'd experienced after Willy's death.

Although her spending money was restricted, Will always gave her some at the start of each semester. He did the family's business because her mother was occupied looking after the house and all the children. Besides, Kate hadn't had time to continue her schooling after they were married, the way Will did. In the evenings he read the *Toronto Star* newspaper or went to the Farmers' Grange, a club in Gamebridge. Will always gave Isabel the money saying, 'When you go to Orillia, you put that in the bank, and then when you need it, you go and get it'. "He gave me enough for board, and there was a little extra for spending, and I was to be going to Sunday School and church, so I'd have to have a little for collection… They never were stingy, or tried to keep track of what I was doin' with the money. But he says, 'All I ask of you is that you keep track of how you spend it'. And so I had a little book, and I put it all down there." This allowance proved to be sufficient. "I could go along quite well with any of the rest of them, even Lil Berry, and she seemed to have as much or more than anybody else in the group that I was with." They had their "little bits of fun", Mom assured me when I interviewed her about this part of her life. After school, she and her girlfriends often went to the Greek restaurant just down Mississauga Street from George's Drugstore, which was on the southeast corner of Peter and Mississauga Streets. "We'd go in there and have a piece of pie and ice cream." The owner was very generous with his ice cream servings for the teenage girlfriends. Sometimes they bought candy at Carter's Candy Palace.

A new girls' physical education teacher arrived at OCI in 1917, a woman ahead of her time. She got the girls playing basketball. "At that time, the girls weren't near the gym… We never even got to look into it, let alone play in it. The boys had everything in the gym. But then, in the fall when she came, we could play basketball outside, so we did." When the teacher thought they were reasonably good, they went through the grades playing against one another, until the team that Kathleen Jackson, Lillian Berry and Isabel were on (they were all friends and in the same age group) came out the winners. The three girlfriends worked together in this way: "I was at the basket end, because I was long in the legs and the arms, to get the ball in the basket. And Kathleen Jackson was my partner because she was a little bit hefty and was shorter. She'd just shoulder the other people away and get hold of the ball, give it to me and then I could reach up and put it in the basket." Lil Berry, tall like Isabel, played center. Lil could assist Kathleen and Isabel at the one end of the court. The teacher arranged to have this team and the other top one play off at the YMCA on a Friday night. When Isabel's team became the school champions, "The teacher wanted us to go on and fight Barrie or some of the others around, but the principal says, 'Nope, they're here to learn. They're here for academic purposes, not for sport purposes'. And so we never did get to do that. But I was well enough satisfied." She knew she and her team-mates had scored more than one victory. When my brother and I (and even the grandchildren) were growing up, none of us had any inkling that Mom had experienced this pleasure and distinction. She didn't usually boast about her accomplishments. I was delighted to get this detailed information on tape and to imagine her slim five and a half-foot body careening toward the basketball hoop, dark brown hair flowing behind her, as she made a successful shot.

Socially at OCI, an 'At Home', the equivalent of today's high school prom, was usually held. An invitation Isabel received as a graduate of OCI appears in Appendix E. But "In 1918, we didn't have the February prom because the war was on, and that was cancelled completely, so we didn't have anything particularly exciting at school. Anyway, after Easter (and things were getting kind of serious in Europe at that time)…the news that we seemed to get out was a little different from when my brother Willy was writing in 1916. He was thinking he'd be home for Christmas; they were making speed and headway getting to the end of what they wanted to get to." Early in 1918, the news was black. "Things were worse and we needed more help and all that kind of thing. And things were bad all over the world, sort of. So the Department of Education decided that anyone that wasn't writing the departmental examinations (those that were set by the Department of Education, which were every second year at that time) could leave school after Easter when the farm work started, if you had good enough marks…" The provincial government realized how badly help was needed on both the farms and in the munitions factories. Isabel would try her departmental examinations the following June, and her marks qualified her to leave. "So I came home and worked on the farm as a farmerette (we were called). A friend of mine, Helen Burnett, she didn't have a farm to go to. She lived in Orillia with her aunts, and so she went to Hamilton and worked in the canning factory, canning vegetables. I remember when she came back to school in September, she never wanted to see another tomato."

Isabel was home from the first of May to the first of September 1918. Her summary: "What a summer that was!" Brother Reid was now in the army; Willy was gone forever. Duncan was married and had his own farm and family. Her father didn't have a son of his own to help with the farming. So he hired a man whom my mother described as "that fool of a hired man". With so many men involved in the war, he was the only one Will could get. The Wallace family knew him because his family had moved into the community around the start of the war. Although this man wasn't exceptionally bright, "he had pretty good muscles". So he pitched the hay, which is heavy. When a wagonload of hay came in from the field, he put the hay into 'sling' ropes in bundles, which were hauled up by pulley to a track in the roof of the barn and dropped into the haymow. There were four big bundles in each load, and these had to be moved around to distribute them evenly. Isabel and Minnie, also working as a farmerette, did this moving.

And then there was the hoeing. "Father wouldn't let us hoe the turnips. We could do the potatoes and corn. And we spent a lot of days hoeing corn, I can tell you… It was all horses in those days—no tractors. So with the horse-drawn cultivator, Father would go between the rows of the corn and then we had to hoe between the corn stalks and [make] sure we got rid of the weeds that the horse-drawn thing didn't." She and Minnie usually wore hats and long-sleeved clothing when they worked in the fields. Minnie, who would be continuing on the farm when Isabel had to leave in September and probably helping with the grain harvest, bought a farmerette suit from Eaton's catalogue. The material was cotton, not quite as heavy as jeans material, with bloomers at the bottom. Isabel wore bloomers and a middy.

Other outdoors jobs included feeding the calves. "And one thing we had a lot of fun about… (Boys and girls nowadays don't seem to get as much fun out of working as we used to.) The calves had a little pasture field of their own. And when the milk was separated to get the cream to send to the creamery for the butter, then that skim milk was fed these calves. You put it in a pail and took it just outside the barn a little piece and they would put their heads through a place in the fence that was fixed on purpose to put their heads into the pail and drink the milk." They had about six calves to feed, all of them named after generals and majors in the army. The calves were easily trained. The youngest ate first. "You'd be surprised how those calves [behaved]," Mom told me. "They weren't bunting at one other at all. And they knew when we came with those pails, the little fellas came up first, and then the next ones… They kind of knew their names, too."

In late August, the big field job was to cut the grain with a binder. "Well, my father's binder wasn't terribly old, but it was old enough that it hadn't a sheaf carrier on it. Since he'd bought this binder, they'd added a sheaf carrier that would carry so many sheaves to make a stook. And he ordered one from the company but of course those orders were all set aside to look after the war orders first. It was so long in coming that we had the harvest pretty well over before we got it." When they'd nearly got the wheat done, the hired man noticed that the spokes of his buggy wheel were loose. He took the buggy to the blacksmith's shop to get the spokes tightened because the tires were steel, not rubber. At the end of a particular week, he was scheduled to pick up his buggy. At that time, when a man hired out to a farmer the agreement was that some wages would be held back until the agreed-on time was up, helping to ensure the farmer had the hired man when needed. But "My Father was the kind that paid as he went. And he wanted his hired man to have his wages, so that he would have enough to pay the blacksmith for his work. So my Father, he really went overboard and gave him quite a bit of money. He didn't keep much back. In fact, it was so little that [the hired man] never did come back. I can see him yet, leading the horse down the road to go to Gamebridge to get the buggy. And that's the last we saw of him."

Looking on the bright side, as my mother inevitably did, that's how Minnie and she got the job of stooking. The hired man wasn't there to do it. He wasn't missed. He'd just sat on the fence smoking while he watched Isabel and Minnie use the pitchfork to pick up the grain from the outside swath around the field. She and Minnie devised their own system for stooking. "I thought it was quite a bright idea," Mom told me with satisfaction—a surprisingly immodest comment from her. She and Minnie each used her pitchfork to pick up a sheaf so that the heads (the grain) of the sheaf were up. Then they decided where to place the stook, putting the two heads together and the butts on the ground. They didn't make round stooks like the ones in Western Canada, but placed them in long lines, almost like a fence. They also had to arrange the sheaves in the barn so that the threshers could easily pick them out to put in the threshing machine when they came to do that job. To help him finish the harvest, her dad hired a man with his own farm who worked out by the day. Mom didn't view this time as a hardship partly because "In the holidays, there wasn't much going on, you see. People didn't have traveling holidays; they were too busy." Farmers and others worked on, although some people had cottages in Beaverton where they'd spend the summer with their families. "Certainly, on the farm, we worked as farmerettes. You know, the Princesses Elizabeth and Margaret Rose did it too." There was a pride and an honour in contributing to the community this way.

Isabel returned to her studies at OCI in September 1918. Those who'd been doing war work were caught up on their schoolwork by most teachers. Pick Lily didn't bother trying to get Isabel caught up in Latin, but this didn't matter much to her because she didn't need Latin for Normal School entrance—just French. She thought she'd study Latin at home afterwards (it was needed for university entrance at the time) but never did. This bit of information made me wonder if that's why she was so upset with me when I chose the business course over Latin in grade 10.

Because the Kilbanks had sold their house and moved into an apartment in downtown Orillia the summer of 1918, Chrissie had a new boarding place—with the Prices on Mississauga Street. Isabel joined Chris there. They'd been there less than a month when they learned that their brother Reid had been killed in action on the Hindenburg Line on August 23. Remembering how long Isabel had had to wait before joining her family when Willy was killed, Chris took the lead and said, 'We're goin' home'. "And so we both went home. Of course, I had to come back. She didn't have to go back, any more than she was supposed to be working on the munitions." Although she made no further comment when telling me this, I sensed my mother's deep regret that, for the third time in her short life, she had missed the full grieving process with her family.

Isabel's well-loved brother, Willy, in April 1916 just before he boarded the train in Orillia for active service. He was killed in France that October.

Reid, Isabel's next-oldest brother, who died in battle at the Hindenburg line in France, August 23, 1918.

At the end of October, the Spanish Flu hit Orillia hard. *The Canadian Encyclopedia* states that the Spanish Influenza "…killed some 21 million people, including about 50,000 Canadians. It demonstrated a perverse tendency to kill the young and hearty" (McGinnis, 881). Mom described the effects on one of her friends, Verva Jackson: "Verva had been home for the Thanksgiving weekend, and she got back to Toronto and she turned so sick. And her mother went to Toronto to see about things and brought her home… But she died because it was the first of the flu and they just went down like flies. It was awful. Really, it was terrible if you lived through it and [were] mixed up with it at all." Another friend lost; another cloud to search through for some silver lining. "Terrible" is surely an understatement of her emotional turmoil. While munitions manufacturing continued during the epidemic, otherwise "Everything was closed—the churches, the theatres—there was nothing, absolutely nothing open, that was public". Churches became hospitals. The layout of St. Andrew's Presbyterian Church, she said, was suited to caring for really sick patients because of the separate classrooms around the balcony. The Sunday School room was the same, while the middle was completely open, a circumstance she described as "just perfect". Nobody was looking for perfection. In any public building "Wherever there was a space it was used. Every square inch, I'm tellin' you." Such emphatic language suggests how traumatic my mother's experience was. The deaths of her brothers were bad enough; now she saw devastation right before eyes, and lost a friend as a result. She must have done some quick maturing. The situation provided a severe test of her ability to turn the clouds inside out.

Of course the closures included the Orillia Collegiate Institute. Students were summoned to the assembly hall by their principal. "And Mr. Lily got up and told us that the school would be closed indefinitely and we would go home because of this flu', and they would let us know when it would be re-opened. We were told it was a good idea to get some oil of eucalyptus and put it on our handkerchiefs so that when you had a cold or were blowing your nose you would get those oil of eucalyptus fumes in your system to avoid the bug that was going to give you the flu'." Isabel and her friends followed this advice. Soon, however, she went home to the farm where she could work and be safer—and where her parents didn't have to pay for her board. She moved right into picking turnips, which she loved to do. Mom recalled vividly for me the day the Armistice was signed, the eleventh of November. "When the passenger train went through our place, the train crew threw off the paper to tell us. That's how we found out, because there were no telephones then in our area. Minnie and I went down to the school and rang the school bell, rang the school bell—they were closed too, you see, there were a lot of schools closed… for the flu'." Then they marched home from the school singing all the patriotic songs they knew. What a bittersweet celebration, as they reflected on the deaths of their two vigorous brothers in this horrific war.

With the other students, she returned to OCI and the usual exams before Christmas. "The teachers were very good. They worked hard to get the whole curriculum looked after before the [school] year was up." So in one calendar year, she had to catch up twice. "After Christmas, things were more or less back to normal at school, and the boys were returning from overseas, not too quickly, because after all it took about four years to get them there, and there was a lot of planning and work to get them back [on the boats]. And they had to be careful about mines and things in the water." Again, no 'At Home' prom took place. Students and teachers were all busy going over the curriculum set by the Department of Education in Toronto, in preparation for June examinations. The Department of Education decided to give students an extra three or four weeks, because of the closure during the influenza outbreak. So exams were scheduled for the middle of July—when it was "good hot weather", Mom dryly observed. Early in February 1919, Isabel was told that Mrs. Glover wished she'd come and live with her. Mr. Glover had died and she was lonely. Since the war and munitions manufacturing were over, Chris had gone home. Isabel was alone at the Prices. She discussed the situation with them, then returned to live with Mrs. Glover, which is where she was when she had to study in July. She liked the house, where she could study anywhere she chose. "Her house was quite an airy one when we were upstairs," so that area was her choice. Often the band concert in Victoria Park provided background music. "Not that it bothered me," she quickly clarified. " It maybe helped me, because the music was good; it wasn't like this shivaree stuff you have to listen to now."

In the meantime, Isabel knew that St. Andrew's Presbyterian Church didn't have a Canadian Girls in Training (CGIT) or a camp of their own. She was pleased when she and another girl in her Sunday School class, Norma McLeod, were chosen to represent St. Andrew's at the Geneva Park CGIT camp across Lake Couchiching from Orillia. She went there before going home for holidays and to wait for the results of her exams, which were marked in Toronto. The resulting diploma gave her the equivalent of grade twelve. She didn't need 'fifth form' (year) for Normal School, where she would get her training to teach elementary school. This, Mom told me in her understated way, was one time she wholeheartedly appreciated the holiday season because it had been such a busy year with so many significant changes.

Mom seldom talked to me about her 'boyfriends', but she did say that she went to a dance with Tom Farrell, a neighbour boy—and a Catholic—at Kirkfield that summer. "It was the Eldon Station baseball boys put on that dance, in order to make money to buy new uniforms." Those boys hadn't been old enough to go to war. The event started with a quilting for the girls in the afternoon; the boys came in the evening for dancing. Isabel's first cousin, Florence (McFadyen) Francis, described in a letter to me another 'date' Tom and Isabel had that summer. My mother, by the way, would likely disapprove of the word 'date' attached to these outings. I suspect that she wasn't serious about a romantic relationship. And I wonder what her Scots Presbyterian family thought of her going out with a Catholic boy. Florence wrote: "Bolsover Sunday School used to take boat trips. So this time it was an excursion to Barrie, down the canal, and across Lake Simcoe. As you know, Lake Simcoe can get very rough and a good many people were sick. But the main story is that [Isabel] was escorted on that trip by the best-looking guy around. His name was Tom Farrell, one of their neighbours." She didn't mention whether Isabel got sick or not, but she did recall the condition of the captain. "When we got back to Bolsover the captain was drunk and ran us onto some sand. So some of the men on shore, including our Uncle John, came out in a rowboat to get us off the boat."

As Mom reflected with me on those 'teen years', she decided they had been good. "It had quite an influence on my life, to be in Orillia for those [years]. It couldn't help but be. At first when I went, it was kind of lonely, being used to having so many around. But then, you see, we'd got kind of acquainted with Chrissie's friends, the Grants. And Mrs. Glover was great to get us to go [there]." Soon she'd made many friends of her own. When Lil Berry and Thelma Littlejohn came to the train station to 'send her off' at the end of high school, she felt very sad. Many of these high school friendships did continue. For years she corresponded with several of the girls. She treasured and kept dozens of photos that portrayed the companionship she and her close friends had enjoyed.

School chums at Orillia Collegiate Institute (left to right) Lillian Berry, Helen Burnett Jessie Greenland, and Isabel Wallace.

Mrs. Glover, at whose home Isabel boarded in some of her Orillia years.

Despite her own bleak times and the clouds that had darkened everyone's lives, Mom could see the benefits of her teen experiences. She realized she had become responsible for herself in every way: handling money, making decisions, disciplining herself to study for exams. She was ready for the next step into full adulthood.

CHAPTER FIVE: I Was Born a Teacher

My Kingdom

Beside the quiet road it stands,
My little school, half hid by trees
That stretch out friendly beckoning hands,
Cooling hot cheeks by kindly breeze.

Sending its summons far afield,
The lofty bell my touch obeys;
In answer to the message pealed,
The children come down dusty ways.

Wee dimpled hands their treasures hold,
Stray flowerets gathered by the way,
Daisies and dandelions gold,
Wild roses, buttercups so gay.

Thus do my subjects homage prove,
And seal their gifts with sweet caress;
I send a silent prayer above,
That God my dear ones richly bless.

Before them lies the busy day,
Each minute to my purpose planned;
Their many tasks, their times of play,
At my behest allowed or banned.

The years will take them far from me,
May strength be theirs to bear life's load,
And treasured in our memory,
The school beside the quiet road.

Lillian Morley

When her father had asked her in 1914, 'How would you like to go to high school and become a teacher?' Isabel felt "… surprise and delight. Well, if you could've seen inside of me, and how the reaction was… I have no idea what it looked like on the outside, but I know what the inside felt like. How would I *like* to? That was the very thing I'd *love* to do! But I hadn't really said to myself, 'I'm going to be a teacher'."

As she looked back on her life more than eight decades later, however, she realized "I was born a teacher". She had often organized her two little sisters to play school. "I was so selfish, I wanted to do the teaching all the time." Her mother had observed this obsession, because "poor Mother had to settle so many arguments when we were kids—Who was going to be the teacher?—when we played school". Her youngest sister Jessie hadn't even gone to school when they started this play and she wanted a turn to teach, but "I'd get so impatient with her, because we weren't doing things the way we should". No doubt Kate had talked to Will about these playtime episodes. Will was a 'wonder' for his upbringing and time. A country lad, he made sure that each of his girls had a profession. Annie became a dressmaker; Viola, a milliner; Chrissie, a nurse; Isabel, a teacher; Minnie a bookkeeper; Jessie, a nurse. His formal education was limited, but he subscribed to the *Toronto Star* and read it faithfully. So progressive was Will that he even voted for Agnes McPhail, the only woman elected to Canada's parliament in 1921.

The First World War period was really the beginning of women getting into teaching, Mom told me. Only a few women were in the profession at the turn of the century. A married woman was not allowed to teach. "They just didn't hire them, because they figured they'd be wanting—now we call it maternity leave. And what's the use in hiring a teacher and she gets pregnant and you'd have to do something about it? And who were you going to get? Anybody that I know that was married when I was first teaching was somebody like Alice Alcock ..." Alice was a friend of Isabel's who taught at the school near the farm where Isabel lived the rest of her life after her marriage. Carling, Alice's husband, couldn't earn a steady income because he'd had one hand cut off in an accident. They were childless. In Alice's case, "The community around hired you. You taught where your husband lived, and he wasn't able. You wouldn't look at the paper and say, 'I think I'll apply for that school...and send out an application'." How fortunate for my mother that times and attitudes were changing. How fortunate, too, that her parents were (as she often mentioned to me) so sensible.

After she had finished high school in 1919, Isabel went to the Peterborough Normal School. "To go to Peterborough we had to get on the train at Beaverton, of course, because I had a trunk and had to get that all looked after...That train came from Midland, and it went as far as Blackwater. And then I had to change at Blackwater and get on the train that went to Peterborough." Isabel could have had room and board with a distant relative, but the Normal School wouldn't allow male and female students to board at the same place. These relatives had a son of their own at home, and they boarded three other boys. That dilemma was easily worked through. She was fortunate to get a good recommendation for a boarding house run by a mother and daughter, both widows. The daughter's two boys attended public school. The father had been killed in a farm accident; the mother had no special training except as a housewife. As Mom told me this, knowing I would be writing her biography, she insisted, "Now I'd like you to put in that word 'special', because I'm not belittling a housewife. A housewife's experience and training is a very important thing. So that was the *special* training she had. And she was a good housekeeper, and delivered good meals and everything." The home was an easy walk to the Normal School. Having her friend, Belle MacInnis, board with her somewhat eased the wrench of leaving home again. As well, "I'd got sort of hardened to it, going to Orillia, so that I didn't seem to mind. And there were two other girls who boarded there, from Fenelon Falls. And they just took us in as a part of the family. If they were having a cup of tea before they'd go to bed, they'd call upstairs, 'We're having a cup of tea' –and usually onion sandwiches (Spanish onions)!" Often Isabel and the other boarders joined them. "They were awfully good to us in every way, and we enjoyed being there."

Teacher training at Normal School included the basic subjects we know today, but some we do not. Each student had a small garden to care for, in an area marked off into plots. With her assigned partner, Isabel hoed and cared for the plants, a project reflecting the importance of agriculture at the time. She had a manual for agriculture, which she gave to her grandson Ed. She gave her sewing manual to a woman who'd made some flannel nightgowns for her when she was ninety-seven. Mom had planned to throw the sewing manual away, but every time she approached the garbage with it, she said to herself, 'I just can't. It's really such a wonderful little book'. When the nightgown seamstress was offered the book and looked inside, she said, 'I certainly *am* interested in this. Isn't this great?'" The various stitches, the needlework, and the instructions for turning corners intrigued her. Normal School students also took cooking. So they learned all the household arts—which were supposed to be taught in public schools. Isabel didn't purchase the expensive child psychology textbook for Normal School, a decision she later regretted. Mr. Kome, who had prepared the writing practice/copy book Isabel used when she was in elementary school and who ran a business college in Peterborough, taught her writing. Their practice book included sayings similar to those her mother Kate habitually used, such as 'Work while you work/Play while you play/That's the way/To be happy and gay'. The student was required to copy the saying on the page below. "And therefore," Mom commented, "you were teaching the children something, as well as how to write, and that's what I claim about a reader, and it's a downright shame to be without a reader." She recalled how "...the little kids, once they got their first reader...carried it home so they could read at home...when I was first teaching. Nowadays, I don't know. They don't even teach them integrity any more, it seems to me." She did concede that things were getting better when she taped this interview in 1997. Even at age ninety-seven, she had a great passion for children, education and teaching.

The Normal School students did most of their practice teaching in Peterborough, with one session in a rural school. Isabel missed her session, which was scheduled for after New Year's. She'd had an ingrown toenail. Because her doctor had removed the entire toenail during the Christmas holiday, she missed ten days of school. She was more than a little surprised that "They never, ever, came to me about it. If they'd looked up my history—I had already taught in a rural school [while the teacher went to Orillia for a hockey game]. Oh that was the good times...when the community was itself, and it knew what was goin' on." And in her characteristic manner, Mom temporarily digressed to this different, but related, story. When she was in elementary school, she and classmate Mabel Ainsworth got to teach when the actual teacher, Annie Murray, went one Friday with Willy and Viola to Orillia for the weekend hockey game, on the CPR 'stub line' that cut through the Wallace farm. She and Mabel opened the school Monday morning. Miss Murray came back mid-day on the train. "So I had my experience." A total of one day! Mom laughed heartily, then rhetorically asked me, "Wasn't it nice that we could do that? That's human and decent, not this, 'Well who do you think's paying you to run to a hockey game, anyway? Whose money's paying that? I'm paying my taxes and I want the teacher in her place'." She delivered these questions in as deep and grumbly a voice as she could muster. She described one incident from the practice teaching that she did complete: "I was teaching in one school, and I had grade eight. I was supposed to teach the Fathers of Confederation." When she got through the lesson and the teacher had come up and dismissed the children, she was criticized for calling one of the men 'fellow', rather than by name. In Mom's opinion, that was a way to avoid repetition and boredom. "You see, all these men you had to talk about, you'd get so sick and tired of the name and what they did, and all that kind of thing, and that's the way it was in the book pretty well." A less self-confident person might have felt 'squashed' by the supervising teacher's petty comment. Isabel just moved on.

Sometime during that year at Normal School, when she had time to reflect, "... it came to me—all of a sudden it just hit me right between the eyes—here I am in Peterborough, Mother and Dad sending money, giving me money, to pay my board and keep me in clothing and all that. And I had to buy books there, and Chrissie was in Toronto training for a nurse." Although student nurses had their food, uniforms, bed and laundry paid for, Chris did need some financial help with street clothes and spending money. Will and Kate also were paying for Minnie's board while she attended high school in Orillia. Jessie was in public school, not working except on the farm. Viola was at home with her mother. Again, like the branch of a tree, another story grew from the main stalk. Mom recalled how one Christmas "[Mother and Dad] bought for [Viola] and I've often thought that was really nice that they did it—and I was wishing I could've controlled myself—they bought her the fur collar (It was wolf, I think, by the colour of it) and a muff, you know". Nearly all the girls around Bolsover had this combination, which was available in Eaton's catalogue. "A well-dressed young lady, that's what she had. And I remember it was lovely. There was always something like that going on, that you could see that they were looking after their family." Then back to the main story she went: Isabel decided she would repay Will and Kate for their investment in her education. When she came home for Christmas from her first teaching position, she gave her dad a hundred dollar bill. "And I said to Dad, you can pay my life insurance premium [which was around twenty dollars] and keep the rest for having paid my board all these years." So every year she did this and "I didn't wait for Christmas".

I wondered what my mother had meant when she said she wished she could have controlled herself, regarding Viola's furs. Did she feel a little envy for Viola and her furs? Did she feel this was an un-Christian emotion to experience? Did she feel especially guilty because this sister had died in Saskatoon, Saskatchewan, of acute appendicitis in March 1929 or because she herself had a muff that she had received in 1915? Perhaps the fur on her muff was not as fine as Viola's had been. I never did see that part of the muff. But Mom kept the 'pillow' portion of it until the day she died. It was small, and useful for putting between her knees to sleep, when she had lost so much weight that the bones seemed to grind together. While she was in Soldiers' Memorial Hospital in Orillia in 1999, one of the nurses was fascinated to see and hear about this muff that Isabel had owned for nearly eighty-five years. And I was delighted to see this nurse take a personal interest in my mother, who had so many fascinating stories to tell those willing to take a little time to listen—and to listen thoughtfully enough to derive from them the message that the story often subtly delivered.

Near the end of her year at Normal School in 1920, the twenty-fourth of May holiday, Isabel and her roommates couldn't go home. To celebrate the occasion, they rode the one-line streetcar from downtown to the outer edge of Peterborough. They went to the end of the line, enjoyed the park in the woods, got on the streetcar and came back. That's all. But for the country girl, Isabel, "It was quite a ride". A day or two later, the little boys at their boarding house broke out with measles. Quarantines for such communicable diseases were still in effect. The boys' mother was smart. She didn't let the authorities know that she had boarders, just got them out quickly to her sister's home down the street, where Isabel and the others spent about three weeks. None of the boarders got measles.

Isabel had written some of her Department of Education "Second Class Professional Examinations" in April, including history, science of education, literature and advanced reading, and school management. Appendix F shows the school management exam. June exams included English grammar and composition, geography, and arithmetic. It was time to celebrate. "To the best of my knowledge, every year, our farewell to Peterborough Normal School was a boat trip from Peterborough to the Kirkfield Liftlocks. To Belle MacInnis and I, liftlocks was 'old hat'." Most of the newly minted teachers, however, had never been on the canal with all its gates that had to be opened and shut. "That was our last fling, our last goodbye. We never went back to the school. There was no graduation, because there was too much war stuff. We'd had no graduation at high school either." Over the summer at home in Thorah Township she kept up her 'friendship' with the handsome Tom Farrell. Appendix G shows the programme from the event she attended with him in Beaverton on July first that year. Was it deep patriotism or sentimentalism that prompted her to keep this programme for the rest of her life?

The little setbacks at Normal School didn't deter Isabel. She got her first teaching position at the one-room rural school in Roseville, a village about three miles west of Uxbridge. (See 1915 map of Uxbridge Township). Isabel described her arrival in August, 1920, in this way: "I came on the train and I got off at Uxbridge station. George Hockley was the secretary-treasurer of the School Board. There were three trustees. And a trustee could do the double job. He didn't make a bad job of it, considering all things." George had a Chevy car and a big family. This included a son Dave and a daughter Charlotte. "Those two came in this Chevy car to take me where I was going to board. And they didn't have trunks in the cars in those days, so my [steamer] trunk was put in the back seat, and I sat on Charlotte's knee in the front seat because the seats weren't wide enough to put three in, and Dave did the driving." She must have been impressed by this auspicious beginning to her career. There were few cars in the country then, even though the area was fairly close to Toronto and the businesses related to Lake Simcoe.

Before she was leaving home, while still applying for a position, her teasing brother Duncan would say, "Oh you'll likely get out there somewhere, you'll be way back in the bush and never see anybody 'till Christmas time." As they drove west on the Uxbridge road, she looked up the fifth concession to the north and saw that it wasn't much more than a trail. Ahead of them stood a 'great big hill'. She wondered whether anybody had driven over the road for the last two weeks. And she must have wondered whether Duncan was right. They got up the big hill, however, turned north onto the fourth concession of Uxbridge Township, and passed the Roseville School, S. S. # 10, Uxbridge Township, to go to her boarding house at Garnet and Ruth Smalley's. "When we turned in that lane, on her verandah [Ruth] had a three-cornered shelf situation where she had plants. And there were these geraniums blooming and other plants that made this bright, you know. I remember what a boost it gave me inside to see those lovely plants there. It looked as though I was getting back into the world again." Later in life, she confessed, "I often would tell myself, I should've shown more appreciation to Ruth and Garnet Smalley…" Perhaps she did, without realizing. Certainly Ruth, who took a turn pouring tea, seemed delighted to be part of Isabel's ninetieth birthday party seventy years later.

As an introduction to the cost of her board at the Smalley's, Mom recalled how her parents were so thankful to get the Beaver School and have their family and all the neighbours' children educated properly that they said they would board the teacher for three dollars a week. "Now that was everything," she explained. "The washing was done. She had her soap to wash herself and towels to dry on. Her bedding was changed and all that. And she had her food. And if the buggy was going anywhere, to town or to church or wherever, she could go along too, if she wanted to." Isabel paid the Smalleys one dollar a day or seven dollars a week unless she went home for the weekend. Not long before that, teachers had traveled around from one home to another within the school section. I know she was grateful to avoid that sort of situation. How could a teacher possibly be sufficiently organized and have enough time to do a conscientious job in such a temporary arrangement?

Isabel had written to the school board in August to ask if she was to open the school on the first day of September or after Labour Day. At the time, not all schools opened on the same date, although the book of regulations stated September first. The board replied that she could suit herself. She decided she had no choice but to declare September first the first day of school.

"That's how I got caught," she noted. "But I was always thankful afterwards because you see it was a Thursday and I taught Thursday and Friday. And then I had Saturday and Sunday to get my head squared around and get a timetable worked out, and that sort of thing. It was really a blessing in disguise." This task gave her a new appreciation for her Orillia Collegiate Institute principal. "And before I got through with my timetable, I said that Mr. Lily (and he got quite a high salary as we thought of it in those days) earned his first thousand dollars when he was wrestling with the timetable." As she worked on it, she was "...part of the time kind of lonely, thinkin' about the fun they were having at home. The other girls would be home from Toronto and, you know, Duncan would be at home and the Matheson boys often would be down there. A lot of people would be around for the holiday weekend." But she did what was necessary at the start of the career she had chosen and that had chosen her.

While boarding at the Smalley's, Isabel often went with the family to Sandford church or to shop in Uxbridge. Garnet's brother Ed took her out a bit, too "but not right away". Often one of his sisters, Bertha or Florence, was with them. But then sometimes "Just he and I would be in the buggy, you see. But I never really had any idea in my head sayin' he was my boyfriend, if you know what I mean. I went for the ride, 'cause he asked me, and I had no other wheels in those days. If you didn't accept an invitation in the community where you were teaching you'd be sitting all the time in the corner." In 1921, Ed's father bought a car, a Grey Dort—"No model T for him. He put a mortgage on the farm to do it." While the car had its benefits for her, she was not impressed by the financial arrangement used to get it. She preferred the less risky financing approach that her parents had demonstrated. But Isabel did learn to drive in the Grey Dort. "And so, it was suggested [by Ed]...well, sit over here and I'll show you how. I don't know how it started. But I was behind the wheel, and he showed me the 'H' [for shifting gears]. And so I did driving enough with it, the odd time—only just very odd—but I knew, and I seemed to take to it..." She said the Grey Dort was fairly easy to drive, with separate pedals for the clutch and brake (unlike the Model T, in which one pedal served both purposes) and a stick shift down near the floor.

She liked her room at the Smalley's house. "That was a lovely warm place because it was a south exposure and all the walls except the one end that had the window in it were inside walls, and they had a lovely box stove right outside the door. It was downstairs, you see." She experienced a marked contrast the next year when she moved after Christmas to Bob and Ethel Hutchinson's, because the Smalleys were expecting a baby and needed the downstairs bedroom, close to water and the heat from the box stove. Mom described this first winter at Bob Hutchinson's as "most terrible". The following story demonstrates just how terrible. One Saturday evening Carling Alcock, Mrs. Hutchinson's half-brother, had gone to a hockey game in Uxbridge with a horse and cutter. "And when he was coming home, it was so cold (You see, Hutchinsons were about three miles from Uxbridge, and then Carling would still have two miles to get home to Siloam) he came in there, when we were all in bed, and put his horse in the stable and came to the door and said that he just was so cold he was afraid he would freeze if he tried to make home. And the horse, he seemed to think, was getting beyond too." Carling said he would sleep on the couch in the kitchen. Isabel's bedroom was off the front room, and the Hutchinson's was off the kitchen. "So Ethel says, 'No, you can get in here with Rob, and I'll go in with Miss Wallace'. So she came in, and I'll be darned, I had on my flannelette nightie, and I had stockings on my feet, and I had what we called a kimono in those days, a heavy thing made out of flannel, on me, and I was in there. Well, I'll be darned, I thought, I'm not going to give my warm nest up. She can get on the other side of the bed, on the other side of me. And so I let her get on the other side of the bed. I thought it'd be good that she'd know how cold it was. They weren't mean about the heat, but they didn't understand." The rooms in those old houses were small, and the bed was placed alongside the window, which meant the wind from the east was right over Mrs. Hutchinson's feet.

She apparently got the message. Soon after, "They got another bed at a sale somewhere—believe it or not, it was a rope bed, but it was very comfortable—and I didn't mind it in the summer. They put me upstairs over the living room. There was a stove down there, but it was an upright stove. They didn't give the heat that these old box stoves gave, you know. But it was all right. It was what was on the market. And the pipe went up. It shouldn't have been too bad, but the house was like a sieve." Their house, on the northwest corner of Roseville, was constructed with board and batten. Typically, Mom gave them the benefit of the doubt: the Hutchinsons had been married only five years, so hadn't had time to do many home improvements.

Isabel's salary for the entire first school year was eight hundred and fifty dollars. The three school board trustees were all local, so "They could make decisions, and they did make decisions. And it was so good at that time, but it'd be a problem nowadays. I'm not complaining about the change there, only that it was such a different way of living," she commented to me in her customary way. "When the taxes were paid in the fall then [the school board] would get their grant from the township, and then they'd pay the teacher at Christmastime for the four months. The Teachers' Federation was trying to get these old country gaffers to pay us by the month, instead of at Christmas, Easter and summer holidays." When she had accepted the offer and the eight hundred and fifty dollar salary, she asked how she would be paid. "I said I'd have to borrow money to go on, to start with, you see, because I had not taught before, and they knew that. So they wrote back and said they'd pay me the end of September. They'd give me the fifty dollars." At Christmas she would get the rest at the rate of eighty dollars a month and at the end of June the remainder owing. She knew she should have been paid more for her position because "They told us at Normal it was around a thousand dollars, and it really should've been, but then I was glad to get a school and get my fingers in, you see, so that I could have experience." Being both clever and a planner, she took a different approach in 1921. When the School Board asked her to stay on, she said she'd like to, but thought she should be paid a thousand dollars, the amount stipulated by the Teachers' Federation. The trustees agreed to pay her one hundred dollars a month. Thinking of the impracticality of receiving a salary for only ten months, she jokingly said to me, "What am I going to do in the other two months? Go to pasture with the old race horses?" She wasn't truly concerned, however, because she could retreat to the Wallace farm. Some teachers went to work at summer resorts to support themselves during those two months. Others went to Toronto or a family's summer cottage as a mother's assistant for the children.

Isabel taught in Roseville for three years. Enrollment averaged between twenty-five and thirty students. She'd arrive at the school at 8:30 a.m. to get organized. She knew, once she got the higher grades busy, she could work with the little ones. "And that's what had me beat at first a bit, because we didn't have very much to work with. It was an old school. They should have had a little more there. They hardly even had a pointer at Roseville, it seemed to me. I'll tell you, for a while it was really something." Her teacher training and personal experience with rural schools did give her an advantage. She had learned from all her teachers, even the bad ones. With so many grades (one to eight) "you had to learn to run classes together a bit, you know, when you could". For example, hygiene (later called health) could be done with grades one to four as a group and grades five to eight as another group. Writing was handled similarly. "We really did do writing then, and you could make out what people were writing. But now you can't make out what they've written." To illustrate, she showed me a letter received in 1997 from a cousin in her late fifties. She could read only about half of it.

The Department of Education encouraged letting some of the older pupils take the younger ones for reading or spelling, but Isabel didn't do that often. "I couldn't seem to work it one way or another, I guess because I never went to school when they did it with me. It seemed to me that I wanted to know what those little ones were doing, even if they were only young ones, you know. And another thing, sometimes you kind've enjoyed the little ones, because that wasn't so serious. It was almost like a rest for you." She managed. She had picked up some good tips in her training. "And of course I remembered in Normal School…(in my own words) when the children have come to school in the morning, they're fresh and their minds are open for things. So mathematics, whatever it'd be, those heavier thinking things, were taught in the morning. [Sometimes] I would give the older ones their spelling words. And I never could understand…why you'd learn to spell all those words in the speller or in your reading lesson, and if you couldn't use them, what was the use of learning to spell them? And so they had dictionaries, and they looked up the meaning of the words, and sometimes they wrote sentences. We did that sort of thing, first thing, for the senior grades." Perhaps partly because of her positive high school physical education experiences, "I always tried to get in a little phys ed., because I thought that was quite important. But you know, they hadn't been used to it at Roseville, and at first it was kind of almost a joke with them. But we kept it up pretty well, just to have a little bit, but not necessarily for very long, just to stir up things." Sometimes the children did exercises in the aisle. Then they had their minds clear and almost rested, ready to complete their work.

She was thankful to have math textbooks for the older pupils. "But you know they didn't for the little ones, like they do now. You had to put everything on the blackboard. It was an awful chore… I often have thought about that. I had quite a bit of [blackboard work] that I had to do that they don't have to do nowadays—it's all ready for you, one way or another." She also had magazines such as *The Canadian Teacher*, "wonderful for the rural schools" because it contained several little sheets and covered all the grades. Another magazine, *The School*, offered updates on education, advertisements of interest to educators, and practical tips. For example, George W. Hoffard, M.A., from the London Normal School, contributed an article called "Agriculture for December", basing his tips on the principle of correlation. The beginning of this article is displayed in Appendix H. Mom said her friend Alice Alcock, who taught for many years at Siloam, the next school west of Roseville, was good at using these resources and providing extras for the children. She taught the children sciences beyond agriculture, and even woodworking—though the latter only to the boys. The girls produced items such as Christmas tree decorations made by crocheting around rubber jar rings. Clearly Mom admired Alice. Our family attended the same church as Alice and her husband Carling, and we visited fairly often in their home. As Alice's pupil, I was a bit uncomfortable, but certainly my mother enjoyed the chance to keep in touch with changes and advancements in the education field.

Her self-image to the contrary, I don't see my mother as a slouch when it came to getting children into hands-on projects. One project she told me about ran in response to the 1921 forest fires in Northern Ontario. "Forests were on fire pretty nearly from one end to the other. It was a terrible fire. We experienced the smoke down here, mind you. They didn't have airplanes and things they could work with, you see, like they do now. So the Red Cross had sent letters around to the different rural schools if they could help out financially for the people that were burnt out. Why, one person that I knew, they had to get down in a well for the fire to pass over them, or they would've been burned… When the fire had passed over, they got out, and everything was destroyed." So when she received the Red Cross letter appealing for help, accustomed to the wartime appeals as she was, she responded eagerly. Still, she weighed the circumstances carefully. She knew that several families had very little to live on. For example, two girls from one family missed school because their mother didn't have flour to make bread for the girls' sandwiches. She considered all the families, asking herself, 'And how could I ask them to bring money to give to the Red Cross?'

Then she realized the people in Northern Ontario needed more than money. "We'll do something—they won't have quilts… This was in the fall. And so I suggested we make a quilt, a 'crazy quilt'. You know, this is what mother used to put us to do when we couldn't walk to Egypt School. It was so stormy, you wouldn't dare go out, you know. You could get lost in a blizzard. And to make these 'crazy quilts', as they were called, you didn't cut the pieces at all. Mother would take the front of a man's work shirt. The back would be all eaten up with the sun and the rain and everything, but the front would be pretty good. And then you'd sew these little pieces of [cotton] print from your aprons and your school dresses onto this patch." When she told me this story in 1998 she still had a quilt that one of the boys had made in 1921 at Roseville. "I couldn't throw it away. Even the boys (not all of the older boys, but some of them), they all took over and made these patches/quilt things." Pupils who had their schoolwork done could work on the quilt. After the patches were all sewn together, she bought the lining and batts, then invited the ladies of the community to come and do the quilting. There was no teacher's room in the school, just an entrance for the boys and one for the girls. In the schoolroom proper, she created a surface for the borrowed quilt frame in one corner by putting boards from the wainscoting on one wall to the other. Fortunately, just the year before, because there were bracket lamps in the new Beaver School, she'd decided a school should have lights. So the children did a programme for the community to raise money for lights. After the ladies had put the quilt in the frame, they worked on it in the evening or on a Saturday.

That's when the inspector decided to come. "And I thought, 'This was down there in the corner, what in the dickens would he think this teacher was doing anyway?'" Mom chuckled heartily at the memory of it all. "I didn't know what he'd say. But he never said a word about it, or else I felt so guilty that I said, 'This is for when our work is done, or in the school at noon hour' (because children would be in at noon hour; there wouldn't be many of them that went home) or recess time." As we were taping these memories, she suddenly seemed to break off discussing the quilt. What follows is a great example of the 'righteous indignation' over injustice (in this case criticism of teachers by people with no knowledge of the profession) that could put my mother into a fury faster than almost any other situation: "But I can tell you a good story for any teacher to know and to carry it on, and don't forget to tell the people that aren't born yet, and tell the people that *are* born to tell the people that aren't born yet. That there were a lot of people that thought a good deal about the teachers, and they wouldn't need to be always printing this, that, and the other how the teachers were overpaid and had this, that, and the other—and all the other trash that they accuse them of now."

Here's the story. "About 9:30 a.m., somebody came to the door and rapped, and I went to the door. And here were two of the ladies that hadn't come [to quilt] the night before. The husband of the one lady was going to Uxbridge with a load of grain to get it chopped for the animals, and the wife says, 'Well, I'll just go over to the school and get off there and go in and do some quilting'. So she called this neighbour a piece down the road…and the two of them came and they quilted. So, when it came time for recess, one of them piped up and says, 'Why you know, Miss Wallace, you never had a minute to yourself all morning'." And how did Miss Wallace react? "Oh dear, did I laugh to myself. And many a time I've laughed since. Did they think that we sat with our hands folded? You see, those poor souls, they didn't know what was going on in school. If some of these critics [nowadays] would get their nose in the place and see what is going on in the schools, they wouldn't be making such foolish statements. You can tell them that story the next time you talk to them," she advised me. As for the quilt—"And where there was kind of a plain patch in the middle, I wrote with India ink 'S.S # 10, Township of Uxbridge School children'." Then the women bound the quilt and sent it to the Red Cross.

To demonstrate that some in the community understood and appreciated a teacher, she told me about an old retired gentleman who lived in one of the houses at the Roseville corner. "There was a little barn with a stable under it, and they had a cow or two. His son was on the home farm, and so he kept a piece for pasture for his cows in the summer, and so he'd bring them up the road [in the fall]—and he'd bring apples to the teacher. It was comical, I thought. Of course, the kids used to bring them, too. But this senior gentleman, you know." Perhaps this man wanted to show his appreciation for how Isabel responded to potato picking time in the community. The older children who missed a few days for this farm task were welcomed back to school without a word. Mom just "worked around it" and made sure that they got caught up.

Another Roseville story captures equally well her feelings for children and their needs. The spring of 1922, a five-year-old boy started coming to school. "Generally, in the country in those days, you didn't start to school until you were six because you had to walk, and some of them had quite a long piece to walk, really, for a child that age. But he didn't have too terribly far to come, and he had these two sisters to come with. And he was forever falling asleep. I didn't bother much with him. I'd been one of a family myself, and I knew that youngsters had to get rested, and it was quite a struggle for him, maybe, starting at five years of age." At the Teachers' Convention in the fall, which she always attended, the inspector asked if the teachers had any questions. "So one young teacher got up and said, 'Well I'd like to know what you could do with a child that's only five years old and starting school and they fall asleep all the time in school with the head on the desk'. Of course, my ears were wide open." The inspector had this to say: 'Just let them have their little rest and when the class is being taught, he'll be with the class, and maybe he'll get something out of it.' "Then he turned to another inspector, 'What do you think about it?' That inspector says, 'I don't know what else you could do, unless you asked the trustees for a cradle'." Mom ended this anecdote by commenting, "Now they're sending them to school at three and four years!" She realized, however, that rest is part of the routine for these young ones, and that the pupil-teacher ratio is now much lower.

These littlest ones weren't her only concern. The following incident speaks volumes about the responsibilities of a one-room rural schoolteacher. "What happened in Roseville was really scary to me. You know, you don't know what to do, out in the middle of a hayfield, as it were, in the country. We had nothing there to work with [no first aid kits]… It was in the wintertime and it was bitter cold. It was too cold to make the kids go outside to play. I could never do that when it was cold weather. I don't know how teachers could. I was writing away, something on the blackboard. And I had still just a little bit to do, and it was recess. The girls were playing in their entryway and the boys were playing in theirs. In the boys' entry, there was the awfullest racket goin' on out there. And I thought, 'Oh my conscience, whatever in the world is goin' on out there?'" She would be ringing the bell in a couple of minutes, so decided to close her ears to the 'racket' and continue. Fortunately, "then I decided I should go. And when I opened that door into that entry, I'll never forget it to my dying day. My heart must've stopped beating. It just went to my boots." Some of the bigger boys had picked up a younger and much smaller one and put him on the top shelf above the coat hooks. "And the bell rope came down in the boys' entryway. They had that bell rope around that boy's neck. I do not know if it was ever tied, or if he'd jumped it could've loosened and he wouldn't have been hurt, but you don't know these things. And when I saw that, oh, I just trembled and I could hardly speak. But when I got the speech out, I said, 'You boys get that rope off that boy's neck. Do you know that, if anything happened to him, it wouldn't be I that'd be punishing you? It'd be the police.' And I turned around and walked back into the schoolroom. I just shook. Well, I was late ringing that bell, I can tell you. And if you ever saw, as meek as Moses, those boys coming up to their desks from that room. I never ever asked them. I never found out. I couldn't bring myself to thinking about it. Wouldn't it be dreadful if anything like that had happened? And it'd all be just in fun and nonsense, you know. I know they wouldn't be doing it on purpose." At that time, especially in a rural school, she could honestly make such a statement.

In 1922-23, the last school year Isabel taught at Roseville, she had seven pupils in the entrance class; in other words, seven who tried their exam to go into high school. "And that was a pretty heavy year, because you've got to spend extra time with those students, and there's no use of kidding yourself. We'd go early in the morning and stay after four, and work when there was quiet and…you wouldn't have any interruption." One student named Walter didn't pass because he couldn't spell. He had so much trouble that "He couldn't spell 'cat' and spell it right. It wouldn't be 'cat'; it'd be 'tac', or something like that. And it seemed an awful pity." Walter could spell, she said, if he'd had a lesson on the word. Very likely he had a learning disability, a condition that had never been diagnosed or even named at that time. Five of her students did pass. "But one we didn't expect to pass, because she just tried because the rest of her family had to try twice, so she thought she might just as well start early! Now that's the truth, so help me." Isabel told the girl that she could try the exams if she wanted to. If the fee was paid, she couldn't be prevented. Her parents paid the requisite dollar. As expected, the girl didn't pass. She did succeed the following year, just as her siblings had.

One of those grade eight pupils, Jean Hosie, wrote a letter to Mom for inclusion in her ninetieth birthday memory book. Jean provided the following glowing tribute: "Isabel was a *born* teacher! Always fair with her pupils and always had their welfare at heart. She tried to instill a love of reading in us all, and one of the ways she did this was to use it as a reward, when we got our other work done quickly and well we were allowed to go to our 'meager' library for a book to read. Another thing I remember was when we reached that awful prospect of passing our 'entrance exam' she came to school at 8:30 in the morning and stayed until 5 p.m. to give us extra tutoring, all with no extra pay for her spare time lost. Over her ninety years her life has touched and influenced many and will continue to do so." That ninetieth birthday morning, I rather shockingly understood my mother's intense physical, mental and emotional involvement with these pupils. While leafing quietly through the memory book for the first time, she suddenly blurted, "Oh, look at all my children", her face glowing with pride and love. Being one of her two biological children, I wondered how she suddenly got so many. She was responding to the photo of her Roseville brood.

As she had planned, Isabel stayed at home with her mother during the 1923-1924 school year. Each of the girls took a turn for a year as her helper, and she hadn't yet spent that year. Helping Kate entailed a great variety of tasks. One was milking. "Two cows I'd milk. And Arthur Belton [Will's hired man] helped with the milking and turned the separator. And then I'd have to wash the separator. We took hot water from the house…and I'd have that to do first thing in the morning and then come back to the house. It'd all be done before breakfast. You got up and did the chores before breakfast. You know, those terrible farmers that were mistreating the animals… It's just terrible. We should be lookin' after it." (her editorial comment on a news story that was current at the time of taping). "We never had a bite of breakfast till the cows and the horses and the pigs and everything else—and the elephant if you had one—would be fed."

When "Arthur and I were in the stable milking the cows… Arthur was the greatest one, you know. He was just like a brother and just like a part of our family, to tell the truth. We'd be milking away there, and Arthur'd say, "How be we have a contest, see who can beat in repeating nursery rhymes?' He'd say a nursery rhyme and then I'd have to say one. Then he'd say another, and we'd go on till finally first one, then the other, would be stumped. You know, I think that was one reason that we didn't do much quarreling and one thing and another, and worked together at home. Mother was a great one to do that—make fun or make entertainment or make something out of your work, instead of grumblin' and growlin', 'What am I doing this for? I don't like doin' this'." The attitude was passed on to her own family. Isabel's children, grandchildren, great-grandchildren, all have a strong work ethic.

That year Isabel also took care of the hens and chickens "…that were always the responsibility of the woman of the house. It wasn't heavy work. I remember Mother said it was the first fall the chicken coops got cleaned out. I just loved working out in the fall at that on a nice day. I had cleaned them all up and put the manure stuff on the flowers. And there's nothing any better. Oh the beautiful flowers—Mother's dahlias. And then you'd have the flower bed had to be looked after a bit. And the lawn had to be cut. We always did it, the girls." Kate baked bread, buns, biscuits, scones, and pies. Isabel made cookies and tarts. She also completed regular housecleaning, washed windows, and washed extra things, such as bedding, blankets, and her father's all-wool underwear, for storage over the summer. My mother refined many of her household skills during this period.

In the spring, when it was time to sell the fat cattle, she had a different sort of experience. " We drove cattle to Beaverton. Dad was in the buggy driving, and Jim Cockburn and I were walking the cattle. And you kept them out of the gates on the [farm] laneways… And then we'd have to turn on the Centre Road, which was a fairly busy road, but we managed. It wasn't too terribly bad—nothing like now. There weren't any cars—next to no cars. There wouldn't be very many cars for the simple reason it was early in the spring, too. [The road would be too muddy.] So then Dad walked a while and Jim went on the buggy. But I walked every step of the way to Beaverton station. You didn't have to go through the town. The stockyard was a little bit before the actual station house. And so that was another way I put in my time—and kept fit." In the summer, she picked raspberries, another outdoor activity that my mother always enjoyed. "Why…every Monday morning, ('cause people didn't go to the berry patch on Sunday) you could just go and fill your [container] just as fast as you could pick them in our own bush, where they'd cut out trees to make lumber to build the house, you see, just a few years before. And all these brush heaps grew up with the berry bushes." She and Kate used the berries to make jam and pies. Her mother also 'put the fruit down' in preserving jars for winter use.

Isabel kept socially fit, too. That summer, the family had a big lawn party for her Grandpa and Grandma Wallace, who had celebrated their sixtieth wedding anniversary in March—an inhospitable time for such a celebration. The summer date was on her Grandpa's eighty-third birthday, July 10. Also in the summer, as she always did, a neighbour, "Mrs. Morrison had a quilt for quilting and the women and girls went to quilt. And then the boys would come at night and dance." Mr. Morrison was almost blind, but a good musician who played the button accordion and the violin. In the fall, a girl about Isabel's age, who lived near Gamebridge, had a Hallowe'en party. She invited the Wallace girls. Viola made a fortuneteller costume by sewing euchre cards on her skirt. Isabel went as a witch and Arthur as a cat. Viola, who was a milliner, helped make Arthur's costume. They wound black stockings around a rope to make the tail. "And we had a lot of fun there, you see. In the country, we made our own fun. There was always something going on." During the winter, various social activities and trips to Beaverton provided diversion. She recalled going to Gamebridge to a young people's concert in the winter of 1924. A neighbour picked up people with a sleigh. The next day, Isabel was telling her mother about the different performers at the concert: "This McQuaig girl, she sang, and she had the sweetest voice. It's to be hoped she gets a little chance to use it, and even if she doesn't get special training," she said to Kate. "And I'd been telling her just before that about sitting beside a Mrs. McDougall, and Mother says, 'Well that McQuaig girl would be her sister's daughter. She'd be that woman's niece'. Well, I said, 'It's a good thing I didn't say what an awful voice [that girl] had, wasn't it?'" And Isabel soon concluded, "It isn't very wise to go where you don't know people too well and start making remarks. A lesson learned. And you never forget when you learn it the hard way—and that's by experience."

Intending to return to teaching, in the summer of 1924 Isabel had applied for three schools. One in Simcoe County had accepted her application. She admitted to being a bit slow in mailing her acceptance letter. By the time the trustees got her letter, they'd had their meeting and accepted another teacher. However, she said, "I didn't worry about it. I'd saved up a little bit of money, you know, when I did have a school. And I felt there's always a school that wants to get rid of a teacher they have, or they find something happens and Thanksgiving time, there's no teacher." If she'd wanted a job, she would have consulted with the inspector available. "Anyhow, it didn't happen. Because just at that time, I went down to spend a few days with [Roseville area friend] Nellie Oliver—just a break and a holiday, you see." She stayed with Nellie about a week. When she arrived back home she got a startling surprise.

Kate had been injured in a horse and buggy accident. Here's how my mother told this story: "Mother had always driven. She used to drive Old Prince before [Will] bought Frank. [Prince] was a workhorse but he wasn't a heavy one; he was kind of more general, in a way. And so he could do pretty well on the road. Frank was a driving horse, a colt with such long legs they thought he would make a wonderful racer. So his owners were training him on the racetrack. But he never won anything, you see. So they sold him [to Dad]" around 1909. Isabel had many stories to tell me about adventures with Frank, as he learned not to be a racehorse. For example, "The first time mother drove him, she went to the Ladies' Aid [meeting] at Bolsover, and she picked up my Grandmother McFadyen on her way, you see. And another cutter came up behind them, and Frank just took off like a streak. And they didn't know what in the world was going on. And Grandmother says, 'Do you think there's a pain in his stomach?' Grandmother was a quiet talker...so concerned about the horse. Well, anyway Mother held on to the lines." At a corner the other cutter turned and went the opposite way, so Frank calmed down a little. Mom described how "...that dear old beast, he would put his head down to help [put the bridle on]. You see, some of them they'd put their heads up. And he was tall; he had these long legs; of course, I had pretty long legs myself, so I was also in the tall area. But down he'd put his head, and he'd take the bit. Now Old Maude, she wouldn't do that, the one we had after Frank. You had to kinda' work with her." Kate was driving Maude when she had the buggy accident. But "Mother always said it wasn't the horse's fault. They'd met a car coming on to our concession off what's now Highway 12 and it was a drover...a man that came around buying cattle in the stable."

Kate was badly bruised from the throw out of the buggy. "So the doctor had come...and fortunately there was a bedroom downstairs where there was plenty of water and things handy to look after Mother. And she was a good patient, you know. She wasn't grumbly and growly. So, anyway, when I got back and Mother was in bed, I never even looked at an ad in the paper until about the last of November." When Isabel began to look for schools, she bought the *Globe* newspaper, because her dad subscribed to the *Toronto Star*, which rarely advertised for a teacher. "And the *Globe* was just full of it. It was a morning paper, you see. The *Mail and Empire* was a morning paper, and it had some in. Well, you see, it was a Tory paper, too, and Uncle John took it, up at the grandmother McFadyen's house. And when I was up there one day I says, 'Oh, here's one. Now wouldn't that be fun? I have a notion to answer it'. It was in the North, you see. And it was something like Crow's Nest, and Annie says, 'Oh my goodness, you wouldn't go to a place like that, would you?' I said, 'Sure I would.'" But Isabel didn't take the paper or the address home with her. That was just as well. Kate was supposed to stay off her leg. She was in bed from September until after Christmas. Still, Isabel kept her eyes open for a suitable teaching position. Finally she saw in the Beaverton paper that Riverview School, close to her home in Thorah Township, wanted a teacher. "So I phoned. They said they weren't having their meeting for a few nights. I sent my application, and I got the school." She stayed with Kate until the new year. "It was a God's blessing in the end [that I didn't get a teaching position earlier], because Jessie could never ever have done it alone in the fall. Jessie was the one that was taking over to stay with mother that year... It was too much for one person, and she was more or less inexperienced, four years younger. The harvest wasn't all in yet, there was threshing to be done, corn to be looked after, and men to be fed—a dozen of them streaming in to the table twice a day for the threshing. There'd be one or two extra for breakfast. They didn't have cars to run around in, so they slept at your house, usually."

That Christmas brought a different sort of guest to the Wallace home. A group of musicians came by train from Uxbridge to put on a program at the Bolsover Presbyterian church. Isabel's sister Annie and Grandma McFadyen were at the farm for the holiday. "We left both Grandma and Mother in bed, you know, and went to the church. And there wasn't any worry about it. Couldn't do it nowadays. Somebody'd be in cutting their throats or something. My father was very fond of music," Mom explained, so he brought the group home to sleep, planning to take them to the train in the morning. When they all arrived at the Wallace home around midnight, the group needed something to eat. The future parents of famous Canadian pianist Glenn Gould were among these musicians. "I remember so well," Mom said, "because Miss Greig [later Glenn Gould's mother] was the pianist and she wanted to make toast. Anyway, I saw that here she was with the slice of bread, putting it on the lid of the stove, on the top of the stove. And I said, 'Oh, just a second' and went in and got the wire toaster. Then she was going to put that on the top of the stove. And I said, 'Oh, well, we'll lift the lid and put it down in. It'll do it better and more quickly'. And so she made her toast then." Once fed, the musicians created a musical evening that contrasted sharply with the one years earlier when Annie had been scolded at ten o'clock for disturbing her father's sleep. "They had all their musical instruments with them, and I'm telling you it was about two or three o'clock in the morning before we got to bed. There we were and Dad didn't seem to mind one bit about the music—never saying it's time to go to bed. Maybe he was more easy-going because he had his family raised. The train left fairly early in the morning; they'd have to get up at about seven o'clock." This story further enhanced my understanding of Mom's attitude towards her father, which differed so radically from mine. I had never gotten past feeling that he was a frightening, stern, rigid autocrat. Of course, I never got to know him as she did.

By January 1925, Kate was much better. Since Jessie would be with her for a few more months, Isabel went with no regrets to teach at Riverview School. She boarded in the community from Monday morning to Friday night. At first, the situation was challenging. The previous teacher was from Toronto. She had wanted to go home every weekend, but she didn't have a car. The train she returned on each Monday didn't get into Beaverton until nearly noon. Meanwhile "The kids were just running up and down on top of the desks—oh, they were really havin' a wonderful time. And so [the school board] couldn't put up with that, and of course they fired her." It took Isabel a while to get the children settled down. She was fortunate that Will had bought a car; she had transportation home for the weekend.

That November, she experienced a crazy adventure with an unforgettable conclusion. Wanting to go to Toronto to get a new winter coat, "I asked the trustees—at first I asked the children to ask their parents at home, if it would make any difference to them if I taught on a Saturday, instead of a Monday. And I'd take the weekend in Toronto to buy a new winter coat." They agreed to the plan, so she prepared to go. Preparations included closing the school on Friday afternoon. "I never left school until all the children had gone. That was one of my policies as a teacher." Often in the rural areas at that time, a set of parents took the caretaker job, but one of their older children did the sweeping. The young girl who did the job, and a neighbour girl who was waiting for her, left the school with Isabel, who locked up. "They went straight on the concession and I turned and went across to my boarding house. I was the last one to leave and to lock the door that Friday night that I was going to the city on the train. I had plenty of time from four o'clock 'til the train left the nearby town, Beaverton, just before seven. "Well, the lady where I boarded (that was Mrs. Dave Ritchie) she *would* have me have something to eat. I said, 'It doesn't matter. I don't need it. I've had a good meal at noon... If I need a cup of coffee, I can get it at Blackwater', because I had to change trains there. But anyway, to satisfy her, I did have [something]. But I had everything ready. And Mr. Ritchie had his Model T car ready. They were taking their children, to go down to her parents' place and stay for the evening a bit."

Finally they got on the road. "We were going in on the fifth concession to Beaverton. And there was a great big car. And this is a disgrace, an absolute disgrace. We were coming along and...it was a bit slippy in the mud. This big car had two men in it, and they were gawking and lookin' at this and lookin' at that and wavin' their arms and goin' on like this. And Mr. Ritchie wanted to go by then, because they would go so slowly for a while. Then, you see, when he'd go to go by them, they'd pick up and away they'd go. They weren't lettin' that old Model T go by them. Once the car kinda' slewed, and I said, 'Oh, Mr. Ritchie, don't try to get by them. If they're that mean, I don't care. I don't want any accident'. So he didn't try to go by them any more." The brakeman was out on the step waving the lantern for the train to go, as they reached the Beaverton station. Mr. Ritchie decided to take his wife and children back to her mother's place and then catch the train at another station. He didn't catch the train there or at any other stations. Isabel finally persuaded him to let her take a taxi to Blackwater. She never did get to ride on that particular train.

What concerned her most about the evening was that, "At six o'clock that night, while we were tearin' through the country in the Model T Ford car, my school was burning down". Mrs. Ritchie phoned her in Toronto on Saturday to say she didn't need to come back Monday as planned. She could stay longer. Isabel's reaction was swift and heartfelt. "But I didn't stay. I couldn't. It was like as if my home had gone. Oh goodness, I couldn't stay. But there was one thing I was thankful for. I used to take some of [my own] *Book of Knowledge* [encyclopedias]…to the school sometimes, but I kept bringing them back to the Ritchie's, because there was no place to put them in the library there. Fortunately I had taken them, just the night or two before, to make sure that I had them all together before I went away." Isabel decided that mice eating matches in the organ had caused the fire. The school was full of smoke, which she attributed to the leathers on the organ. The only salvaged items were the teacher's hand bell, which had been on the windowsill, and the big iron poker for the stove.

It was an old school. In fact, it was so old there wasn't a separate entryway for the children. Everyone had to hang all their belongings inside the schoolroom. The only toilets were outdoors. "As Mr. Ferguson, the inspector, said, 'It was a blessing in disguise'. I had to agree with him. But I never got to teach in the new school." Her job, however, continued. The community soon figured out a quick solution. Mom filled in the background: "I had some pretty good trustees there—a little more educated than the ones that were in Roseville when I came there. Dave Ritchie and Fred Clayton were two. And I don't know who the other one was now…" She thought their decision was a good one. The trustees' meeting was held soon after she got back from Toronto. She and most of the community attended. Some wanted to volunteer for most of the work to build the new school. Fred Clayton moved that they issue debentures and start right from the bottom. His argument was that the volunteers would consist of four or five people, who were there that night, and who would do most of the work. "And he was right," Mom commented.

The school's location made temporary arrangements relatively easy. "It was a little village, in a sense. There were a lot of people around that corner. Years before that, at one time they had a Sunday School." Near the school stood a driving shed for horses to rest in. Since the studding and the roof were good, the school board decided to fix it up as a temporary school. Fortunately, Mom noted, the open part of the shed was facing south. People with window frames or windows to spare were asked to bring them in. "There were storm windows on the old part of the [Wallace] house that had never been used since they built the new part because you had central heating, and it was upstairs. And so I asked Dad if he'd like to lend one of these," she said. The shed was insulated with sawdust, "…and it was the warmest school I ever was in," she declared. The west end of the building was already fixed up for a woodshed. At the east end, the men put a window that could be opened to let the air circulate in hot weather. In colder weather, "it was a nice warm school, and lovely sunshine coming in those [south] windows. I used to love it, to tell the truth." Somebody lent them an old-fashioned pot-bellied parlour stove. Someone else donated her small pedestal desk. The trustees did buy new seats and blackboards, items that could be used in the new building.

This new situation led to another. "I went home to Ritchie's for lunch…instead of staying at school. Nowadays you have to stay at school, or else when you got back, everything'd be smashed and broken. But then, there were civilized people that went to school, believe it or not. And now they're not civilized." Such an editorial comment, so typical of my mother's lively involved mind, often punctuated one of her stories. She would then continue; in this case, " So while we were still eating, one of the youngsters came rushing in, 'The school's flooded; the school's flooded'. We'd had some nice weather in March, and there'd been quite a bit of snow, and it had piled up in the yard." The school was indeed flooded; it had to be closed. Later, she was told that the children had started the water coming in, but more came than they had expected. Isabel never told the trustees about this rumour or tried to verify it. She decided if the trustees wanted to find out and call damage, fine. She wasn't going to sort out the situation—and then have to discipline for it. Very wise! Mom often said (about a politician, most often), "If they had an ounce of common sense..." She had it in pounds.

Another Riverview story came out of an exceptionally cold winter day. A girl who was carrying the family lunch pail froze her fingers white. First, Isabel put snow on the fingers to ease the pain. Then she told the girl, 'Now you stand behind me and put your hands under my arms 'cause it's good and warm under there. And then wiggle your fingers'. "We didn't get school called until about ten o'clock, partly because of that. And the school was kind of cold anyway…" The girl's fingers peeled later, but they had been saved. Common sense at work again.

Mom also shared this delightful memory: One June day in 1926, she was standing behind her desk, teaching, when "I looked out the window and I saw these women down around the corner there. I thought, 'That seems funny. They're carrying baskets. You'd wonder if they were going to town for eggs or with eggs…'" As it turned out, the mothers of the school children were collecting at the corner to come into the school, arms laden with gifts for her wedding shower. "Actually, it was the only shower I had, because you know I was away from home so much, and there weren't that many people my own age. They were really from the whole school section. I didn't know a thing about it. I had a lot of lovely nice gifts, [including towels with hand crocheted edging]." These lovingly crafted towels were such treasures that Mom seldom used them. Some of them are now in my linen cupboard—still treasures, but for a different reason.

Isabel (kneeling) with Roseville pupils

Isabel (back, right) and Riverview pupils

After Isabel married on September 22, 1926, she was not allowed to teach, according to the regulations. But Mother's Day 1928 combined with much earlier circumstances to turn this cloud around. To her, being barred from teaching was unfair, a waste of one's education, and a personal trial for someone who'd truly been called to the profession. On top of that, she wanted to get her five full teaching years, so that she could apply for her pension. She and her husband Walter Beach, who lived in Uxbridge Township about an hour's drive from Isabel's original home, had gone to the Thorah Township farm for Mother's Day. "And while we were there, Miss Furniss phoned to say that she had the mumps and couldn't come back the next day to teach [at the nearby Beaver School]." The school board needed a replacement—quickly. This was the opportunity Isabel had been waiting for. She'd missed a semester the fall she stayed with Kate after the buggy accident. "But then I taught in Egypt School, supplied for Bessie Carson in '24 from Easter to summer holidays. So when I went counting it up, I counted it up from…Easter to summer holidays and September to Christmas, and called it a school year. It had to be month for month."

Isabel seized the moment and phoned Billy Miller, chairman of the school board. "I said we'd got word that Louise [Furniss] phoned to say that she can't come to teach tomorrow. And we probably were in Bolsover Church that morning and Mr. Miller would know that I was there. I didn't have to do a lot of explaining. And I says, 'Well I'm just here, and I wondered if you were going to get a supply teacher, why I'd be available'. And he said, 'Well, I don't know what we'll be doing, but I'll remember that'." Isabel had an ace up her sleeve. She knew the Millers had a soft place in their hearts for her. Their son Gordon was born the spring of 1915, the year she was home before going to high school. Mr. Miller had asked Kate if she could spare one of the girls to do light housekeeping. Isabel got the job. "I didn't do any baking [for the Millers]. I did do a little bit in the line of cooking… I do remember doin' the meat, because Mrs. Miller had it salted away, you see. That's the way she was keepin' it. And she fried it out—pork—in milk, and then threw the milk away. And that took the salt out, or a lot of it. And then, you see, you cooked it. Ever after, I was their pet, in a sense, but never anything ever said, and I never said anything. They appreciated it, and they never forgot it." She and Walter came home that Sunday in 1928 because they had to look after their livestock. Soon after, she received a phone call asking her to supply teach for Miss Furniss. Of course she boarded with her parents. And of course they didn't take any money for board. Isabel supplied for a month. Miss Furniss had the mumps on one side and was just ready to return when the other side broke out. "So she was three weeks, anyway, and there was an extra week. And I said to Mr. Miller and the rest of the board that I would stay on to the end of the month, and they didn't need to pay me. It wouldn't matter. What they paid me for was three weeks." She stayed partly because Miss Furniss had been teaching fifth form (first year in high school, which Isabel wasn't qualified to teach) to two girls, as well as the entrance class. When Miss Furniss came back, Isabel said to her, 'You take those two students in the teacher's room and I'll look after the other children that I'd been doing, to finish off'.

At the end of that extra week, the months added up. Isabel qualified for her pension. "I applied. I thought I had a perfect right to apply for my pension fund when they wouldn't let me teach because I was married. What was the use of leaving pension money in the pension fund, you see? If you taught for five years, you could get it back but no interest. But I wasn't worrying about the interest. It wouldn't amount to that much, in those days. And so the people in the pension place, it was none of their business whether I was teaching for nothing or not. They got their pension money. And I was teaching for a month… So, when I got that [pension] money, I made up my mind to buy [the living room suite] because we didn't have anything for the front room. So, anyway, I thank the Lord for that, and I'm not sayin' it flippantly. I was very thankful for that, because [the opportunity] came so early, and everything was so easy." Through quick thinking, a bit of luck and clever planning, she'd easily turned this cloud inside out.

Although she'd had this work after marriage, Isabel felt she couldn't send out an application to teach, with a Mrs. before her name. But her teaching career was far from over. In 1930 she found out that her niece Winnifred (who'd been a last-minute attendant at Isabel and Walter's wedding) wasn't well. She'd been staying with her grandparents to go to school. Her mother, Bertha (wife to Isabel's brother Duncan), had been a teacher herself and so appreciated the importance of education in a child's life. She asked if Isabel would take Winnifred to teach at home. No problem. Isabel saw that Winnifred was in a similar situation to her own when *she* was ten years old and concluded, "What Aunt Tene and Uncle Jack did for me, Walter and I could do for Winnifred." She did this home schooling under the supervision of the inspector, with permission granted by the Provincial School Attendance Officer, J.B. MacDougall, in a letter dated February 9, 1931 (Appendix I). The arrangement didn't last as long as it might have, because Isabel became pregnant with her and Walter's son Beverley, who was born on January 31, 1932. Short as it was, this experience made a significant impression on Winnifred, who later wrote in a letter to Isabel, "One of the happiest years of my young life at ten was the year you taught me at your home. The very special attention that I received then has stayed with me. Some of my friends who I've told about that year were almost envious of my 'home teaching'. From those special times and many others, you have won a very large place in my heart. It was great, it is great, to be able to discuss with you any topic on this journey of life. Your common sense approach to life has been an inspiration to me. When I have been asked, 'Who would you say were significant people in your life?' you are one of my choices." Winnifred and my mother were special friends from 1931 on. When Win was in the army during World War II, she often took her leaves at the Beach farm—a quiet country retreat from the stresses of that time.

A few years later, Mom had another teaching opportunity. She said, "They wanted me very badly to go to Roseville the year [Walter and I] built the barn." It was 1946. Beverley was going to Stouffville High School and I had just started at Siloam Public School. The proposed plan was for Beverley to drive the car, drop me off at Siloam, drop our mother off at Roseville, and drive himself to Uxbridge High School. Mom explained to me the attraction of the plan for Bev (aside from the driving, of course). "And he wanted to take typing. And they didn't have it in Stouffville. I was kind of sorry, but we couldn't do it unless he just switched and that didn't seem very sensible. You could teach yourself to type. Hundreds and hundreds of people have." What bothered her most was that the barn wasn't finished—and wouldn't be by September. There'd be men working on it and needing to be fed. "I couldn't manage to swing that sort of thing," she concluded. "There'd be something that wouldn't be done enough, properly, efficiently, or 100 per cent what oughta' be done. And which was gonna' drop, you see? And maybe both would drop. You know what I mean—the home and the school too." My mother's finely-tuned conscience made the decision for her.

There's no doubt that she had the ability to teach. Florence (Harrison) Kemp, a niece of Walter's and mother's helper in our home for the summers of 1945 and 1946, experienced some of Isabel's teacher qualities. In 2003, she told me about some of her experiences with my mother. Florence said, "She really explained things well, when she wanted you to carry out a task of some kind. 'You'll find it here, and you do [such and such]', which is the schoolteacher, I know now, since I have been one. She was very distinct about how she enunciated her words. There was no sort of slip or slur." Another teacher's habit. "And she used her hands sometimes when she was explaining things. I remember her pinching her fingers like this… She was smart. There's no two ways about it. I just felt she was a good mentor." Isabel told Florence about her own teaching, especially coming to her first school at Roseville. Florence could tell from these stories that Isabel loved the profession. Possibly she even had some influence on Florence's decision to become a teacher. Isabel and Walter shared this interest in education, which Florence probably realized too. For years, Walter served on the local Siloam School Board, often as the chair. The last few years Walter was on the Uxbridge Township School Board (in the 1950s), Isabel took on the secretary's role.

As I reflect on all that I know about my mother's life, it strikes me that she spent as much time turning someone else's clouds inside out as she did finding the silver lining in her own. Such efforts in her last two paid teaching experiences also brought clouds into her own life. In 1955, she supply taught at Garibaldi School, about two miles south of the Beach farm, when the teacher took maternity leave. She had a difficult time with several students, particularly one girl in grade eight. Mom kept confidentiality while in the job, but years later discussed how rude and disruptive this girl was, and how the girl's mother supported her—not recognizing that she was ruining her daughter. Isabel could not 'in all conscience' pass the girl. Even after school was over for the summer—and Isabel did not return in the fall—the girl tried to cause trouble, often concocting stories about my mother. The Garibaldi period was difficult in other ways. Isabel hadn't taught school on a regular basis for over twenty-five years. "I know she spent many late nights…correcting and planning," my sister-in-law Norma said. At the end of the term, Isabel was 'wiped'.

At the same time, I'm sure she was excited about being in the mainstream of teaching again. From July 2 to 6, she attended the Social Studies Conference in Toronto, sponsored by the Federation of Women Teachers' Association of Ontario, with her friend Alice Alcock. She may have taken her sister Chris into her confidence about the difficult teaching situation, or maybe Chris could just see that she needed a break. Later in the summer, the two of them spent a few days in western Ontario where they saw *The Merchant of Venice* at the Stratford Theatre's Third Annual Festival, a treat my mother thoroughly enjoyed. The names of the actors in the play, many of whom later had distinguished careers (program in Appendix J), help to explain why. I had just completed grade nine that year, so was deemed old enough to look after my dad, which principally involved preparing his meals. Mom left plenty of cooked food in the refrigerator. Along with the lessons on how to cook oatmeal porridge and fry cooked potatoes, I was ready for the job. She'd been gently trying to get me, the bookworm, interested in household arts. When they were tied into looking after my dad and 'running the household', I got interested.

When my brother Bev and sister-in-law Norma's children were all in school in the 1960s, Isabel taught briefly at Siloam School, situated a mile and a quarter north of the Beach farm. The request for her services came after Thanksgiving. The teacher had gone to Toronto for the weekend. She phoned to say she couldn't come to teach because she'd fallen down a few steps and hurt her back. "Well that was all logical, you see, and we accepted it," Mom commented. "And maybe she did fall down the steps, and maybe she was having a bad time with her back. But she was also having another bad time. She'd found out she was pregnant." —a classic case of poor judgment in choosing a male friend, combined with over-heated hormones. "She would have been pregnant when she was hired, but she didn't know. She was going out with this guy. And she was stupid enough to let him use her body, for which I would've given him a kick in the pants. And he was coming to the school." Isabel didn't think this young teacher wanted him there. "And that guy came to the school when I was there. He didn't know that she wasn't there. I thought that was great. When he left, I had a good laugh." Such judgments of someone she'd call "a silly fool" were not uncommon with my mom, yet she had a high degree of tolerance for many people and situations.

As chair of the school board, Walter decided to go to Uxbridge to talk with the parents of the pregnant teacher. "They wouldn't come clean," Isabel said. " We didn't know what was at the bottom of it for quite a while. And there were the trustees and they didn't know what to do. Were they going to get another teacher, or what were they going to do? And I didn't want it very badly, because it just seemed as if I didn't need it at that particular time." While in Uxbridge that Saturday night, at the same time as Walter was doing school board business, Mom decided to use the public phone booth to call her sister Chris in Toronto. "Nothing would work right. It was out of order, evidently. Well, I had taken my wallet out of my purse and put it on the little shelf. And I had the money out. When I was leaving the telephone booth I had my purse, but I didn't pick up my wallet. And when I came out and was walking down the street (and I didn't close my purse), I put my purse on my arm, and I guess I was so puzzled, so much on my mind, 'Where was Walter, he wasn't coming back, and it was getting around 11 p.m., and what in the world was I going to do?'" She knew where Walter was, but she didn't know where the family lived. With purchases to pick up from the grocery store, she was concerned that it would be closed before he came to pick her up.

As she walked along, she saw a parked car with some teenagers in it, laughing and having a lot of fun, she thought. When she noticed her purse flopping open, she thought they were just making fun of her. She closed her purse, then continued up the street to Bronscombe's clothing store, where she was well known. She asked to use the phone. Naturally, Dora Bronscombe said, 'Sure.' In an aside Isabel commented, "Isn't it wonderful when they can do things like that, but you can't any more, hardly. I don't think you'd ever trust a person. I don't know whether you would or not." When Isabel went to pay her, Dora said she would let Isabel know the charge when her phone bill came. "And I would gladly have paid more, to be sure that she had enough, because I needed to call to Chris." But she couldn't pay a thing. She discovered she didn't have her wallet. Back to the phone booth she went. The teenagers had left; the wallet was gone too. She had used most of her money for groceries. With part of the remaining five dollars she did what many teachers still do—went to buy something for her pupils, in this instance paste to stick pictures from catalogues on their projects. After that purchase, her wallet contained two $2 bills and some coins. Concerned about her drivers' licence, she went to the police station to report the lost wallet. She mentioned that the laughing young people could see that the wallet was still in the phone booth.

Next morning, an Uxbridge woman phoned Mom. Her young son and his friend had seen the wallet in the phone booth. Her son had brought it home. His mother told him they'd have to find its owner. Isabel went to the woman's home to get the wallet. When she opened it, she saw that everything was there. She said to the boy, "Well, Sonny boy, there's two $2 bills in there. So there'll be one for you and one for me." She wasn't sure that was enough to give him (he seemed to be around ten or eleven), but also felt she wasn't that rich. Then she went to the police station. Nobody was there. So on the door she left a note stating that her situation taught a lesson: we can't blame people until we know what's going on. She'd misjudged the teenagers and certainly regretted the error.

Isabel's granddaughter Joanne also had a mixed blessing memory from that Siloam teaching experience, which was my mother's last professional time in a school classroom. Joanne said, "I can remember being so excited thinking, 'Oh, Grandma's going to teach me at school'." Some days, Isabel walked to school with her grandchildren. One day the creek near the school had washed out the road. Planks lay across the road to form a bridge. To walk across them alone was a scary prospect for Joanne. "It looked as if I'd drown if I fell in [the water], you know. And I remember having to hold hands with Grandma to walk across the plank to get to school." She reassured herself, saying, 'That's OK. My Grandma's getting me across'. When the pregnant teacher hadn't shown up after about a month, another teacher took over. Isabel didn't want to stay until Christmas. "I just didn't feel equal to it," she told me. She was in her early sixties. I can understand why she was having trouble. My mother and I are similar. Her physical energy likely couldn't keep up to the ambitious mental and emotional sides.

Both of Isabel's granddaughters, Joanne and Marilyn, remember with fondness going into her part of the double farmhouse to do their homework because Isabel owned something their parents and the parents of probably all of their classmates did not—a complete set of the *Book of Knowledge*, 1920 edition, that she'd bought to enhance her teaching resources, and that had escaped the fire at Riverview School. The girls took from the glass-door cabinet whatever volume they needed, lay on their stomachs on the living-room floor, and researched their project. Joanne said her grandmother's teaching background influenced her profoundly. "Because there were three kids in the family, when we'd have our homework to do, Grandma's half of the house was a sanctuary. Even though some people might think those encyclopedias were ancient, to us they were full of knowledge, because we didn't have them in our side of the house… And I can remember just laying them down on the floor and stretching out on the floor in Grandma's side of the house and doing my homework, and not being bugged by my brother and sister. It was your own little room to do your homework without being disturbed, and you still knew that if you wanted to ask a question, you could ask Grandma for sure, because she was a teacher. She knew the answers to everything."

Marilyn expressed her memories in this way: "If I was having trouble in school, I knew I could go into the other end of the house, take out those encyclopedias. Those things were just a treasure. We thought we had the world by the tail with those encyclopedias. It's too bad that those things are outdated." Later, she observed how her grandmother "wasn't one to do sewing or knitting or crocheting or that type of stuff. Her skills were in putting skits together, and the readings. And she always read out of the *United Church Observer* for the devotions and planned programs, which I guess is part of the teaching." To Marilyn, it seemed "She was never afraid to get up and speak in front of people. And she never stuttered and 'ur'd and 'ah'd. That was just the way they were taught, I'm sure, years ago—or she might have had that natural ability or at least developed it as a teacher." Marilyn admired her grandmother's career as a teacher and had hoped to follow in her footsteps. That didn't happen. "But I guess I'm a teacher in my own way," she said. "There's always teaching. We can always learn."

Probably Isabel's last formal connection with any of these schools that had meant so much throughout her life was the Siloam School reunion in 1986. She assisted the planning committee as a consultant. Being a former teacher (even though for a short period at Siloam), she was well respected in the community. She spoke at the reunion ceremonies, one of the seven former teachers in attendance. Appendix K displays the formal afternoon program and history of Siloam School, S. S. #8, Uxbridge. Another more famous teacher who was there, and with whom Mom and I (as a graduate) had our photo taken for the *Stouffville Tribune*, was Luella Creighton, author of *High Bright Buggy Wheels* and other works.

My mother was never my teacher in the professional role, but of course she was. She couldn't help herself. Some of the teaching was of necessity, such as how to wash all the parts of the cream separator—a job that I did in the summer from about age twelve on. She also showed me how to dust, sew simple articles, do laundry using an electric wringer washer, set the table, plan a meal, and on and on. Of course I didn't realize at the time how beneficial these teachings would be. When I had my own home, I already knew all the basics of running and maintaining a household. She always explained the why, the reason a task was done in a certain order or a certain way. Her logical and highly organized approach to any task sank in, too—though I didn't recognize this trait in myself for decades.

Through observation and exposure to her habits, I picked up many other skills. I learned that leftover food is to be used again, sometimes in imaginative ways; that a vegetable garden provides inexpensive nutritious food for several months of the year; that story-telling can be an effective way to prove a point; that books provide hours of entertainment and mountains of information; that children can learn from simple materials such as homemade flour glue, blunt scissors and an Eaton's catalogue. The freedom that I had as a child is breathtaking to contemplate in this twenty-first century in North America. Particularly in the summer months, I was outdoors for hours on end—playing in the sandbank beside the road, picking wildflowers in the bush across the road, picking pussy willows in the swampy area in the ranch next door, exploring the back parts of our own farm, or lying on a blanket on the lawn watching clouds. Guidance from a distance was enough.

Isabel's life demonstrated beyond question her interest in and understanding of education, a field that drew her in like a magnet. Her collection of newspaper clippings also attests to that interest. In a *Stouffville Tribune* editorial, the writer quoted part of an interview with Professor T.H. Symons of Trent University: "An education consists of broadening the mind, stocking it with useful ideas and using it. For this, you don't need a B.A. and having a B.A. doesn't necessarily mean any of these things have occurred" (1972, n.p.). This comment matched Isabel's own response to the province of Ontario's Department of Education legislation in the early 1970s that required all elementary school teachers to have a university degree. She adamantly maintained that, "If you're a good teacher, you're a good teacher, I'll be darned if you never saw inside of a university, if you have your teacher training after your education in high school."

Those who knew Isabel well would say she proved herself right. I think they would also say she used her teaching skills to perform her life roles of farmer's wife, mother, grandmother, and community leader with equal competence.

CHAPTER SIX: Why Wouldn't I Marry a Farmer?

No Occupation

She rose before daylight made crimson the East
For duties that never diminished,
And never the sun when it sank in the West
Looked down upon work that was finished.
She cooked unending processions of meals,
Preserving and canning and baking.
She swept and she dusted; she washed and she scrubbed,
With never a rest for the taking.
A family of children she brought in the world
Raised them and trained them and taught them.
She made all the clothes and patched, mended and darned
'Til miracles seemed to have wrought them.
She watched by the bedside of sickness and pain
Her hand cooled the raging of fever.
Carpentered, painted, upholstered and scraped
And worked just as hard as a beaver.
And yet as a lady-of-leisure, it seems,
The government looks on her station
For now, by the rules of the census report
It enters—NO OCCUPATION.

originally published in the *Farmer's Advocate and Home Journal*, June 10, 1910; reprinted in the *Free Press Report*, date unknown

Walter had bought the Beach farm in the spring of 1926. Isabel always knew when he bought it, as explained in this conversation she related to me: "He came up to Mother and Dad's place one weekend, you see, and he was askin' me if I was sure that I wanted to marry a farmer. And I says, 'Why wouldn't I want to marry a farmer? I'm not marryin' a farmer, I'm marryin' Walter Beach. After all, I was born and raised on a farm, and I taught school in the country and enjoyed the farm life', and this sort of thing." She also knew he was going to buy the farm because Arthur Belton, her dad's hired man, regularly teased Walter with 'Now ya' know, Walter, you want to get the cage before you get the bird'. And so, she concluded, he intended to 'have the cage before he had the bird' (a home before Isabel became his wife). The 'cage' became available because Walter's mother, Roseanne, had had a stroke the winter of 1926. When she decided to give up the farm, Walter was ready to buy it. "But he didn't want to buy it if I wasn't gonna' be happy about it," my mother explained. "But he didn't ask me, you see, if I'd be happy if he bought the farm. He just asked if I was sure I wanted to marry a farmer. And of course, he had mentioned before that, 'We don't have to live on a farm, you know. I could get a good job, I know very well, in a garage…' because he was mechanically inclined and he had learned a lot about the mechanics of a car. He could take a Model T apart and put it back together, and goodness knows there were hundreds of them on the road. But I didn't want to go to the city. Heavens to Betsy! You didn't have all the noses out of Queen's Park and Ottawa and all the places stickin' into your business. 'How many licences have you got?' 'How many years' experience?' 'Did you go to university?' and a whole lot of messin' around like that, you see. If you were a good mechanic, there's your job. That's the way they hired them then. And they *were* good mechanics. And if they weren't, they fired them. And now, you can't fire them, no matter how rotten they are," Isabel observed, bringing the topic up to date with her editorial comments.

Walter made that farm purchase in the spring of 1926, but the story truly begins in August 1920, when Isabel went to Roseville to teach. From September 1920 to January 1922, she boarded with Garnet and Ruth Smalley, with whom she attended Sandford Methodist Church in the morning. Sunday School came first, then the church service. "Then in the afternoon," Isabel recounted, "they'd get ready and drive with the horse and cutter or horse and buggy, as the case may be, and go to visit with her parents. She was one of a family of about five..." Ruth's sister, Florence, and Isabel would often go to church in the afternoon, have supper with Florence's parents, and then come home after supper. One Sunday in February 1921, Florence and her brother Ed were talking about going to a dance that Friday night. "And they turned to me and said, 'Would you like to go too?' So I said, 'Well, yes, I wouldn't mind'."

The dance was in Del Badgerow's home on the town line (now Durham Regional Road 30) of Uxbridge Township. One room was prepared for dancing by removing most of the furniture. Isabel explained how a house dance worked: "In those days, you didn't take a girl and dance with nobody else, like they do now. It was a community thing and you danced with anybody. You knew all the people who were there. Of course you danced with the person that took you, naturally...but you changed around and you didn't think anything of it. You'd think it queer if you didn't." She and Florence were in the kitchen when a young man approached them and spoke to Florence, who turned and introduced Isabel. His name was Walter Beach. He lived on the second concession of Uxbridge Township, just one concession east of the Badgerow's. Apparently he was smitten on the spot. "He asked me to go to dance, when he should've asked Florence, really," Mom commented. "So we went out and danced together." It strikes me that my dad wasn't in that kitchen by accident. He'd soon recognize a new girl in the area at a house dance. Maybe he'd asked who she was that night. Maybe he already knew. What I'd bet on with my life savings is that he was captivated by her sparkling brown eyes, her stylishly bobbed hair, and her trim five foot six inch figure clad in a flapper dress just short enough to reveal the curve of slim strong legs.

Then there was her dancing. People brought their own instruments to these house dances. At this one, there was a fiddle. She and Walter danced to "The Irish Washerwoman", among other tunes. They danced several square dances but also participated in the circle dance where partners change each time the music stops. "When you danced with them, you knew those that knew their music and those that didn't, too. And then the waltz." Suddenly, as my mother spoke into the tape recorder, we moved from a description of that event to reminiscing: "And as far as I'm concerned, there's nothing in any dance any more graceful than the waltz. Walter and I danced the waltz so often. And when they'd play "When It's Springtime in the Rockies", we were out on the floor, just like that. And then there was the one-step (I never was much good on a one-step thing) and a fox trot... And the two-step. I could do the two-step, but not with Walter. He never seemed to get it so well." She went on to recall other dancing experiences. "I couldn't take the man's part in a dance, like some women could. I knew the woman's part all right, but I couldn't take a man's place so I couldn't help [Walter]. But I could do the military schottische." One man from the community, "As soon as they'd start up the tune [for it], (he knew Walter didn't dance it) he headed for me. His wife Ethel couldn't go to any dances and he liked to dance, and he went to the dances. So that'd help out people like me that were single. So he and I always did the military schottische together, and we could do it, I say perfectly, but then somebody sittin' on the sidelines might not think it was perfect." I wish I could have seen her doing that dance. I don't recall ever seeing her on the dance floor, though I must have when I was quite young. But my nieces and I (and others too, I'm sure) did see her in her sixties, seventies, even eighties, spring to life and action when Celtic fiddle music played on her kitchen radio. That music was part of her DNA .

The Methodists were opposed to dancing, Mom reminded me, and some Presbyterians, too, her dad much more so than her mother, but her mother—like her father—was both Presbyterian and Scottish. "And they had their dances, you see. That was part of their life [and the Scots' culture]." The English, especially the Wesley brothers that brought the Methodist Church into England, were opposed to dancing. Therefore, "There weren't that many people around Sandford that did the dancing, really, nor in a sense at Siloam. But I wasn't going to Siloam church at first. I was going to Sandford." Regardless, she and Walter "…got along pretty well dancing together" the night they met. "And so we had two or three dances together. But then I went home, the brother and sister took me home, and that was it." She thought.

"Well, about maybe two weeks or three or so after that…the phone rang, and it was for me. It was the Home Telephone Company from Uxbridge. It wasn't Bell. And I thought, 'This was for me? And who was speaking?' I couldn't hear him any too well. I was kind of upset…because it was long distance and me getting a phone call." She thought it was bad news about her grandmother McFadyen, who hadn't been well. Keeping in touch with her family by telephone was a complicated procedure. If she wanted to phone home, she could phone to the Uxbridge butcher shop run by Percy King. He had a phone from Bell, and also a local phone for his business. He took the message on the local phone, then used the Bell phone to relay the message to her parents. Walter King was a butcher in Beaverton. She thought the caller said his name was Walter King. But the caller was Walter Beach, the young man she'd met and danced with at Del Badgerow's home, calling from the store at Siloam village. "We finally got it sorted out. There was a dance at Sandford Hall…so he wanted to know, would I like to go to the dance at Sandford this week with him. And so I said, 'Yes, I wouldn't mind'. And so he came and took me to the dance, and from then on, we just went along." In today's terms, they were 'an item'.

Before that, Garnet's brother Ed, who was single and younger than Garnet, had been 'taking her out', as he thought. Really, Mom said, he was helping Garnet and Ruth who had got pregnant again and therefore weren't going out as much. Often his sisters went with Isabel and Ed. Her view on these outings was entirely practical. She went because it was a ride to town. She had no serious intentions, and she didn't expect him to, "because I didn't give him any encouragement". She realized later, "I'd never've made a wife for him. I could be with him, but I couldn't have lived with him because our ideas and everything wouldn't coincide at all. You see, Walter was raised more like I was raised—in a big family. And you shared and all that kind of thing. And [the Beach family] didn't seem to put as much emphasis on money as the people around Sandford did… If one person got something, the other person had to have something." She found out, when she started seeing Walter on a regular basis and driving with him around the countryside in a horse and buggy, that some people thought he wasn't good enough for her, coming from a poor-looking farm as he did and driving only a horse and buggy. That spring of 1921, Mom said, "I hadn't been out with Ed for a few weeks. He hadn't asked me to go anywhere. And I maybe hadn't been out to town…but I know what I did that spring. I needed a new hat, and there were no two ways about it. I had to get to Uxbridge in the daytime. Going at night was no good for me. So I asked the mailman if I could have a ride with him into town. And I walked home. It was about three and a half miles, not much more than going to Egypt School…"

Ed didn't ask her out any more. Isabel went home to Thorah Township for the summer. She did see Walter, however, because he bought a model T Ford in Barrie that summer. He asked a neighbour, Bristol McGuigan, to take him to Barrie in the horse and buggy, which Bristol drove home while Walter drove the car. "And they'd have to keep together, it was secondhand, you see, and he wouldn't know whether his Model T would hang together until he'd get home or not. But I guess it did, as far as I know." A short time later, when he'd got it in fine running order, she recalled, "And if he didn't show up with this car. I was just a little wee bit provoked at him, because that summer holiday Lil Berry invited me to come to her place for a visit…for two or three days. I never told him I was there. How did he know that I was in Orillia? And where I was and everything? And to this day [July, 1998] I don't know. Every time I asked him, I could never get a satisfactory answer, or else I'd get such a stupid answer, I'd just laugh and go on…" When Walter showed up at the Berry's home, "I couldn't ask him in, and he wouldn't understand, and I couldn't explain to him. Lillian and I were friends, but Lillian's mother was very 'politically correct'. Anyway, I wasn't going to let him break up my visit with Lil, and I wasn't going to ask Lil to start drivin' around somewhere, wherever he thought was a place to go. We had a bit of a visit and then he had to come back home, because he'd have the chores to do." What a woman she was! She knew the circumstances, knew her mind—and spoke it.

Isabel didn't see Walter again that summer because her holidays were nearly over by the time he made the jaunt to Orillia. In September she returned to Roseville and the Smalley's. He didn't come to see her for quite a while. "I was beginning to think 'the heat was off', as it were. And he showed up one night, to go to Uxbridge on a Saturday night." He'd been busy threshing his own crops and helping neighbours on the concession. She and Walter started seeing each other regularly again. "And I tell you, I had no time. I had seven students in the entrance class. And that's not a very easy job in a rural school with eight grades and goin' into town to take exams; it wasn't exams I'd set. We did go out to a dance or two." Evidence exists (Appendix L) that she attended a Women's Institute fundraiser evening that fall—no doubt with Walter. They socialized with Walter's family, too. Beach family members are listed in Appendix M. Isabel had first met Walter's mother in June 1921. Siloam Church always had a strawberry supper, to which Walter usually took Roseanne. He wanted to take Isabel too, so he introduced them and the three went together. Since the church had no basement, the supper was on the lawn of someone's home. Tables were set up with plates, cups and saucers. People brought their own flatware. The supper, a variation on the church picnic, was another affordable social event.

In January 1922, Isabel moved from Garnet Smalley's to Bob and Ethel Hutchinson's to board. She started going with the Hutchinsons to Siloam Methodist Church, three in a buggy or three in a cutter. Since this was the church that the Beach family attended, she and Walter saw each other nearly every Sunday. "And then, you see, Sunday afternoon after church, we'd —in the summertime, not in the winter 'cause it'd be dark and dreary—go to his sister's, the Lazenby's, quite a little bit, and to Frank Beach's and Joe Harrison's. And we did go the odd time to George Harrison's—Lizzie's. Laura and Lizzie and Lettie. Bill and Oliver, goodness sakes' alive, we would've been there that first fall, too, for some place to go visiting, just the same as we went at home. That's the way it was done." In this way, Isabel met most of Walter's family and spent time with him in a home setting too.

That September, back for another year of teaching in Roseville, she had begun to think that maybe Walter was 'leading her on a string'. He didn't come to see her for quite a while. Because there was no phone at Hutchinson's, he couldn't call her—difficult to comprehend in this age of cell phones attached to nearly every young ear. Again, he turned up, and they continued going to church, dances and other inexpensive social outings. "Usually we went to town on Saturday night. Everybody went to town Saturday night in those days. That's the way it was." Mom nearly broke down when telling me about these courting experiences. She felt so bad that she couldn't take Walter to her own home. Instead of going to a home, they drove in the horse and buggy, sometimes stopping to talk or … Though she never mentioned hugging or kissing, I'm sure it happened. My dad was 'crazy' about her. As a youngster I saw this best when, on the occasional Sunday morning, they would take me into their bed to snuggle with them. The love that I saw for her in my dad's hazel eyes was a silken cocoon embracing us all.

In the winter of those courting days, on occasion they went for a cutter ride. "And Walter had the loveliest chime bells. You know, sometimes people that built the cutter had bells on the shaft of the cutter (The horse is in the middle, and the bells on these shafts) and sometimes you had a whole string around under the stomach of the horse. And then there was a band of bells over the [horse's] back, on the harness." She remembered listening for him to come through the swamp that was just before the Hutchinson's home. In addition, "Walter was an awfully good skater, and he loved to skate. But, you see, I was a poor skater because my ankles were so poor. We did skate a little bit at the arena in Uxbridge. And at that time, Uxbridge was pretty strong in the hockey, and so was Markham. And they were at loggerheads, you see, as to who was going to be first. Between the two, they'd be one time over at Markham having a game, and the next week or two weeks back at Uxbridge. And so we would take in these hockey games occasionally. A special train would go from Uxbridge to Markham for the game, sometimes… but we didn't go on it because maybe it wasn't on a Friday night, and I couldn't go anyway."

So when did he pop the big question? I was curious to hear her answer, because of all the stories told in our household by both my parents, this one never had been. Mom told me, "You know, there were a lot of hints going on. He'd evidently made up his mind I wasn't going to leave Roseville without his ring. So if I went to another school, the guys would see, they'd better stay in their own corner." Christmas 1922 at Bob Hutchinson's, Walter was with her one evening in the 'front room'. "And that's when and where he 'popped the question'." She had her answer ready: "'Well, I don't mind accepting your ring, 'cause I've enjoyed your company and that sort of thing, but I'm not ready to get married, and I'm going to teach for five years. I promised myself I would.' So he agreed it was all right. And, of course, you see, I didn't have any pressure like sometimes when I have thought of somebody that had no home, like, or that sort of thing. But [Walter] was with his mother, and his mother needed him to run the farm." And so he agreed that it would be five years. He wasn't going to pressure her to get married. "No use," Isabel emphasized. "He wouldn't need to think he could pressure me. He couldn't. But he didn't. So, if that's the way I wanted it, why that'd be the way it'd be." What an interesting coincidence (if that's what it was) that I told my husband-to-be much the same thing when he wanted me to marry him in my first year of university. I said, "No, I'm getting my degree first." In her circumstances, Mom had an additional factor in mind. All of her older sisters had stayed home with their mother to help her for a year. Viola had filled in for her since June 1922, so that Isabel could teach another year at Roseville. In June 1923, she intended to begin taking her turn.

In the summer holidays after she left Roseville, Walter occasionally drove to see her at her home, staying for a few days. He came by train once during the winter. Arthur Belton, the hired man, went to meet him with the horse and cutter. "Even the highways, you know, they weren't open for cars… There weren't enough of them, and [the highways] weren't built for them either. Even the year we were married," Mom recalled, "Number 12 wasn't paved. It was still called the Centre Road for Ontario County. And then the government took it over. They got it, finally, as a provincial highway because it was all the way through Ontario County, from Lake Ontario to Lake Couchiching, really. So you see, [the highways] wouldn't be open at that time." Isabel took her term helping Kate from June 1923 to September 1924, but stayed on until Christmas because her mother had been injured in a buggy accident and couldn't run the house, even with Jessie's help. Isabel then got a teaching position close to her home at Riverview School, where she worked until June 1926. Having put in most of her five teaching years, she agreed to marry Walter that September.

Isabel hadn't had much experience with weddings. She was the first girl in her family to be married. She was probably eight when she attended her Aunt Tene's garden wedding; perhaps that's why she wanted a similar one. When she and Belle MacInnes were rooming together in Peterborough, they went to a wedding in the church they attended, just before Christmas. "It was a *beautiful* wedding. The Christmas red velvet, and, oh, they had matron of honour, maid of honour. And instead of having flowers, they had muffs. And it was really a beautiful thing. So that was my second experience with a wedding. And I had a few after that, one way and another." Often then, the couple just got married in the manse with the required witnesses.

Her dear sister Annie, a dressmaker by trade, made the wedding dress, a matching slip, and "because you weren't supposed to have a bust or a waistline in those [flapper] days, she also made me a chemise". A family friend tatted lace for the hem of the chemise. To go with her flapper dress, she purchased a long veil with embroidered edges at Eaton's. It was twirled about her feet for the ceremony and photographs. The veil was fastened to a circlet of beads and artificial orange blossoms. Oranges, I learned from Lipton's "Gentle Orange" tea bag box seven decades later, "…have long been a symbol of fertility because of the orange tree's unique ability to continually bear fruit, flower and foliage. Brides in historic England wore the fragrant blossoms beneath their veils in hopes that they would bring good luck, happiness and many children". But Isabel wasn't aware of this symbolism. The style just happened. "Well, they had these things made up. You could choose which you'd take, which you preferred. It wasn't anything in particular."

Then there was the matter of the officiating clergy. In June 1925, seventy percent of the Presbyterian churches in Canada had joined the Congregationalist Union of Canada and the Methodist Church of Canada to become the United Church of Canada. Bolsover, where Mr. Burkholder was the minister, had voted to stay Presbyterian. "Well, in the spring of '26," Isabel recalled, "he decides he's gonna' leave Bolsover. Because at Easter time, when I was home from school and at Bolsover church, I says, 'A fine thing, the trick you're playin' on me, leavin' just when we thought we had somebody…' indicating we were expecting to get married. 'Oh,' he says, 'I'll come back for that'. He was only going down to Morrisburg, so he could come back." Later she'd met him in Toronto when they were both shopping. "And he assured me that he had it in his mind, when we'd set the date and everything." In the meantime, Walter sowed fall rye on the farm. He also planned to plough the fields. "He wanted to do everything just as if he'd go straight on farming the next spring, instead of leaving it lying out, you see." This activity affected the wedding date. "So it kept goin', before we made the final decision, gettin' a week later and a week later." When she met Mr. Burkholder again, he wondered where they were planning to go on their honeymoon and she told him Muskoka. "I wasn't like some, that I thought I had to go to Niagara Falls for my honeymoon. I thought I'd rather go to a place like Muskoka, or some place like that. 'Oh,' he says, 'it's too late to go to Muskoka. Why don't you come to Morrisburg? We've got a big manse there. It'll be fine.' So that's how it ended up that's what we did do…but we branched out from there. We weren't just sitting on their back door all the time, and in the way."

Isabel's sister Minnie, her bridesmaid, had recruited a Toronto friend, Eva Burroughs, to orchestrate the wedding feast. "Minnie had great faith in Eva as a manager in the kitchen and that sort of thing. Of course, she kept house for that man for years. I don't know whether he was gay or not, but anyhow, he had adopted this boy, and the two of them were in this home in the east end… She had her own quarters in the house. It was kind of in Rosedale, in a way, but not actually Rosedale. Anyway, she was there, and she was running it, sort of. And of course, Viola, she could do anything in that line. She did jellied chicken in little dishes, and turned them out, individually." Some of the aunts contributed food, as well. Viola planned to prepare all the individual plates in the basement, then take them up to the dining room for the wedding feast.

Isabel and Walter finally decided to be married on Wednesday, September 22, on the lawn of her parents' home. "So Mr. Burkholder said he would come on the train the night before, and we would have the rehearsal then. Well, that rascal, he didn't come until the morning of the wedding on the train, and I was quite put out. But I held my temper. That was a pretty big job for me to do, I can tell you… I don't know how we did it, but we did it." Her cousin, Bruce Wallace, who often came to their place because he'd had a heart condition for many years and wasn't able to work much, was invited to the wedding. "So he was around, helped to do a lot of things, when we didn't have a brother. Bruce fixed the arch with the fall leaves, where the wedding was to take place." Walter and his groomsman, his nephew Angus Harrison, had arrived the night before for the rehearsal. This situation had its pros and cons. "Well, they had the privilege of getting in the bathtub if they wanted to, and they did." But, "You know, my sisters would be sayin', 'Now you mustn't be lookin' at the bride before the wedding day'. On the wedding day in the morning, 'You mustn't be lookin' at the bride. It's bad luck to look at the bride'." Walter must have been an anxious one! On the wedding morning, he had to be chased away from the kitchen where Isabel was dicing potatoes for salad.

As with many weddings, the guest list proved a puzzle and a small problem. The list started out with the aunts and uncles. Then the two oldest McFadyen children of each family were invited. Aunt Tene later expressed some disappointment that her daughter Christena wasn't invited. She was pretty young, Mom later commented, but at the same time she was a girl and Aunt Tene's only girl, and as a youngster Mom had attended her Aunt Tene's wedding. Her brother Duncan's daughters, Kathleen and Winnifred, *were* on the list. Six-year-old Winnifred, however, got more from that day than she expected. Isabel recounted her grand entrance as the bride from her parents' home and Winnifred's involvement in it. While coming down the front stairs inside the house, her veil was causing a little anxiety. "So, I imagine it was Annie, but I'm not gonna' say for sure though she was with me when I was getting dressed and she was kind of looking after the thing in a way, [who said], 'Oh there's Winnifred. She'll hold the veil'. And so Annie fixes the veil. And so Winnifred, bless her little heart, she took the veil—Annie showed her, got her hands fixed, you see." Stepping out onto the verandah, Isabel saw her family on the chairs borrowed from Bolsover church. "And mother and Grandma McFadyen (Grandfather was dead) were sittin' on the verandah, and Walter's mother. And Grandma and Grandpa Wallace. They had prime seats." Then she noticed Walter, standing with his best man at the arbour. The young people that she had been socializing with had said, 'Now be sure to tell your groom to be smiling when you appear, because you don't want a gloomy-lookin' groom'. She had passed on this advice. "And so, Walter was grinning from side to side, a big smile, when I go down those [verandah] steps, you see. And along comes Minnie behind, 'cause Minnie was the maid of honour. But when I was comin' down the steps, the wind kind of caught the veil. And I often wondered how many people in the guests noticed that I paused and kinda' turned, because I thought it was going to take the thing off my head, you see." (This comment intrigues me. Was she worried that someone—even Walter—would think she was about to make a mad dash for freedom?) Ultimately the veil settled down, as did the bride—for a short time.

When Isabel stood beside Walter, and Annie wound the veil around her feet, "I don't know what went on after that, because I nearly died". Mr. Burkholder told the wedding party to face the guests, when Isabel thought she'd have her back to them, as was always the case in an inside church wedding. Still upset that they hadn't had a rehearsal, this unexpected situation upset her more. She couldn't even remember her dad giving her away. As a teacher who was used to planning each day and taking control, she may have been more disconcerted than some would be to have such a surprise sprung on her. The distress in her voice as she told me suggested disappointment that her wedding wasn't the lovely event she had hoped it would be. In the end, her inclination to look at the silver lining inside the cloud led her to realize, "It didn't make much difference. We were outside and we could make our own wedding, and we did make it, and everything went off all right. Only, I was so nervous, and I was holdin' my flowers so tight to me, like this, it held up my dress and made my slip show a little bit in some of the [pictures] that were taken." This was no worse, really, than the famous (in our family) bridal party photo (page 73) with Winnifred yawning broadly while her bloomers drooped below her hemline.

The ceremony was blessedly short. The social part, the photo-taking and congratulations, were more relaxing. For the wedding feast in the dining room, the table was angled from the outside door to the living room door. "And so we seated, you see, the bride and the groom with our backs to the window…and Mr. Burkholder was at the head of the table. And the others were down the other side, and I don't know who was at the other end. But Mother kind of stayed with Grandma McFadyen, too, you see, so Dad filled in, I guess, wherever he fit. It didn't matter exactly. That's the way the whole thing was, anyway—wherever you fit." There were no place cards with names on them, no formalities, though of course a grace was said for the meal and a prayer for the happiness of the bride and groom. She concluded, "Oh, it went off all right, and we lived happily ever after as the story ends." A newspaper account (source unknown) of this union, which certainly struck *me* as a happy one, appears in Appendix N.

In concluding this wedding day story, my mother's focus again was on turning her dark clouds inside out, as she remarked, "Of course Walter and I were *so happy* to have a home of our own. We didn't have to go out driving somewhere and let the poor old horse stand a while, while we sat in the buggy and talked and everything, and then we'd drive a little more, and then that's the way you'd spend your evening. I was boarding, and for all I could've taken him in, I guess…I never felt free to do that sort of thing. But of course, we had lots of invitations from people in the Siloam church group. And Mrs. Hutchinson did have him in sometimes…from church—if he was a good boy and came to church," she concluded with a twinkle in her eye.

In preparation for their honeymoon, Walter had decided to put a padlock on the box he'd constructed under the seat of his Model T. Then "…we put in a second nightie and pyjamas, and a second outfit of clothing and that sort of thing in a dress box…thinking if they got our suitcases, at least we'd have something under the seat of the car. And the car was put in Dad's garage. And he was keeping the key ready for when we were going away." When she and Walter were ready to go, Isabel got the garage key from Will. They got away with no problem. As the car picked up speed, they heard bells. Someone had fastened sleigh bells for a horse harness, cans, old boots –a "nice collection" Isabel called it, underneath the Model T. When they were out of sight of the house, Walter, who was quite the practical joker himself, got out of the car, removed the "collection", and threw everything in the ditch. "But there was one bell we could not find. And the only time we'd hear it, maybe you'd turn a corner, and maybe just the way you'd turn. We'd [planned to spend] the night in a hotel in Whitby. It was the closest one to home, and we were anxious to get going. You didn't have much highway in those days, or anything else. Number 12 wasn't there. That was a gravel road full of potholes. And so, anyway, I think he found it the next morning, in the daylight, and took it off before we left Whitby."

But, the *pièce de résistance* was revealed on their wedding night. "When we went to get our clothes out of the box under the seat, if there weren't thistles in there! How did those thistles get in?" Two years later, when Isabel and Walter attended the wedding of Walter's brother Jack's oldest daughter in Barrie, the answer suddenly appeared. Mom told me: "Laura, Walter's sister, and I were goin' around…and Laura says, 'What can we do, to put somethin' in the…whatever?' I didn't know what we were going to put it in. She was doing all the suggesting. And she says, 'I wonder if there are any thistles around?' And I says, 'Aha! I know now how the thistles got into *my* nightgown'." Laura told all. Isabel's sister Viola had taken out of the garage a window that couldn't be seen from the house and then crawled in the window opening. Since she was a big girl, Isabel didn't know how she ever got through that space!

After Walter and Isabel's honeymoon, which was less than a week, "It was pretty well night when we got to my parents' home. We were ushered to the spare bedroom. The clothes cupboard door was open. And you went to close it, and behind the clothes cupboard door sat Isabel, all dressed up and on a chair. And you turned to close the door when you came in, you see, and behind the door was Walter all dressed up, in these clothes that he'd come in, you see, the night before [the wedding]. So we had great old howling laughter over that. And that was better than puttin' thistles in your bed." Walter wasn't alone in enjoying a practical joke, as long it wasn't a mean-spirited one.

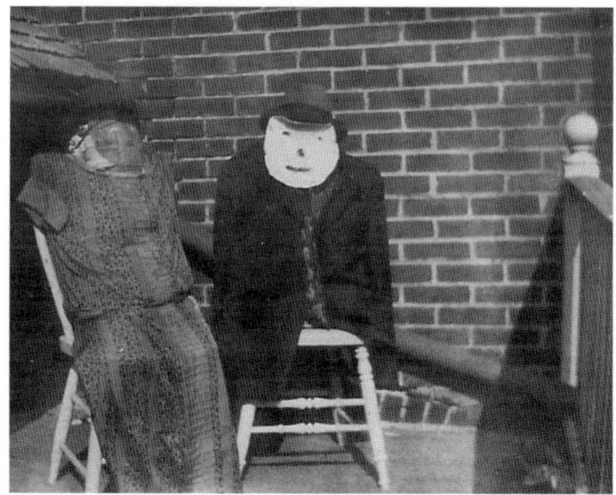

After their honeymoon, Walter and Isabel found that their pre-wedding clothes had taken on a life of their own.

The wedding party on September 22, 1926, (left to right) Angus Harrison, Walter Beach, Isabel Wallace, Minnie Wallace, and Winnifred Wallace.

Walter returned to the Beach farm in the Model T the next day. Isabel arrived there the first day of October from her parents' home, where she'd spent time collecting what she owned. "I had a bedroom suite. The girls all put their money together, you know, and bought that bedroom suite (that Walter and I always used), everything but the mattress and the springs. And the washstand, you know, because you don't have a washstand in a display in a store at that time." She also had her steamer trunk, purchased for her when she went to Orillia, and a black leather rocking chair—their wedding gift from her Aunt Minnie and Uncle Hugh. Mrs. Beach had furniture in the house when they came, as well: an extension table, some chairs, a sideboard, and a cookstove. After her stroke early in1926, Mrs. Beach had hired a Mrs. Lepard from Mount Albert to work for her. Isabel described how "They just went through the house, and everything was in place. Walter's mother had it all cleaned up, you know. What she didn't want was thrown away, and things that she would sell, that's all right. We'll keep them and we'll put them in the sale. And she had it all in her head. She was a wonderful woman. She was a great person. She really was." As I considered this comment, I was reminded of the saying, 'It takes one to know one'.

Walter got a neighbour with a ton truck to bring their belongings to the Uxbridge Township farm. "That was a big truck in those days… They came with the truck to bring me and whatever I 'cabbaged' from home. And mother gave me a chair. Mother and Dad asked me about what I'd like, and I said, 'Well I hope I can have a sewing machine', because I did do sewing—and mending was so important. And by hand, it's terrible. Well, they didn't know if they could afford to buy a whole sewing machine, but they gave me fifty dollars on it. I think I had to pay about twenty dollars or so [extra]. It was less than a hundred, anyway. So I got my sewing machine. But I didn't have it then, you see." All of the newlyweds' joint belongings went upstairs in the Beach house. "And then that evening, Mrs. Lepard went home. That was a Friday. And the next day was Saturday, and Markham Fair. And we went to Markham Fair. Of course, Walter's mother was no sissy. You know, she could look after herself for a while. And Warren was here. It was Walter that made the decision. I didn't know much about Markham Fair. We didn't stay real late. We had supper there, though. The church used to put on the supper, after the fair—the United Church." This day trip seems to have set a pattern for their marriage. When I was growing up, Markham Fair was like an institution, and my family's attendance a tradition. Our family went on many other annual outings—the Uxbridge Santa Claus parade, the Mount Albert Sports Day, the Brooklyn Fair, The Canadian National Exhibition in Toronto and several more. I'm grateful that, as a farm girl with few companions, I had the opportunity to mingle in the community, meet people, and expand my horizons.

When speaking about her life as a newlywed, Mom emphasized that she came to a household at the Beach farm. She and Walter lived with his mother, Roseanne, and his brother, Warren, from October first, 1926, until January first, 1927, because in the agreement drawn up around the sale of the farm Walter's mother requested the crop from 1926. "She said she would have possession till the first of January because she had planted the crop, and then she'd have to have a sale. Walter was paid by his mother, you see. And he was paid his wages until the year was up…" Working for his mother was a great advantage to him: he was thoroughly familiar with the farm, so he just kept on working when the ownership changed. As for my mother, "You might say I was working for Walter's mother, because I took Mrs. Lepard's place… I had nothing to do outside the house. But of course she didn't pay me. I wouldn't take it anyway." Isabel and Walter's belongings stayed in the large bedroom upstairs until January 3, 1927. Naturally, my mother had to make some personal adjustments in this living situation. The pantry had no table or other flat workspace, just open shelves. She hated (because she never was used to it, she said) preparing everything for meals and baking on the extension table that they also ate at. "I found that the most difficult part for me. But then, I could do it." It was only three months, after all—just a little cloud.

Meanwhile, "Walter's mother prepared for a sale in November. And the girls did help for that, of course—Lizzie and Lettie. And we went up home [to Thorah Township] for Christmas. And Walter's mother sort of went right along with it and almost insisted that we go. And she and Warren'd get along all right, you see. I don't remember if we stayed all night or not that time. I don't think we did…because you'd have to have somebody come and do the chores, you see." Keenly aware of her own position, Isabel kept a low profile. "I was keepin' pretty quiet, you know. I didn't want to get them thinkin' that I was bossing the thing or anything like that—which I didn't need to do. And the boys were so good to help—Walter and Bill and Oliver and Warren." Roseanne planned to live on the proceeds from the sale of the property and her farm and household goods. She intended to pay five dollars a week to stay wherever she went. Early in January, Roseanne went to live with her daughter, Lettie, in Siloam.

Finally, Walter and Isabel had the reins in their own home and with their own farming business. They decided to make their changes, too. In 1927, they opened a joint account in the bank that had just started coming twice a week to Goodwood village (which was about three miles from the farm), from the Stouffville branch (which was seven miles from the farm). The bank staff traveled to and from the village by train. "They had [the bank] in that old hotel that was on the corner. And Walter liked havin' it down there, because if he wanted it in a hurry, he'd just jump in the car in everyday clothes. Or if he'd take things down to put on the train (potatoes or anything like that) he'd be in his everyday work clothes from the barn, and he didn't have to dress up to go to the bank. It was a very sensible idea."

The first full week of January 1927, Isabel went to Toronto to buy items she and Walter needed for their household. She went two or three more times, into February. At Eaton's August sale she got the living-room suite, after applying for and successfully getting her teaching pension. In 1929 they bought the bedroom suite for the south bedroom, at that same annual August sale at Eaton's. This provided a place for her parents to sleep when they came to visit. They had sold their farm and moved to Toronto in 1928. Walter went to the Goodwood railway station to get the suite. Everything but the bed was assembled. When they removed the crating, they discovered one piece was chipped a little, but they kept the suite anyway. Perhaps with a new bride's pride of ownership, perhaps with the sense of history that was always with her, my mother wrote on the back of one of the little jewel box drawers in the dresser: 'This belongs to Mrs. Walter T. Beach, R. R. No. 3, Stouffville, Ontario', as I discovered in August 2004 while cleaning the dresser. She had taken such good care of this dresser—as she did all her belongings—that the original manufacturer's label was still almost perfect. It declared that the set had been manufactured by the Knechtel Furniture Company, Limited, makers of Quality Furniture since 1867. The (south) spare bedroom became mine when I was about ten. I grew quite attached to that bedroom suite. In 1962, the set was split up. Her sister Chrissie and I got all of the pieces but one. Mom kept the most elegant—the dressing/vanity table—for her home because the low mirror allowed her to see most of her outfit at once. She never owned a full-length mirror. There was little 'vanity' about her. She just wanted to look respectable. In 1999, the suite was reunited in my home. That dressing table, a constant gentle reminder of my mother, is my favourite piece in the set.

Although Isabel felt the Beach house was in much better shape when they went to the farm than the barn was, she and Walter did some house renovations right away. Originally it was a small pioneer home that had been expanded in the late 1800s to make way for the large John Beach family. It wasn't a model of carpentry skills. "They said that whoever built the house to begin with had neither a level nor a square. And besides, in this particular house, the joists were not strong; it'd be a plank sort of thing, about two inches thick, and maybe six inches down." The dining room ceiling was always 'shaky', Mom told me, because originally there was an east-west partition through it. Moving the partitions had been a bad idea; the partition downstairs was supporting the upstairs. Walter decided to rectify the situation. In January 1927 he worked on their bedroom (which was directly above the dining room), as well as the upstairs hall and the living room. "So he tore up the old floor [in our bedroom] and he tried to level off, but of course that wasn't much of an advantage for the depth of those [joists]. But what he did, was he took two by four scantlings and cut them to fit…to make it so it didn't shake so much. Then he laid the old floor down on top of it, you see." They hired F. A. Forsythe, a well-respected carpenter from Goodwood, to lay hardwood flooring in all three areas under renovation.

They decided to put the cheaper second grade flooring upstairs. Mom verified that even it was good quality flooring. She knew F.A. wouldn't settle for anything less. "But it was first quality we put down in the living-room, and we bought the stuff from Schell's Lumber in Stouffville. And [Schell] told us how to finish it." The living-room floor had been in especially poor condition. It was one-inch tongue and grooved maple. Having been finished with the wrong kind of oil, it was very dark. The oil had been used to fill in the grain, make the boards smooth. The boards were also varnished and waxed. As a result, the floor never looked clean. "So we just put down oak, right over top of it. And you always put the grain/boards the opposite direction." While F.A. and Walter were working upstairs she heard F.A. say, 'Well, I'm tellin' ya' I wouldn't wanna' be puttin' hydro in this house'. At that time, some Goodwood homes were getting hydro. The wires were being installed under the flooring. Luckily, by the time Isabel and Walter got hydro, installation methods had changed. They finished the new living-room floor themselves. First they sanded. Then "You used cornstarch, mixed up with paint oil and turpentine. You put that on the floor. And then you took a brick and wrapped it in a strong cloth, and you rubbed it into the grain of the wood…and if there was a little crack or that, it would fill that too." They avoided varnish and went to the final step, waxing. Walter made a polisher for Isabel from a wooden box containing a large rock. They wrapped the tail of an everyday shirt around the bottom of the box. Walter attached an old broom handle to facilitate pushing the polisher. I remember that homemade polisher very well. It came out of the upstairs closet every year for the spring cleaning ritual. My mother never owned another floor polisher.

In 1930, she and Walter fixed up the south bedroom as the guest room, and put in two clothes cupboards. One opened into the hallway, the other into the bedroom. F.A. did that work too. They also built the outside cistern to hold rainwater. Before that, their soft water was available in a barrel in the basement. "And I loved the cistern with the soft water. Oh my, oh my. I wish I had it now. It was easy to work with, and goodness sakes' alive, the water was handy and everything. But it didn't run." So "You had to pump it, but then what's that? That gives you muscle." Cloud-turning again. The soft water pump was located in the summer kitchen, with a sink, a built-in cupboard and a window to the west. After they got the clothes cupboards done, Isabel had wanted F.A. to build cupboards in her pantry, but he'd promised the Goodwood Baptist congregation he would put cupboards in the church basement. Later, he wasn't feeling well. Anyway, she reasoned, the pantry cupboards couldn't be done until the farm was paid for.

"You don't put a lot of money into buildings on land that you don't own." In fact, very little money was available for house improvements over the next ten years. Other circumstances also intervened, as Mom so aptly summarized: "Well, you see, the Depression came, and Beverley came, and the war came, and Catherine came. And so we went on, as we do."

Looking after the farm business required time and money too. Spring arrived early that first year they owned the farm. "The first Monday of April, we had a load of hogs (at that time you sold your pigs by the penful, not by two or three pigs at a time, not the way they got when they started to grade them—grade A, B, and so on)." When they sold a penful, "Some would be a little too fat, and some would be just beautiful, and some might have stood another week. And you had a stock rack which you put on the wagon or the sleigh." Walter had bought the stock rack, the wagon, and some animals at his mother's sale the previous November. My mother seemed to question some of his judgment when she told me about another of his purchases, but at the same time she understood his motivations. "He bought the old grey mare. So, Walter thought he'd raise some colts like his mother was doin', you see. Anyway, I suppose he had felt towards that old horse…because Walter had been with his mother for about twelve years, I think, before that. We started out, you see, with two bay horses and this old grey mare. And Walter had a driver, of course, but then he was kind of an expensive driver for people that didn't have much money, so he sold him. We bought one cow that was a good milker and the calf at its side. I think he had two cows after the sale. Then that winter, you see, we had milk right away from the one that had a calf, but the other one had to have a calf. It'd be after Christmas before it'd have the calf, I guess. And that's pretty well what we had for cows."

Walter desperately needed equipment to operate the farm. He had bought his mother's binder for ten or twelve dollars at the sale. "He knew what was good on it, and what had been fixed and what was likely to go on it… And then in the spring, he was at another auction sale, and there was a binder being sold that was exactly the same, made the same year, and everything (maybe he bought it for five dollars) and he brought it home to be pieces to fix the other one. So he started out with a binder—I know it was less than twenty-five dollars. But then, he was kinda' mechanically inclined and he enjoyed doing that sort of thing, and he didn't mind fixin' at it, you know." Mom recollected a remarkable amount of detail about the beginning of their farm business. At other auction sales, Walter bought a bucket or an old pail filled with nails and screwnails, fence staples, etc. Such items had all been sold at his mother's auction. There'd been no such sale after his father died in 1901. "Everything went on the next day, just as it would've the day before. There never was a spade or a shovel, a fork or a thing [sold]. And it was right. That was the right and proper thing for her to do, because that was what her money was invested in, and she needed her money to live on. And all that was gone. Walter had to start buying."

Through her own upbringing, discussions with Walter, and reading the farm magazines, Isabel became quite knowledgeable about farming. When their wedding didn't happen as early in September as they'd originally planned, she understood that Walter had to plant the fall rye crop, which always was sown in September or October. Walter tried growing wheat sometime in the late 1930s, but the crop was poor. Uxbridge Township's sandy soil wasn't suitable. Sometimes he planted mixed grain for feed (oats and barley and spring wheat) or just oats for the horses and barley for the pigs and cattle. She continued, "And then you'd have to sow the clover seed with the grain seed, in order for the grain to be the nurse crop for the hay. And about that time, just a little earlier than that, the sweet clover got going, and that was a wonderful thing for this kind of land, because the roots were so sturdy and went into the ground and gave the right nutrients.

They made good soil… And then you'd have it mixed, too, and so you'd have timothy…and a grass seed…and alfalfa." Hay had to be cut at just the right time. If it got too old, especially the sweet clover, the stalks got too woody. "You had to go by the moon," she said. "The hay would go on for two or three years, and then you'd have to rotate it, you see. At that time, we didn't put in any corn. We didn't have a silo." They did grow turnips and plenty of potatoes, good crops for the sandy Uxbridge soil. Of the fifty acres Walter planted in crops, usually five or six were in potatoes. "Everybody grew fields and fields of potatoes. Ike Smith…used to dig the potatoes with a fork, you know. And Walter went behind with a pail and picked them up. Of course it's hard to farm on the hills with the implements they had in those days, because they didn't build the implements for hills. So, while some people that had more level land had diggers before he did, eventually he got one."

Isabel and Walter worked as many acres as they could manage by themselves. They never did have steady hired help. Walter hired Ike Smith, who had worked for Roseanne in the same way, by the day. That's how Ike preferred to work. He lived at home and he ate at home. Isabel soon noticed, "He'd come over here, you know, and you'd know very well he hadn't had too much breakfast, in a sense. He'd have plenty of bread and butter (I don't know about the butter; they said he used lard) and tea. But he wouldn't have a good meal to stick to his ribs. And Walter had said he'd be here (when he hadn't been for a long time—when the spring work would start) two or three days before he'd be able to do what he should be doin', because he wouldn't have the food. But he was *very* independent. It's too bad there aren't a few more people like him now, you know, that would have a little pride in their independence." This was a telling comment. My mother valued independence as if it were gold. Independence, combined with hard work and intelligent management, had allowed her and my Dad to develop the farm and its auxiliary businesses to such a degree that it supported two families comfortably for nearly fifty years. In proud independence, she refused to apply for the government supplement income after my dad died, even though she qualified. It just wasn't right, she argued. She didn't need it.

Isabel helped with quite a bit of the farm work, especially before she had a child. But "I never picked the potatoes. I remember I said before we were married, 'I'll pick turnips any day and every day, but I will not pick potatoes, 'cause every time you move your pail, it's heavier than the last time. And with turnips, the horses are drawing them'. You bend over to get them, but that's all right. My back wouldn't carry those potatoes. I wouldn't try it. So I never did, except when he and Ike were doin' it in October." The early crop was harvested in August to provide spending money. The late crop was stored in the basement to be sold in the winter when the price was generally better. If frost was expected when the late crop was dug and bagged in the field, Walter went to get the horse and wagon to bring the bags to the barn. She took his place then, picking behind Ike until Walter arrived with the wagon. Turnips were a different story. "I picked turnips every year, and I just loved it because it was outside in the beautiful fall air, and the leaves were coloured and we'd just come to the barn with a load and then go back. Oh, it was good. I liked it. I had my overalls and an old shirt of Walter's, and there'd I'd be." Her voice resonated and her face shone in the memory of this exhilarating experience.

She knew the benefits of a buckwheat crop, too. Sown in July, it was used in any field the farmer wanted to clear of weeds. "So, we did put in buckwheat some years—almost every year later on. I remember Walter always liked to use the buckwheat chop to fatten the chickens in the fall, because the meat'd be so white. And if you used the corn, it made the meat yellow. You'd take your own fowl…they had the market you know, in Uxbridge at that time, and Stouffville too." After Isabel's parents moved to Toronto, she and Walter acquired several Toronto customers who loved to get a fowl direct from the farm. Isabel's mother had given her about twelve pullets from chickens that were raised at her home in 1926. "Where'd we get the rooster? I think Laura gave us a rooster, if I remember right." Then giggling, she said, "And then in the spring, you see, the old hens'd sit on the nest and say, 'Come on, come on, I gotta have some eggs'." And she giggled again, pleased with this natural reproductive process, while perhaps at the same time recalling her and Walter's own participation in the ways of nature. "Put the eggs under them and then you have some chickens, and the hens, 'Cluck, cluck, cluck, cluck'."

At first, the chicken house was just across the laneway from the house. Isabel didn't like it there because the chickens usually strayed into the yard. She realized, however, that Walter's mother had found this location convenient for looking after them. So Walter fixed a place for the chicken house behind the woodshed, a little further from the house. When the young chickens had grown enough, they went with the hens south of the house into a field where they caught insects among the crop of grain, hay or potatoes. They never went into the yard. "So, I'd always set enough hens to fill that [chicken coop]. You'd set three hens at the same time, so that if the chickens came out well, you might have two hens lookin' after them. And if you had a poor hatch, one hen would look after them all. And then you'd set three more. It took three weeks for the chickens to hatch. And then, some years you had quite a few roosters, you know." As with most farm wives at the time, Isabel used the egg money to buy groceries and other household goods. From dependence on this income, of course, came the saying—well-known and oft-quoted by my mother— 'Don't count your chickens before they're hatched'. In the late 1980s she read to me from her accounts book and marveled at some of the egg prices: "In 1929, twenty-nine cents a dozen, thirty-five cents a dozen." In 1931, she received a dollar and eighty-six cents for seven dozen eggs. "Now," she noted, "we pay that for one dozen—exactly. One eighty-six they are right now down in Stouffville—large ones." She went on to look at the list of prices received for a dozen eggs, once just thirteen cents. "They graded them on me," she explained with a wry smile.

Isabel also helped with milking the cows and processing the milk. "Walter'd milk two; I'd milk two. And then he'd milk three if we had five." They sold their cream for butter-making, so they had a cream separator. "At first we had an old separator. We didn't always have too good a test. In a way sometimes the test wasn't high enough, but it was hard to get it much better. That was the test of how much fat. The cream man would…leave his can, and then you'd put in the cream and then he'd pick up the can. Then the next time, he'd bring the money for the previous week and take that can, and so on." Each day as she added cream to the can, she stirred to prevent the cream from souring. She never added warm cream to cold. Isabel's sharp observation and reasoning skills were at work here—because she did so naturally, but also because the cream was another important part of her household income. "It could be that the flavour would not be so good where people weren't careful about things like that. Because there could be a little bit of mould get in the sour cream if you didn't keep it stirred. We had a good cellar, and if you used your head, it didn't really get sour. If you poured it into hot tea it'd maybe go like sour cream, but it was all right for the butter flavour. And when you think of what money we got…" Again looking over her old record book, she exclaimed, "Goodness sakes' alive, when I look at it here—a dollar seventeen. But then, we didn't have as many pounds then, either." Appendix O shows an Uxbridge Creamery envelope from 1956, when she received five dollars and one cent for twenty-six pounds of cream. "Of course we never did have more than five cows. If you had eight cows, then you'd have to pay somebody to come and milk, and they wouldn't be happy about it." With Beverley's help later on, they milked cows and sold cream until the mid-1960s.

Sometime in the thirties, she recalled, a man moved to the second concession of Uxbridge from Toronto, thinking he would farm—and maybe thinking he would survive better there than in the city. "And he never did stay long enough to become a part of the community, and he wasn't very much for mingling, you know. Of course, at that time, if you were gonna' live in the community and farm, you had to be neighbourly or you didn't have anybody to help you thresh and that sort of thing. But I guess he didn't find farming just what he thought it was. He was only there about three years." This man had apparently had enough money to buy equipment. He'd purchased the new binder that was in the auction sale when he left the farm. And Walter bought it. "And he really got a good deal on it. I remember he and Warren came home from the sale talkin' about how stuff really went kind of cheap, considering it was so new." In a reflection of the economic times, the Dirty Thirties, "It was the first time that Walter had ever bought anything and didn't pay for it right then. And you see, at that time, at these auction sales, they would take your cash or cheque or a promissory note. [Walter] hardly knew how I'd react to it, as if he wasn't sure he should be tellin' me he gave a promissory note on that binder. I think it was a hundred and twenty-five dollars; two hundred and twenty-five should've bought the thing brand new at that time, I would've thought. And I don't know that he paid anything on it. But my goodness, I told him, nobody needed a binder any worse than he did. And so, anyway, we got it paid for."

As far as Isabel was concerned, 1931 was their worst year because there was such a spread in the prices. They didn't have much of a cash flow either, but they made do with what they had. "And of course you know the way we did, and I keep saying that's the only way they're going to get back out of this mess they're in now, in the country, and in the families, and in the businesses. And there's no use in them thinkin' they can do it any other way, because they'll never succeed. They simply have to use the money they have in their mitt—and forget about the rest. That's the only way they're gonna' get it. And that's what we did." To the day she died, my mother was opposed to credit cards. She knew that disciplined spending was much easier when you didn't use the plastic card. During the Depression, she exercised that discipline on a trip to Watson's store in Goodwood with her basket of eggs. "You used to go down, when we were first married, and you had ten or twelve dozen and they were thirty cents a dozen or something, well you knew how much money you'd have. [In the thirties,] you'd go down with the same number of eggs, and you didn't know how much money you had. But, whatever you got, that's what you spent. Then you put your groceries into the basket the eggs were in. And I remember quite well, [the store owner] Charlie Watson didn't want me to take anything out of that basket, you see. Of course, I'd have some cash from the cream, I suppose. However, I didn't have enough that day with me to pay for all that. And so I just said, 'Well I can take something out of the basket'." The 'something' was possibly rice or raisins; they could live without it.

The cream and egg money provided a steady cash income. Occasionally they'd sell a pig. "We only had two sows, so you see that'd only make about forty pigs a year. You see, ten dollars a hundred pounds, goin' down to Toronto…two hundred pounds is what you'd figure they should weigh when you'd be sellin' them. So you'd see how much you had. And then if you had to buy feed for them, there'd be a certain amount of stuff you'd have to buy—for one thing, salt. All animals had to have salt. And then there were other things that they had to have sometimes too. Once in a while the vet had to come around, you know, if the calves got scours or something." When I asked about clothing, Mom said she and Walter bought very little in the Dirty Thirties. "No, we didn't, but you know, we had Eaton's catalogue. And I must admit, you know, that I don't know what people would've done without that Eaton's catalogue. And if you happened to be able to go into Toronto, which I was at the time, on account of Mother and Dad living down there, and you'd go to the Annex at Eaton's—it was really a caution what you could get. I'm tellin' you, there's a family name that should never be forgotten in Toronto or Ontario, is the T. Eaton Company. They were the first people (so I read before now) to put on their catalogues and [sales slips] 'Goods Satisfactory or Money Refunded'. They were the first to do that, and you would send back anything, there never was a thing said about it, no matter what it was."

Mom was fortunate to have another way to temporarily access the silver lining of this dark cloud that hovered over much of the world in the nineteen-thirties. She could visit her parents and sister Chris in Toronto. When my brother Beverley was young, perhaps in 1935 (which was two years before her mother, Kate, died), Mom took a few days to go to Toronto for such a visit. She was welcomed warmly and pressed to eat some of the many treats prepared for her. But she responded with, "I don't want anything to eat. I'm stuffed. I just want a good laugh." And one of them said, "You're in luck. There's a Charlie Chaplin movie just down the street." So she got her antidote to the Depression blues.

Overall, surviving the Great Depression was easier for farm people than for many. Still, the question arises: How did they manage? Life was definitely simpler then. The technology that now gobbles up so much of our time and money didn't exist. Farmers had little time for entertainments outside of church, community, and family social connections—where admission charges were low or non-existent. Besides the meat, vegetables, fruit, milk and eggs produced on the farm, they had wild berries and morels that grew abundantly around the area, speckled trout from a neighbourhood stream, and maple syrup processed from sap harvested in their own maple bush. With a little ingenuity, a farmer's wife could provide hearty and nutritious meals for her family. I think my parents did brilliantly because they became experts at how to handle money and be resourceful. Planning carefully, scraping by, they made it through one of Canada's darkest times in the twentieth century.

Then in 1939 came the Second World War.

CHAPTER SEVEN: We Worked for It

Still Plenty

Rations of meat, rations of cheese,
Rations of bacon and ham,
Rations of margarine, rations of milk,
Rations of sugar and jam,
Rations of fruits, rations of lard,
Rations of butter and tea,
Rations of clothes, rations of boots,
Come and go shopping with me!
Unrationed sky, unrationed sea,
Unrationed sunshine and breeze,
Unrationed stars, unrationed clouds,
Unrationed beauty of trees,
Unrationed peace, unrationed power,
Unrationed pardon and love,
Unrationed faith, unrationed grace,
Free from our Father above.

Author Unknown

During the Second World War (1939 to 1945), of course both domestic and wild farm produce was still available. Flour, sugar, tea and other staples, however, were rationed. Each family could buy only a limited amount, using ration tokens. The poem reproduced above, published in a 1943 issue of the *Free Press Prairie Farmer*, captures well how Isabel carried on. Her strong connection with nature combined with a deep faith to provide nourishment and strength for turning the clouds of her life inside out once more.

In January 1939, opportunity for a new business venture literally arrived on the farmhouse doorstep one Monday morning in the person of Mr. Scott and a younger man from the Canadian National Railway. "They'd got off the train at Goodwood and skied up here through these hills. Now just before that, I guess maybe a year before, Dagmar [ski area near Uxbridge] had started, and the CPR was just havin' a wonderful time having excursion trains out from Toronto to Dagmar (and making money hand over fist, I guess), so the Canadian National thought they'd have to have a little bit of competition in some of the Uxbridge hills here. So, this Scott was quite high up on the executive of the Canadian National… He thought if they got running out to Goodwood on the CN, why then they might work up a ski resort around through these hills." Since it was almost noon and dinnertime when the men arrived, Isabel invited them to stay. She even remembered the menu on that surprising day. "And I had put potatoes in the oven to bake, you see, so I didn't have to take time to peel them. I had spare ribs with dressing in them that I had made for New Year's Day, and so we were to finish that, and I had the Christmas pudding on steamin' to finish it. I might have had turnip or something on top of the stove." The men accepted her invitation to stay for dinner. Not much choice of restaurants! Mom quipped. "I went to take the potatoes out of the oven when they were cooked, and Mr. Scott says, 'Oh, don't take them out. Leave them in there; they'll be nice and hot'. I guess he was nearly frozen." She and the CNR men were discussing the proposal when Walter came in for his noon meal.

As they ate, an agreement was reached. The skiers would come on Sundays, not the best day for a family that usually attended church, but in the winter it didn't matter, Mom commented, because often the roads weren't ploughed. She and Walter decided they'd go ahead and see how things worked out. First, Walter had to find out if any neighbours would object to the skiers being on their land. Nobody did. The property available to the skiers included the Carmody's 200-acre ranch just south of the farm. Walter and two neighbours, Morgan Degeer and Bristol McGuigan, were to take their sleighs and teams of horses to meet the skiers at the corner of the second concession and Highway 47. And so the CNR started bringing out the skiers, many of whom were CN employees. Mom's job was to provide food and beverages at noon and before they headed back to Toronto. The noon meal was a full-course dinner. I can assure you from personal experience that it would have been a good one. Often she prepared roast beef, which could be ready the day before. For dessert, she might make mincemeat or raisin pies. If the skiers couldn't come because of poor weather, the pies would be fine in the corner cupboard in the farmhouse summer kitchen, which wasn't heated in the winter. "And I'd cook up potatoes and vegetables, and have pickle. I remember putting that ripe cucumber pickle on, one time, and one of the girls was sayin' to the other, 'What is it?' And the other one was sayin', 'I don't know. It might be pumpkin'. So of course I heard them and I said, 'No, it's ripe cucumber'. And, oh, they thought that was awful good pickle. They sure gobbled it up. And Mr. Scott, he noticed I didn't have much help in the house, so he was helping, goin' into the little pantry/kitchen to serve. He always came." Isabel received one dollar for each person's meal. Just before they left, she set out milk, sugar, and cups for coffee, tea or hot chocolate. Each person paid twenty-five cents for a hot drink and snack, such as tea biscuits. Isabel couldn't recall what they paid for the sleigh ride. Possibly the CN paid that bill.

Walter and Isabel didn't have a telephone then, even though Walter was an Uxbridge township councillor. They had had a telephone in 1932 when Beverley was born, but "…in 1933 [when we were feeling the pinch of the depression] Walter had said, 'Well we'll have to do without either the car or the telephone, I guess. We'll have to cut back somewhere'. I said, 'Well it seems more sensible to do without the telephone. You need the car to run to town for a little bit of pig starter for the baby pigs, or anything like that'. So that's what we did. When the fall came, the car keys were thrown in the dish up on top of the cupboard and we weren't running the car in the winter 'cause they never kept the roads open." With great enthusiasm for the whole enterprise, Mr. Scott had offered to put in the phone that Monday in January. It would be needed to give information, make the arrangements for the horses and sleighs, and find out how many had signed up for a particular Sunday. But Isabel and Walter decided to pay for the phone, as they really needed it for themselves.

Nineteen thirty-nine was a poor year for skiing. Many weekends, there was rain. The skiers came several Sundays as long as they could. "But then it came a fairly early spring too. I mean March was not good; lots of times you have good skiing in March. And then, you see, it was just whatever the weather made. It wasn't like these places now that have groomed trails. But they had a good time, anyway, and a lot of fun." Other glitches occurred. Mr. Scott, "so full of pep and energy", unfortunately had a stroke on one of the return train trips to Toronto. "He didn't come out of it well enough to be ever out of the hospital. He overdid it, I guess. And the CN wouldn't allow them to stop at the end of the concession. They had to go to Goodwood. But then, you know, the people liked the sleigh rides, and they were dressed warm for skiing. That was part of the day."

The winter of 1940, the Second World War was underway, "and it just went flat, because the young people weren't there to ski. And, really, Dagmar went pretty flat there too for a while. And after the war, see, Dagmar kept theirs up a little bit…it wasn't much of a thing [in the fifties] but then it got built up more. I think it was more because there were highways and they kept them open for people to get there." To me, it was a shame that this side business was so short-lived. The hills on the farm and the Carmody ranch were wonderful for skiing. With some of my Toronto cousins or on my own I spent many hours skiing those hills when I was a teenager. And, like the skiers in 1939, we enjoyed hot drinks and Mom's wholesome homemade food when we got back to the house.

One lasting benefit did result from the CNR skiers. Mom described how "After [the skiers] were here a time or so, we were talkin' one day when they came in to get their hot drink before they'd leave, and they said, 'We should have a name for this, you know'." They had called one spot on the Carmody property, where a single pine tree stood at the top of a hill, 'The Trail of the Lonesome Pine'. "And so we were muddlin' around about names, and it happened that I was the one that said 'Echo Valley', for I says, 'You know you never know where the sounds are comin' from in this blessed place. There are echoes all over the place. I guess Echo Valley is what you'd have to call it'. 'Echo Valley it'll be,' they said. And then, we got usin' it too, you know." The first farm truck was green with Echo Valley Farm painted on the side. Some people said that the name had to be registered to put it on a vehicle, so "… the next truck we didn't have it put on, and it wasn't on after that. But it didn't matter, anyway. It came to the point where [Beverley and/or Walter] weren't too fussy about having the name on anyway. It was none of the other guys' business. They were too nosey." But the name stuck. Today it is proudly advertised with a large sign on the front lawn, *Echo Valley Farm, established 1876.*

Walter and Isabel weren't able to make changes or expand the barn until 1946 because of first, paying off the mortgage, second, the Great Depression, third, the Second World War. "And in the meantime, it was a bad time to keep the roof from leaking," Mom told me. In the early 1930s, Walter put a tarpaper product called Ready Roofing over the existing roof and sealed it with tar. The second time the roof needed attention, Walter ordered a barrel of tar to seal it in the bad places. "So it came on the train to Goodwood, and Walter went after supper down to Goodwood to get this barrel. And at that time, we had a Model T 'runabout' car—there was one seat in it, you know, and there was a back in it, like a buggy back, sort of. And so, he was gonna' bring it—took a rope and that to put it on the back of that runabout." When he didn't appear in a reasonable time, she "…was at home here havin' a fit, wondering where in the world he was, not gettin' back. And the chores weren't done, and I usually helped with the milking, you see. And I thought, 'Well is he in the ditch somewhere? Maybe upside down in the ditch, and all this'." She decided to walk across the sideroad to join him. About halfway across to the next concession, she met him. And she chuckled at the thought of what he'd done. "Well, somewhere over on the third he hit a bump and the blooming thing fell off, and some of the tar ran out, you see. So he was busy scoopin' it up… He'd picked up all he could get of the stuff (and it didn't matter about havin' sand in it; for the roof it didn't make any difference)." This patching got them through until the mortgage was paid. Materials were hard to get during the war, anyway. If a person wanted a keg of nails, "You could get some this week, and next week you'd need more and you'd go to get them and they wouldn't have any, you see. They were short. Of course, things like that weren't rationed. It just wasn't there."

In 1939, Walter and Isabel did manage to build a free-standing garage. The original garage attached to the north end of the house had long ago been commandeered for winter wood storage. The new garage, "We only built for one car. We didn't look far enough ahead. But we had it with a hip roof, and Walter had steps up there, fixtures and a workshop up there, see. And the verandah wasn't on. And so F. A. [Forsythe] came to put on the verandah and to build the garage, and the doghouse, with the scraps left from the garage." On the twenty-fourth of May, all work stopped for the holiday. "That's when we appreciated our holidays the right way," Mom interjected. This one was special, a highlight of her life. She and Walter went to Toronto to see King George VI and Queen Elizabeth, later known as "The Queen Mum" and one of my mother's heroes.

A few years later, the house got some extra attention. Florence (Harrison) Kemp, a Beach niece born in 1935, whom I interviewed in September 2003, came to help Isabel the summer of 1945, when I was five years old. "And we housecleaned," Florence said. "I remember the one big closet…[in the hall] and taking all the stuff out of this closet, cleaning it all out, dusting everything off, puttin' it all back. And we painted and papered. It was upstairs. We did that hallway going upstairs. We didn't do their bedroom. We did the spare room, in which I slept. I was just a mother's helper. I was just sort of an extra hand. I was old enough to hold the end of the paper." Basically Florence was there to keep me occupied so that my almost forty-five-year-old mother could get her work done—or maybe even have a rest. Florence recalled, "She was having a bit of a difficult time. She was having her sweats and her time. I'm sure it was because she was in her menopause. I didn't know too much about menopause at that time, but anyway, I learned."

Certain aspects of Isabel's personality left a deep impression on Florence, including her organization and orderliness. She said Isabel "always wore her apron from the afternoon and evening before" in the morning. She'd dust and clean and scrub the vegetables while she had on the 'dirty' apron. "And then she always put on a clean apron for lunch. There was a little sort of washstand off the summer kitchen. There was a basin in there, and water…a little sort of cubbyhole. And she always went in there and got her face done and fixed up, put on a clean apron, before lunch. And she'd have me go in and do my hair. She thought it was important that you wash your face and hands and do your hair before the men (well, it was only Walter and Beverley) came in for lunch. That was a ritual she did every day. I don't remember her fussing up so much before dinner/supper at night, but I do remember it at lunch, for some reason. You should look your best." This ritual was news to me. I have no memory of that cubbyhole or its exact location in the summer kitchen, though I do recall from later years that Mom still habitually combed her hair and made herself presentable before sitting down to a meal.

Sometimes, that summer, Florence was sent to pick berries that often went into a 'fruit cobbler' dessert for the evening meal. For berry-picking, my mother always put on an old pair of Walter's overalls or dress pants and one of his cast-off long-sleeved cotton shirts. Ordinarily, my mother never wore pants. She did have a pair of shorts that she wore on extremely hot days, but not to the table for a meal. She also wore to the berry patch a straw hat securely tied with a belt from one of her old housedresses. Florence said, "I had her hat on, because of the sun. But I think I had on my ordinary jeans. She might have even had me put on a long-sleeved thing to keep from scratching. It might have even been one of Beverley's shirts." To add to the larder, Florence recalled, Beverley sometimes went fishing on a rainy day in the brook that ran through the nearby Wees' property. If he brought home brook trout, Isabel often cooked them for supper. Whatever was harvested from the country around, my mother always accepted and used with respect, be it a few wild blackberries, the wild mushrooms called morels, or a bouquet of wild flowers I'd found on my childhood wanderings. We were all treated democratically.

The routines of this now well-established household stuck in Florence's mind too. "I remember goin' down to Goodwood to the little store to shop—Charlie Watson's store—to do some shopping. And then we went over to Uxbridge, or maybe Stouffville. We used to do a big shopping [there]." Saturday night shopping in Uxbridge was close to a ritual for my parents. "And through the week, if there was some little thing, down to Goodwood we'd go… I can't remember going to Siloam store, but maybe we did." Florence enjoyed this time in the Walter Beach household because "I came from a family where there were so many of us, and then to be sort of just a few, you could take note of a lot of things."

That fall, Walter started looking for a barn to buy. The timbers in the old Beach farm barn were still good, but too few to make a larger barn, and he wanted to lengthen it. Mom recalled its good features: The stable was all cement; there were two pigpens at the north end, then the cow stable. But Walter needed more places to tie up cattle. He also needed somewhere to put the young cattle. They could run in the box stall sometimes, but it was needed for the mare when she was going to foal. The other three stalls were for the team of horses and an extra one. Walter found a barn about the size of theirs at Brown Hill near the south end of Lake Simcoe. He consulted Morley Simms, who was the best barn-builder through the surrounding countryside. They decided it could be used.

The day Morley's men and about half a dozen men from around the neighbourhood, including Jack Sheehy, went to tear down the barn, Isabel packed them a lunch. Jack never forgot that lunch. Neither did my mother. Forty years later, she described it for me. "I made scalloped potatoes, and put them in the oven in the morning. I probably peeled them the night before. I never thought anything of it 'cause that's the way I was raised on a farm. And you made do. Whatever was necessary to do, you did. And I thought, the men had no hot meal or anything, you see, when they were up there. And you gave them, like they do in the shanties or in the bush, a honey pail and they'd make a fire and they'd steep their tea. And that was the only heat they'd have, because there was nobody livin' on the place, you know. And then I had ham sandwiches, 'cause we'd butchered, and there was the ham of the pig. And so I'd cooked it, and it was cold. And I put in pies. But it was the scalloped potatoes. And I thought, 'Mercy, by noon they'll be gettin' cold, won't they? Whatever could I do to make them hot?' And we used to put bricks in the oven and heat them to drive to Beaverton, and roll them up in paper. And so, I thought, 'I'll use my smoothing irons, you see'. There was one the handle came out of…and so I heated the smoothing irons, and I packed them in paper and put it in a wooden box, and then these scalloped potatoes." Years later, one time when she met Jack Sheehy, he said, 'Mrs. Beach, I'll never forget those scalloped potatoes'. "I guess he was about half frozen when the time came. And to take those hot potatoes out of that box made his day." This story is one of my favourites from all of the taping Mom and I did together. I love her ability to see what lay ahead, to use creative thinking, to problem-solve, to care for others.

Another factor in the decision to build the barn in 1946 was that hydro service was coming to the second concession of Uxbridge Township. Isabel and Walter's closest and most affluent neighbours, the Weeses, had wanted hydro a few years earlier. Several people on the concession would have to take it, however, before the hydro company would put it in. Wilf had said he'd pay for two if the Beaches would agree. But Walter wasn't anxious to install hydro until he rebuilt the barn. So he suggested to Isabel that they put it in the house only, leaving the barn for later. This plan wasn't carried out because, when Wilf joined the army, he and his family went to live in Ottawa. From there, he was sent to England. After the war, the Beaches were ready for a new barn and hydro. In December, Walter and a neighbour, Wilfred Mantle, hauled the timbers from the Brown Hill barn to the Beach farm by horse and sleigh. In the spring of 1946, Morley Simms began to work his magic. In her own vernacular, Mom called him "one of the best barn-builders that ever stood on two legs". He sorted out the material from the old barn, measured it, and laid it out for the frame. The new timber came from the farm's own bush—some pine and some ash. All that spring and into early summer, Morley Simms and his gang worked at making the new stable, extending the stable, putting on boards and preparing the roof.

The Beach Farmhouse, fall of 1939

Barn Renovations, new stable on left, 1946

"We had the barn-raising in June, so that we'd be able to have the hay in. You see, for the barn-raising, you have to have the barn boarded up and a lot of things like that, and the roof put on. And raising was just to put the timbers in. The frame was put up on barn-raising day. And all the neighbours helped. They put it together and put it up by 'bents' or sections. The timbers are fitted in for size and shape and everything. See, the old barn didn't have a hip roof. This barn has a hip roof. That makes for extra space for the grain and hay." The Weeses were back at their nearby property on an occasional basis when the barn was under construction. Walter and Isabel hadn't thought to tell them when the barn-raising would be. Mom felt sorry about this situation and said, "Frances, in particular, felt kind of hurt and badly that they weren't here the day of the barn-raising. But if they'd said anything, well we certainly would've let them know." Neither Isabel nor Walter would have intentionally slighted their neighbours.

Meanwhile, plenty was happening in the house. "The cellar was just the sand; it was not cemented. And so Walter very fortunately thought of that and said, when they were stirring up cement [for the barn], 'We'll just cement that floor'." He also white-washed the walls to make a clean space for extra food at the time of the barn-raising. "You had so many pies and cakes and tarts and all that kind of stuff that you made. So I had a table in there, the card table, 'cause the space wasn't that big, in a way." Florence Harrison came back that summer. With her help, Isabel managed to cook for the men who prepared the barn foundation. As I sat with Florence in her spacious kitchen nearly sixty years later, she shared vivid recollections of the food aspect of her duties: "And I remember she used to make a lot of upside down cakes. She'd put the fruit on the bottom and then put the cake on the top. We had a lot of those. We had every kind of berry and then peaches and blueberries and whatever was in." Isabel canned many fruits and vegetables for the winter. Most of these came from her huge garden, where Florence remembers seeing many raspberry, gooseberry and currant bushes. "The canning was just sort of starting as I was leaving at the end of the summer. But then, another thing she used to do—she'd make quite a few pies at once. And you know that screen cupboard in the basement? She'd have me run down to the screen cupboard and take these pies down. They'd stay cool in that cupboard, uncovered, but insects and mice couldn't get at them."

When Morley and his carpenters came to lay out the barn ahead of the actual barn-raising, Florence's help had to be augmented. "I'd have the table stretched out for about a dozen, ten anyway," Mom explained. "And that's when it began to be a little bit of a burden, to have enough food ready and to clean up after and get the next meal ready, and everything. It was such an awful time to get anybody, because there was nobody around. Everybody'd been working on war work, and women were doing what had been formerly men's work, and the men hadn't all got back by any means from the war. There were shiploads that came after that. There just were not the people to do it. Finally…my sister Chris came and helped, and Mrs. Tom Wilson came. I was so thankful, because you know, you'd peel a bushel of potatoes pretty nearly, for every meal." One neighbour who'd offered to help for the actual barn-raising got a rather interesting culinary assignment, which Mom described: "And of course the war was just over and lots of things were still rationed—sugar was one. And lots of other things were scarce. So, I had made a kind of a light flat cake. This was an idea that I got out of the Homemaker Page in the *Globe*. Beat up the white of your egg, and then put your own homemade good jelly, you know, in it and beat it up, and use that for icing on your cake. And it was wonderful. But it wouldn't last too long. It'd be all right the next day, but not like a sugar icing would last. And so, I planned to use that on this particular type of cake I made…and that had to be done the last minute, sort of, on account of the white of the eggs."

To help with cooking these vast amounts of food, Frances and Wilf Wees had lent her their Quebec heater, which burned wood or coal and had an oven. Dozens of people used such a heater for their extra space in the winter in those days. Some people closed up part of their house to heat just a few rooms. The Wees' model was bigger than some. So Isabel had two ovens. That, too, she considered a blessing. "It was very thoughtful of them, because I could put a roast in the oven in [the main kitchen], 'cause it's a slow fire, and then do the baking [in the cookstove in the summer kitchen]. And then it didn't heat the upstairs and the rest of the house much because you only had a bit of fire, to keep the meat cooking. It was really a wonderful idea. And then you could use it full force if you wanted to." June fifteenth, the day of the actual barn-raising, everyone washed up and ate outside. Well over fifty people turned up that day. "The women and the family all came. Anybody came, you see what I mean? There always have been farmers, some of them would be retired, maybe… Oh yes, they'd come from all around [to the barn-raising]."

I had never heard mention in my family of a barn dance in connection with the barn-raising, so I asked. "Certainly it was a standard thing up around where I was raised," Mom answered, "because they were Presbyterians and Scottish people and they had the bagpipes and the music in their bones. I can't remember a barn-raising that I ever was at…that there wasn't a dance, up around home. But, you see, it was different here because it was a Methodist community and settled by English people. You see, they weren't dancin', even when I came around here in 1920. But, of course, where I was raised, there were more house dances that you went to." In addition, the flooring in the old part of their barn wasn't good enough for a dance, nor in the new part, as it was secondhand. Some of the flooring was just one inch thick, too thin to support a lively crowd of dancers. She and my dad certainly did have something to celebrate.

"Believe it or not," my mother proudly announced, "[the barn] was paid for in December '46. Because then we had to save our money, you see. Because that's why we didn't 'go to the wall'. We never did these things until we had the money—not every cent of it, but pretty well. And so, each time, you knew that you had the wherewithal to accomplish what you set out to do." Somehow, I learned these financial lessons. It's hard to figure out how because I was so young when this project was accomplished. Osmosis? Dinner table conversation? However it happened, the lessons have been a great gift all my life.

She went on to express her views on how people handled their finances in the late twentieth century, a popular topic for her to expound on. And no wonder. Now most people go for credit and quick results, just the opposite of my parents' approach. "But that's what people don't understand now. You see, there'll be people, if they knew, if you told up this story, they'd say, 'Well, weren't they lucky to have all that money and they didn't have to borrow money from the bank'. Well, they had it because they planned, and they didn't spend what they didn't have. You know, if they'd pay attention to old Stompin' Tom Connor—'buyin' up the bargains with the money they ain't got'—I'll never forget that till the day I'll die. You'd see it on TV every week, and yet they couldn't get it into their stupid heads. And that's what they were doing, spending money they didn't have, and then thinking they were getting a bargain. Well, anyway, that's the way we got it. And don't think we didn't work for it. We worked for it; but we also planned for it. The working doesn't mean anything if you don't do a little planning with it."

In September 1946, Beverley started attending Stouffville High School. He left at Easter, 1949, when he was in grade 11. He wanted to work the land, especially because Walter had bought his first tractor, a 1948 Ford, from the dealer in Zephyr in the fall of 1947. A few complications arose in this first tractor purchase. Isabel recalled how "[Walter] gave a cheque for it, and a few days after he gave the cheque, they phoned from the bank in Stouffville that he didn't have quite enough money to honour this cheque. Well, it wasn't very much we were short—less than a hundred dollars. 'Well,' he said, 'that's all right. I'll be down to fix things tomorrow'." The bank didn't charge for the NSF cheque. "They just informed Walter, and gave the man in Zephyr his money, and nothing was said." Dad had uncashed cheques in a drawer, likely payment from the sale of pigs. He just hadn't gone to put them in the bank. Mom provided her customary comment on the situation: "But, you know, that's what I mean when they talk about 'the good old days'. And now…oh, they're so mean and so ugly [in the banks], and they don't seem to realize that you've been in the country [for decades] and nothing had gone wrong and you'd been an honest person. It's a poor way to do. It's no good at all, as a matter of fact."

Thanks to the larger barn and the tractor purchase, diversification and expansion of the farm business naturally followed. "When we got the Wees' land [forty acres rented in 1950], we had more young cattle. You could sell them as feeders to other people that had more barn space to feed them. That's what Walter did. Sometimes at a sale in the spring he would buy some of these feeders and then put them on the ranch, whatever many you thought you could manage with. You had to go according to your amount of feed you had in the ranch. There was no use of exceeding your capabilities and space and so on." She didn't remember how much rent Walter paid. "I didn't handle the money nor keep the books, as it were. Walter kept the books in his head. He did! He had a good head to do it, and I didn't." This disclosure surprised me. I'd thought Mom was an excellent manager, in many spheres. She certainly liked to record the information.

When hydro was installed at the barn and house in 1949, she had cupboards built in the washroom, where the soft water pump was, and in the little pantry/kitchen. A young returned soldier did the work. Rubber tile floors were laid in those areas and in the dining room. Painting the cupboards took her a long time. She remembered working on them in 1953. The summer of 1952, she and Walter did extensive house renovations, because Beverley planned to marry Norma Jean Jordan and live in half of the farmhouse. In the washroom, "We had to take some of the broom cupboard away, in order to make that door to go out into the back porch. And I didn't want to do without a broom cupboard, for some reason. I guess I should've stuck it behind the door." The resulting cupboard for hanging coats was a bit awkward, and "really a mistake" she realized afterwards. She *was* glad, however, that her vacuum cleaner fit in there. A second storey containing two bedrooms went over the summer kitchen, and the back porch was extended to make an entrance to the little kitchen (once Walter's garage/woodshed) in this new part of what had become a double farmhouse. Isabel clearly recalled when the student minister, Victor Wood, came calling. "We had to walk a plank, over the cellar steps, to get in the door." The picture this conjured caused her to chuckle. "And he and his wife came in, and I thought, 'Oh dear, can they walk over that plank or not?' But they did." The renovations weren't quite done when the wedding took place on August twenty-third, 1952. Bev and Norma completed the work after their honeymoon.

When I left in 1959 to attend university, Isabel and Walter traded ends of the house with Beverley and Norma, who, with their three young children, found the north end crowded. They started the move before Christmas but the exchange wasn't completed until mid-January, 1960. Both families still heated their home with a wood stove. Mom got a wall oil furnace installed in the north end of the house in November 1964, shortly after Dad got home from the hospital, following his surprisingly strong recovery from a cerebral hemorrhage that August. She kept track of the cost of fuel oil for heating the house because "Walter thought, you know, it would put us in the poorhouse buyin' fuel oil, and all those good hardwood trees in the bush. Well, I can understand it. And after all is said and done, there's nothing nicer than a good wood fire, with good dry hardwood." However, they managed financially and were quite comfortable. Another record of prices, dating from 1965, reflected Walter's part of the farm enterprise—trucking and selling the calves and similar activities. "He and Beverley did have slightly different arrangements after he was sick, because he couldn't do that much. And they had to hire a little help more, you see."

Bev and Norma stayed in the south end of the house until November 1967, when they moved a short distance down the second concession to their own bungalow. One of Mom's darkest clouds descended abruptly in early December. Dad suffered a massive heart attack. Within hours, her farmer was gone. She was, to use one of her dozens of expressions, 'such a brick' during the funeral time. Aware of every detail, as always, she counseled me to buy a black dress because "…that's what your Dad would want". I was stunned by this death. Like so many young people, I'd been busy with my own family and community life. I'd taken my parents for granted. Sitting beside Mom at the service in Uxbridge, I was the one who broke down. Gently, she put her hand on mine. Three months later, another funeral loomed, this time in Orillia. The infant daughter of our close friends had died. My husband and I were their main Orillia support. We wanted to be with them the entire day of their daughter's funeral. But our son James needed to be cared for, and so did our friends' son, who was six months older than James. I asked Mom to look after the boys for the day. As I talked to her after the service about the deep sadness around the event, of how the child's father had converted himself into a walking statue to cope with his sorrow, she began to cry. It was my turn to be the comforter. As I put my arm around her, we wept together.

Mom continued living in the north end of the farmhouse and for much of the time rented the south end. She hadn't planned to do so, but circumstances led to people coming to ask if they could. She needed that help with her cloud-turning. The summer of 1973, the house was again a busy place because her grandson, Edward, who was now part of the family business, planned to marry Pamela Forsythe in October. Renovations were underway. This time my husband, Vern, who'd just begun doing renovations, did the work. In Mom's part of the farmhouse, he transformed part of the back porch into a small kitchen, complete with cupboards and a double sink. He put the bathroom in a space partitioned off the larger of the two upstairs bedrooms. Indoor plumbing! Believe it or not, Isabel had been using an outdoor toilet or a pot under the bed and carrying drinking water from the well all those years. She was seventy-three when she got to flush her own toilet for the first time.

This circumstance and many others might prompt the question, 'So was she happy she'd married a farmer?' Not being one to speak directly from the heart, Mom never really said. However, these comments about coming to live in a lonely—though beautiful—valley in Uxbridge Township, made as they were sixty years later, probably provide the answer: "When I came here, I couldn't see a neighbour that had a chimney with the smoke comin' out in the morning, ever." Her mother-in-law, Roseanne, had made similar comments. When she and John Beach bought the farm in 1876, no roads had been cut through the hills. "And [people] didn't go up the hill. They just rambled through the bush (It was pretty well all bush the way that Roseanne spoke to me about it) and wherever the trees had been cut." A sandy sideroad was the only road into the valley. "The sideroad stopped at the Beach property," Mom said, "and does to this very day. The right of way was never used to put it through [west] because it led to the town line. And the next part was York County, and they started their sideroad themselves and had nothing to do with Ontario County here. So, if [the Beaches] had to leave here, when they first settled, they had to drive out this sideroad to go east, in order to go south, and then when they got down to the next sideroad, go west. And that happened to be where [Roseanne's] parents lived [at Lincolnville]. And she'd get so homesick and so lonely here that she told me John Beach would hitch the team to the wagon—now that's all the transportation they had—and take her to see her mother." Today, she could make the trip on paved roads by car in about seven minutes.

My mother had her own way of coping with the isolation: "And I don't know if you know how I made up my mind that I wouldn't be so terribly lonely as Walter's mother or not. Well…if the old shelves were in that kitchen place, I could just show you where I tacked up things, sayings and verses such as

To every man there openeth
A way and ways and a way
And the high soul climbs the high way
And the low soul gropes the low
And in between on the misty flats,
The rest drift to and fro;
But to every man there openeth
A high way and a low,
And every man decideth
The way his soul shall go.
"The Choice" by John Oxenham

Things like that, and another I think about now when so many people are so particular about what somebody…will say about this and that and the other that you do, you know. And I hope I can say it right. 'If I put a rose beside the three-legged clock on the shelf/It matters to nobody but myself.' I know that was the ending. And so that's just what I had in my head. And then, of course, it was a little different, because we had a Model T for the summer and a driver and a cutter for the winter."

For forty-one years, Isabel lived as a farmers' wife, an integral part of the team that ran the farm and kept the family functioning. In 1991, she commented in conversation with me, "Farmers were always proud of their land. When you loved [farming] and love the country, you were just in heaven." I think the answer is 'Definitely happy'. After my dad's death, she received invitations and offers from other men, but paid little attention to them and rarely spoke of them. Her many friends and family members cared about her, offered assistance, and extended invitations. So she went on, taking a daily interest in the farm comings and goings while living on her own in the north end of the house for another thirty-two years.

Though she lived in a lonely valley, her spirit took the high way.

EIGHT: Like One of Their Own

Can we live to ourselves and never share
A moment of joy or a time of despair?
As we travel along life's lonely road
Do we need no one to share our load?
In time of sorrow or joy without end
We all need someone we call a friend.

Mrs. W.J. Aubrey

Family and friends were important to Isabel, just as they were in the Wallace family in which she grew up. At their home, grandparents, uncles, aunts, friends and neighbours thought nothing of dropping in for a visit. Relatives from Toronto came for a weekend. With such a large family, you'd wonder where the space was found. It always was. A verandah stretched across the front of their newly renovated house in 1911. The family got an expandable couch with a flat mattress. "Three people could sleep out there. We used to sleep out there in the summertime," Isabel recalled. In the cooler weather, "We always had a spare bedroom that was used continuously for a period of time. You had to have a spare bedroom as there weren't any hospitals. You needed a place to put anyone who was sick and needed to be segregated. That room was called Annie's, but she was away working."

One particular surprise visit resulted from weather conditions. When the Wallace children got up one morning, the Munros (friends of the family) were at their house. They had been driving by horse and buggy to Kirkfield. "It had started to rain when they were coming home after having supper with someone in Beaverton. They could hardly see where they were going, and of course they didn't have headlights. They had to depend on the horse. When they came to the tenth concession, Mrs. Munro says, 'Dan, I think we'll go up and stay with the Wallaces till morning and go in the daylight to Kirkfield'." The Munros weren't highly educated, but traveled in wider circles than most of the Wallace family did. They brought to my mother's childhood home something different, a type of education for everyone. In the environment of this busy and interesting family life, Isabel grew—and learned the potential beauty of human relationships.

When Isabel was in her late teens, her Aunt Minnie (Kate's youngest sister) decided to go west with Isabel's sister, Annie. Hugh McIntyre had been courting Aunt Minnie, but "she wasn't too sure she wanted to marry him, anyway. And I understood that he was a little too fond of the drink, of the liquor business. Aunt Minnie wasn't marryin' anybody like that. And so, I guess he knew very well why she went west and why she wouldn't have anything to do with him, see." Another man was interested in her too, so there was some competition. "Well anyway, when Aunt Minnie came back from the West, Hugh McIntyre was right there at Grandma McFadyen's. He was gonna' have Aunt Minnie on the string again." This time he succeeded. "Hugh and Aunt Minnie were married in 1921. When they were setting up their house, some agent that was selling pianos got hold of it—of course, you know, that's the way they did a lot of it, in those days—and they wanted to sell them a piano. Well, at Grandma's house, they did have a piano. Anyhow, they bought the piano. And the guy said, 'Now if you can find anybody else that'll buy a piano, I'll pay you well'. And they gave him my name."

At that time, Isabel was teaching in Roseville, newly engaged to Walter, and boarding at Bob and Ethel Hutchinson's. "And I thought, 'Oh, I could handle the price and everything with my salary…' I forget now how much it was and all of that. But anyway, I bought it." Isabel asked Mrs. Hutchinson if she minded having the piano at her house. She didn't, so it was delivered there. Isabel was expecting to go back to the Hutchinson's in September. Mrs. Hutchinson didn't play, but she came from a musical family and had a close friend in Uxbridge who played piano beautifully. When Isabel wasn't returning to teach that fall (1923), she would have left the piano with her, thinking Mrs. Hutchison would enjoy it. But she didn't want to keep the piano. "So Walter brought it over to the farm and put it in the living room." And, Mom explained, "That's why the varnish got cracked so badly, because you see it was too cold, because they didn't keep a fire all the time, but they had a pot-bellied parlour stove in there and they'd have a fire sometimes." This piano is another family treasure that sits in my house today. Mom passed it and the matching bench on to me in the early 1990s. Although she seldom played the piano, as a teenager I used it to practise for lessons and try out popular tunes. She had kept it tuned and in remarkably good condition through the intervening years.

Following the custom of the time, when Isabel married Walter in 1926, and even when they were courting and then engaged, he took her to visit various family members. "The Beaches just took me in like one of their own," my mother told me, a hint of wonderment in her voice. "You know, I never had any problem at all with the Beaches, except [Walter's sister] Lizzie… And Walter had nothing to do with her, anyway. Although he did take me [once before we were married] to visit George Harrison's one Sunday…" Lizzie was married to George Harrison. They had several children, some preschool, some school age. On this particular Sunday, "Lizzie went to the barn to help with the milking. So there was a sofa, as we used to call them, that was in the kitchen at Lizzie's house and we were sitting there. I was on that couch and Walter was on a chair somewhere… And Walter was foolin' with this little boy, you see, like you do with kids, one way and another. And then when he went to sit down, instead of sitting on the chair, he sat on the couch beside me…and when Lizzie came in from the barn and saw us two sittin' on the couch, she was just furious. And she up and said something about—now I can't remember her words 'cause I was flabbergasted—as if she couldn't turn her back 'till they'd be doin' things they shouldn't be doing. And all these other kids there, and it was just playing with them, you know. Now that was ridiculous. Oh, awful."

She didn't see much of Lizzie again until the fall of 1926 when Roseanne was preparing for her auction sale of farm and household goods. Lizzie did considerable work to help. Isabel was glad she did. "I didn't have anything to do with it…and I was glad for her to come, bake pies and tarts, and stuff. Oh, dear me, I was awfully happy. And Lettie came over and helped a bit too." Lizzie had older girls who could help at home, so she stayed overnight at the farm, but Lettie had to go home. "And I'm tellin' you—Walter's mother was sleepin' downstairs there, and Walter and I, we slept in the south bedroom, you see. And so [Lizzie] talked and talked away to her mother, away into the night." In the morning, "I know from what Walter's mother said—and I can't tell you one word—I know she was upset about things. Maybe she wondered if we could hear her upstairs, but I certainly never heard anything and I don't think Walter did. Anyhow, she was tryin' to put nasty things in her mother's head about me." These were along the line of 'watch that she doesn't be getting her hands on things', and 'whatever you don't take, she will take'.

Isabel had no intention of taking anything. Her sense of fairness and habit of honesty made her extremely indignant, an emotion that spilled over as she talked to me about this stressful time at the start of her married life. "Now I can't tell you one word because I wouldn't allow my mind to take it. I was not going to accept it, because if she said it, all right; she said the wrong thing, and her mother wasn't payin' any attention to it, and I certainly wasn't gonna take anything from Walter's mother. I mean, if she was giving me a gift, that's one thing. But we weren't going to leave her high and dry, that's for sure." Isabel felt that Lizzie thought Walter was getting too much for nothing. But, still indignant, she said that she knew "He wasn't gettin' it for nothing. He was workin' for it. And he paid for it. He paid for the farm, as far as that goes, and the running price of farms at that time."

Walter and his brothers, Oliver and Bill, bought several items at the sale in November 1926. Still on the defensive, Lizzie thought they were buying too much, discouraging other people from bidding. She said Mrs. Beach would've got more money if they hadn't bid. Isabel didn't see things the same way. For example, Walter bought the old grey mare. "He was used to having her around, you know, for a third horse. And, my goodness, I don't know who would've paid any more than he paid for it, and I don't remember what he paid. Ten dollars would've been a pretty steep price for her." Another next to useless item he bought was a three-cornered cupboard. "The bottom was good, but the top part was just full of mouse holes. And they just boarded them up with shingles." Isabel kept it in the summer kitchen, but didn't use it much. "I kept food in the bottom of it in the winter, for storage, when it wasn't too cold. But the top part, I didn't use for anything. The middle shelf I'd put newspapers on, 'cause we always got a daily."

Fortunately Isabel found Walter's sister Laura the opposite of Lizzie. "Why you could just go up to Joe Harrison's and Laura's place and enjoy yourself and have a lot of fun, come home happy." Laura took a different approach to the sale, too. When Mrs. Beach and Lettie sorted out the furniture and things, "Laura wouldn't have anything to do with it. They started with the idea of sorting it, each one having what they'd like, and so she didn't want any part of it. 'Anyway,' she says, 'the whole thing isn't worth more than a hundred dollars.' 'Would you take your share of a hundred dollars?' says Lizzie. Laura turns to her, 'Sure'. So they handed over Laura's share and she was glad to be done with it." Isabel found it equally enjoyable to visit at Lettie's, noting that unfortunately "…she allowed herself—and I guess [Walter's brother] Bill knew it, 'cause he was in on the ground floor—to be twisted around Lizzie's little finger, and for why, I don't know. Bill Beach says, 'Lizzie made the snowballs and Lett fired them'. Lizzie wouldn't put a bad name to herself, you see, but she'd get Lettie to do the bad work." Isabel stayed as far as she could from these family politics, though she couldn't help but know what went on.

Alone with my paternal grandmother as she was for a few months, my mother (always a history fan) enjoyed learning some of the Beach family background. Roseanne spoke about her loneliness when she and John first came to the farm in 1876, three years after they were married. They had one son, John (Jack) then. They must have planned to stay because they purchased and registered the land, Lot 26, Concession 1, Uxbridge Township, in their name, as shown on the 1877 Uxbridge Township map. Their pioneer home had two rooms downstairs and a loft. Any time Roseanne couldn't take the isolation any more, John took her to her mother's house at Lincolnville, in Whitchurch Township, a little west of Uxbridge Township. (Rusnell descendants are listed in Appendix P.) "And she'd be pregnant, you see, I suppose. So, this got to be too much of a strain, I guess. And, anyway, John Beach didn't have a very good heart, unfortunately. Now when it showed up, I don't know. But anyhow, they left this place. He probably got a chance to rent (or whatever they did in those days—squat, some of them did) a house." Within two years of coming to Lot 26, they sold the property. On the 1895 map of Uxbridge Township, the property belongs to I. Connor. They moved to an old pioneer house at the corner of the current Highway 47 and the second concession, so that Roseanne would be closer to her mother.

The rest of the family (except Walter) was born in that other house. Warren was three weeks old when they repurchased and returned to the Lot 26 farm.

After Roseanne's stroke early in 1926, her situation, as described to me in an interview with one of my Uncle Bill Beach's daughters, Grace Thompson, was this: "And this lady looked after the house and looked after Grandma, because Grandma wasn't able to. I don't know whether she could even dress herself for sure, because her one arm was affected by the stroke. She could still talk, very plainly. She could walk. I think she walked with a cane, because she would go out and sit underneath that [apple] tree that was at the northeast corner of the house...in a rocking chair." When my mother was first married, she had her own special experiences with Roseanne sitting in a rocking chair. "I was so sorry that she didn't live longer, because she had lots of things [to share], and she was great to talk. She'd sit back in that rocking chair and she'd pull it over to the couch sometimes and have the Eaton's catalogue on the couch. It was heavy, you see. And then, when she'd get tired of lookin' at it, she'd lean back and then she'd start to talk." Mom soon developed great admiration and respect for Roseanne. When my father, Walter Thomas, was born on December 24, 1897, she had borne eleven children. Less than four years later, in March 1901, John Thomas died after falling into the cold spring creek on the adjacent property. Roseanne continued to run the farm with the help of her older sons. They managed with what they had. Isabel thought "[Roseanne] certainly made out well with her children. They should not ever have felt cheated. They had their friends come here, and she welcomed their friends. And she only had one big room to welcome them into at one time." When a large group was there, she put chairs around the circumference of the room. People took turns sitting down.

The conversations ended in January 1927 when Roseanne went to live with her daughter Lettie. Mom recalled so vividly for me, "When she was leaving (and I was in the room, too, you see), packed and leaving to go to Siloam, I was there to hear her say it. She turned to Walter and she says, 'Now Walter, when Isabel wants to go to see her mother, you be sure to take her'. I knew [why she said this], because she told me this other story so often. She'd be rockin' away…and then she'd come up with something about how lonely it was here, so very lonely. You couldn't see a chimney smoke, you couldn't see a thing from anybody else." But conditions were better for my mother. There was a road through those hills on either side of the valley, and Walter owned and drove a car.

One day early in April 1927, Lettie and her husband Wilfred Lazenby drove into the farmyard with Roseanne. She had come back to live at the farm. "She wouldn't stay [in Siloam]. But Lettie didn't treat her too well, I'm sorry to say. It's awful thinkin' of anybody bein' rude to their mother like that, you see. But Walter's mother never said a word about it when she came here in the spring, and I never asked her, nor would I ever bring it up. There was something that she and Lettie weren't agreeing about, anyway. And the day that they drove into the yard with her, Walter had taken a load of hogs to market, to Stouffville. When they brought her in, they said, 'Now, you don't have to keep her, but she was determined to come so we brought her.'… I let them come in and welcomed her in, and they could leave her; they didn't have to take her back against her will." Her daughter Laura, whom Mom enjoyed so much, often said Roseanne had come home to die. Apparently that was true. She died there near the end of June that year.

Warren, Walter's brother who stayed on in the house but worked away from the farm, was to pay board once Walter and Isabel officially owned the farm. Determining the amount was a tricky matter because no one knew where he would be at any given time. For example, "Warren'd take the circular saw, and away he'd go. And he'd be up and down the town line doin' pretty nearly everybody's pile of wood, you know. And sometimes he'd stay overnight;

sometimes he'd come home to sleep, but then he'd be off in the morning. And then maybe he wouldn't be there all day and some night about 5:30 he'd walk in for supper." When the three of them had their discussion on the subject, Isabel mentioned that she knew of a widow who paid her son a hundred dollars a year to live with him. That amount didn't sound like very much to her, but Walter and Warren thought that it would be fine. After recording the number of meals she'd served Warren, Isabel decided the charge for board was too low. She and Walter didn't want to make money by having him, nor did they feel they should be keeping him when he had "plenty of money and plenty of health to earn more to keep himself".

A year or so later, they raised his board. "So then he paid a hundred and twenty-five dollars a year, and that's all he ever did pay. But, as I say, he was away so much and he wasn't a person who grumbled or growled, and whatever was put on the table, he ate, and he didn't make remarks that anything was wrong with the food. The only thing that was hard—he had terrible smelly feet, you know. And he wouldn't buy enough socks and keep enough socks. But I never darned his socks. When he got holes in them, he could go and buy new." Sometimes she washed his greasy overalls but not often. She felt he needed to learn that he wasn't paying for that service or for soap and towels. And he did learn to quite an extent, she felt, before he was "married and away". Married and away didn't happen until 1937. And even after he and Donalda Wilson married in December, they stayed with Isabel and Walter at the farm until March 1938, because Carling and Alice Alcock were living in Warren's house in Siloam. The Alcock's lease hadn't run out. Warren and Donalda had no other place to go.

Throughout her life, family on both sides figured prominently in Isabel's life. She had all sorts of experiences to recall—some happy, some troublesome, some amusing, others disturbing. She tackled them all.

Some of her family felt so welcome that they came into the house even when no one was there. Her mother, dad, and sister Chris came unannounced one Sunday when Isabel and Walter had gone visiting and for supper after church. When they came home to do the chores, they found *their* visitors. "You see, Chris came in that little window in the pantry. So, they had their supper here, and ate my applesauce that I put cinnamon in," she told me in mock horror, laughing heartily.

In 1928, Isabel's sister Viola came to visit. She photographed Walter and Isabel sitting on the old wooden stoneboat under the apple tree, their dog beside them. Because Viola was borrowing Isabel's camera to take west, they had to finish the film before she went. That was the last time Isabel saw Viola. She died of acute appendicitis in Saskatoon, Saskatchewan, in 1929.

Although Isabel was just twenty-nine herself at the time of Walter's sister Laura's death in April 1930, she took charge like a professional. In July 2001 Grace (Beach) Thompson told me about this response. Laura's son, Angus, and Walter were almost like brothers. Angus had been Walter's best man in 1926. Perhaps this is why, Grace said, Isabel "…was up there helping for two or three days. And, you know, she just took charge, and it was just no bother to her at all. Everything just went smooth, and the boys, of course, certainly were feeling bad about losing their mother. If they came along and said something, she'd always have an answer for them, and it seemed as if it was enough to satisfy them and, you know, made them feel better." Grace went on to tell how, "Everything seemed to come easy to her. It probably didn't. Probably she had as many stresses in her life as anybody else. But they didn't show. Maybe, her being a teacher, she seemed to know what kids needed. Somebody else might go in there, but they wouldn't know what on earth to say to the kids. But [Isabel] seemed to have the right attitude." She was a natural.

Later that year Isabel felt her own deep sorrow. In July, her and Walter's first pregnancy ended in a miscarriage. Grace was part of this experience, too. "That's why I was there, to help her to do the housework. Her sisters [Chrissie and Jessie] were there too, a lot of the time." More than sixty years later Isabel provided some of the details. The baby was in its third month. She had been painting one of the rooms that was renovated in 1927-8. " I was workin' away at it, stupidly thinking, (I say stupidly, just because I didn't know any different, and yet in another sense, I'm sure that other people never stopped for being pregnant). This is what Dr. Darling said: the lead in the paint probably brought on the miscarriage. Then Dr. Darling says, 'Well, hurry up and get pregnant again. That's the way to get 'em'." Isabel chuckled softly as she recalled this advice. Then she went on, "Well we didn't hurry very much. The hurrying part didn't work out, because it was 1931 before I became pregnant."

In connection with this first pregnancy, she recalled an awkward situation with her parents. Her dad had bought a new Chevrolet car in 1927 and moved to Toronto. "And they were driving from Toronto to the Wallace farm, and from the farm to Toronto…staying on Number 47 and Highway 12, naturally. And I didn't tell them. They didn't know I was pregnant until I had the miscarriage." Isabel and Walter had visited them in Toronto in the spring. She was wearing a coat she didn't like, never felt comfortable in. Walter had suggested she put the coat on before they left, because they had an open touring car, which had no side curtains on it—leaving the passengers rather exposed at that time of year and day. She didn't see her parents again all spring and into the summer. "And you didn't phone like you do now, because it cost money to phone. They didn't have cheap rates at all. And so I said, 'Well I just thought, you didn't come around, I'd wait till some day you were there and I'd tell you'. I didn't mean it in a sense as seriously as it sounded, or as seriously as they took it." They got the situation resolved, one of her family even commenting, 'We just wondered about you having to put on an extra coat, that you might catch cold'. The 1931 pregnancy, however, was successful. Beverley Wallace Beach arrived on January 31, 1932, in the living room of the farmhouse. Isabel and Walter had finally started their family. Isabel's sisters, including the eldest, Annie, wanted to help. Isabel said, "I remember when she wrote here and asked me if I needed help when Beverley was born. Grandmother had died, and she wasn't needed there the same—and I think she wanted a change, anyway. I said to Walter when we were discussing it, I don't know how I could turn her down because she really was like a mother to us younger ones." So Annie came for a time.

Since they had both grown up in large families (Isabel had eight siblings; Walter had eleven, two of whom died before adulthood) they had probably wanted a large family. They were used to and enjoyed the busyness of such a household. However, this was not to be. Later in the 1930s she had another miscarriage, and then no more pregnancies. She and Walter had given up hope. They were seriously considering adoption in the summer of 1939, when Isabel became pregnant. Since Mom was such a great admirer of Queen Elizabeth, the Queen Mother, I've sometimes wondered whether seeing her and King George VI in Toronto that May provided such a 'lift' that she got inspired. Whatever happened, this pregnancy took them both by surprise. They hadn't been using birth control. Almost sixty years later, she confessed to me, "Walter never did like those French safes." Born in the living room "around suppertime" on April 20,

1940 (assisted by my mother's two nurse sisters, Jessie and Chrissie), I was named Catherine Rose in honour of my two grandmothers. Since Grace was married and busy with her own family, her younger sister Evelyn came to help with the housework. Though she was initially less than ecstatic about my late arrival in her life, my mother never breathed a hint of that until the 'French safe' remark. She must have quickly accepted that her life would change again, and decided that she could manage the change. Never once did she make me feel unloved, unwanted. My dad, I'd always known, was thrilled 'over the moon' to have a baby girl. Wilf Wees loved to tell how Walter appeared at their cottage around 5 a.m. the next day, banging loudly on the door in his excitement to share the news.

Family friend Polly Herd (left) with Isabel and Beverley, circa 1938

Cousin John Craig with Isabel, Annie (right) and Catherine, circa 1948

The Second World War in progress at this time was a world-shocking event that affected everyone. As Grace pointed out, "You know, the visiting kinda' stopped when we got rationing—when gas was rationed during the war. You didn't like goin' visiting and eating up somebody's rations that they needed for the whole week." Luckily for Isabel, her son was too young and her husband too old to participate in this war. Besides, everyone who was actively farming was exempt; they were needed to keep the country fed. So she was less personally touched than during the First World War. Niece Winnifred, whom she'd home-schooled and who was in service in Canada, took some of her leaves at the newly-named Echo Valley Farm. Winnifred's brother Billy, however, was a casualty. He had signed up for duty but was killed in a mining accident in Sudbury on November 20, 1942, before going into training. Mom and I happened to be visiting my grandfather and Aunt Annie when word of Billy's death came one evening. Mom was asked to drive her brother, Duncan, to the train station so that he could go to Sudbury to claim his son's body and bring it home to Gamebridge by return train. Again she willingly took the opportunity to help others with the dark cloud in their lives. An amusing family story even resulted from this event. She had parked our family's car in front of my Grandpa's garage when she returned from the train station. When I went to bed, the car had been in the garage. Just two and a half years old, I got up next morning, looked out the upstairs window, and called out, "Mommy, come quick. The car jumped out of the garage!"

Walter and Isabel continued visiting Walter's siblings, particularly Oliver's and Bill's families. When they went shopping in Uxbridge on a Saturday night, they always dropped in to Oliver and Edith's house. Sunday afternoon and evening was the more likely time to visit at Bill and Lizzie's farm, which was west of Walter and Isabel's home, in Whitchurch Township. They usually went once a month. Bill and Lizzie's daughter, Evelyn (who had helped in the house when I was born), recalled in a conversation with me how much Isabel and Lizzie enjoyed talking to each other. She said Aunt Isabel was interesting to listen to because "…she talked about different things than farming". Possibly she even had some influence on Evelyn's decision to become a teacher.

In her interview, Bill and Lizzies's daughter Laura described a particularly special evening. It was 1944. All of our family was at Lizzie and Bill's for supper. "And, of course," Laura said, "we always cornered Aunt Isabel to read our teacups. And she usually gave in. She'd read my teacup and she said, 'You're going on a trip'. Well now, you can imagine—twelve years old, out in the country, I mean how far a trip am I goin' to take? Am I goin' to Stouffville? Or am I goin' to school, or maybe goin' to Uxbridge? But later on that evening," Laura continued, "Mom and Aunt Isabel got talkin'. Of course, Aunt Isabel always had her 'duty shoes' and she got them in Toronto. Her duty shoes were her everyday shoes she had to work with." They were, in fact, the equivalent of today's orthotic shoes. My mother had worn such shoes from her early teaching days. When she learned that Lizzie was experiencing foot problems, she suggested taking her to Toronto to her shoe store the following week. (Appendix Q shows a 1972 receipt for two pairs of those 'duty shoes'.) Laura saw opportunity in this shoe-shopping plan. She wanted a 'perm' in her hair. So, "Somehow or other, between the Sunday and whenever it was (Tuesday or Wednesday), I had Mom convinced," Laura said. "I ended up takin' a trip to Toronto. I never forgot. I thought, 'Anybody that doesn't believe in tea leaves…' And Aunt Isabel had no way of knowing when she was telling me I was taking a trip that I was going to be part of that trip they took." Laura, an impressionable young teenager, was awed by her 'trip'. Toronto was a big adventure for this country girl, with the bonus that she saw Eaton's Christmas window display.

I'm intrigued that the Wallace side of the family has never mentioned Mom's teacup reading skills. Just how and why did she acquire them? Her extensive clippings collection offers some clues. A series of articles from the *Canadian Countryman* magazine explains the principles, gives the meaning of over one hundred and fifty tea leaf symbols, and provides four sample interpretations of teacups. The writer states this empirical evidence: "Generations of spae-wives have found that the recurrence of a certain figure in the cup has corresponded with the occurrence of a certain event in the future lives of the various persons who have consulted them" (November 21, 1936). Maybe my mother looked on this activity as an inexpensive form of entertainment in the harsh depression times. Perhaps she was encouraged to adopt the practice through one article's reference to "…the [Scottish] Highland custom of examining the leaves of the morning cup of tea in order to obtain some insight into the events the day may be expected to bring forth" (October 31, 1936). Whatever the reason, she studied the details and practised them on her Beach nieces, an entirely captive and credulous audience. Using the information from the articles, I suspect what Mom had seen in Laura's teacup was a straight line of tea leaves, said to indicate "a journey, very pleasant"—which Laura's trip to Toronto certainly was.

Shortly after the war ended, Isabel suffered a deep loss when her Aunt Tene, who had taken her into her home when she needed a shorter distance to walk to school, died on January 7, 1946. My mother's most striking recollection of the funeral focused on the community's respect: “When the McFadyen family came by Argyle School for Aunt Tene’s funeral, the teacher had the children lined up outside paying their respects to the cortege of people coming for the funeral. Now when do you see that nowadays?” she wondered. “You couldn’t possibly, such an interruption it would be.” Now, she said, children never have it enter their heads that the people before them ever did anything. All of Aunt Tene’s family had gone to that school, and her daughter-in-law had taught there. “And,” Mom added, “Aunt Tene and Uncle Jack had paid taxes there ever since they were married, and therefore they were worthy of this respect—and that was teaching those children respect for the elders and for what they had done.” This community response was a common custom at the time. Just as we now pull over to the side of the road if a fire or police vehicle is coming, if there was a hearse coming, everyone showed respect by giving the funeral procession space. “I’m sorry to say that our own Canadian people have let down on some of these things that they shouldn’t have let down on,” Mom said, concluding with the observation that sometimes immigrants are more respectful in such situations.

Later in 1946, family came to Isabel’s rescue when she and Walter tackled expanding the barn. Florence (Harrison) Kemp, another of the many Beach nieces, spent that summer at the farm keeping me occupied while Isabel cooked and served meals to workmen and did the regular household chores. Florence saw then—and remembered—how much family mattered to Isabel. She noticed that although the household was small, it was busy. She remembered Isabel’s sisters Annie, Jessie and Chrissie coming to visit. Minnie was not among the visitors simply because she had married in the 1930s, stayed on the family farm with husband John for a few years, then gone with her family to Los Angeles, California, where John worked as a surveyor. Florence also saw that the Walter Beach family was a happy one. “I don’t remember them ever having an argument over anything while I was there,” she said. “It was pretty much easy-going.” My memories are similar to Florence’s. If Mom and Dad did disagree, they held off on the heavy discussion until a more private time after dinner. Usually dinner table talk was interesting—probably much as it had been at the Wallace table when Mom was growing up. Politics, religion, farming, community events, storytelling, and the neighbourhood were popular topics. Often, on weekends the table was crowded with friends and/or relatives. Perhaps this background explains why I so enjoy sitting down with friends and close family, chatting and listening while consuming good food. And why I always insisted that my own family sit down together at the table for the evening meal.

Her little family and the farm continued to keep Isabel busy, but she characteristically reached out beyond. One Sunday in 1952, Grace (Beach) Thompson and her family, our family, and Grace’s cousin Dora and her family had supper together at the Thompson’s farm where, Grace told me in 2001, Isabel said, ‘You know, there’s so many of us, we never see each other. I think we should have a get-together of some kind’. Soon after, while they were together again at Dora and her husband’s farm, the discussion continued. Dora mentioned that they could easily host the get-together on their large lawn. “So,” Grace explained, “this is what got the [annual Beach family reunion] started. I don’t really think it was planned that it was going to be that way.” Another factor that year was the expected visit from the West of Dora’s sister, Lauraine, and her family. A family get-together would help them see and visit with many of the extensive Beach family. So they gathered on July 27, 1952, for the first annual (as it turned out to be) Beach Family Reunion with all descendants of John Thomas Beach and Roseanne Rusnell welcome to attend. Isabel served several times as president or secretary for that annual gathering

and seldom missed attending, well into her nineties. In the photo on the left she is visiting with her sister-in-law, Lizzie Beach (at whose home our family had often visited) at one of the Beach reunions. The reunion was held in July for a number of years, then switched to late June. As the Beach tree grew, this gathering outgrew a home setting and was usually held in a public park. To this day, Isabel and Walter's descendants seldom miss the annual Beach Family Reunion.

August of 1952 was another busy family-focused month. On the twenty-third, Beverley married Norma Jean Jordan. The wedding ceremony took place at Stouffville United Church parsonage with another young couple as witnesses. The reception was on the lawn of the farm where Norma's parents worked. Over the summer, the Beach farmhouse grew into a two-storey double house to accommodate the newlyweds. When Norma came to live in the smaller part of the house that had been readied for her and Bev, Isabel shared with her the Electrolux vacuum cleaner and the Beatty electric wringer washing machine. Always aware of new advancements, Isabel was amazed, Norma recalled, "When Edward was born [in 1953], they'd started making these Curity diapers, and how I could get them washed and out on the line, and dried so quickly, instead of the old-fashioned flannelette… And they didn't stain as easily. She thought that was one easy thing to what she'd had." When I was using disposables for our sons in the 1960s and '70s, Mom was even more amazed, but also environmentally and economically conscious enough to agree with me that disposables should be used mainly while visiting or camping.

Norma started going to the United Church Women's Association meetings the month after she became Mrs. Beverley Beach, in September 1952. Isabel had wanted her to go to a meeting the day after they got back from their honeymoon, but Norma was busy moving into her and Beverley's part of the farmhouse. However, Norma commented, "I never missed a meeting when Edward was born. We went to the homes and I went to the July one and see, he wasn't to come until the end of August, and he came early, and your mother had the August meeting at her place, and so I sat in." Over fifty years later, Norma still attends the United Church Women's organization. "So I guess she was quite an influence in my life that way." Church and the wider community were always important for Isabel. She naturally wanted to share that aspect of her life with her daughter-in-law, feeling that it was right to include her.

Mom was always conscious of giving Bev and Norma their privacy. An important house rule was to knock on the door between the two parts of the double house before entering the other section. "And if one or the other had company, we didn't interfere," Norma explained in our interview. With just one phone in the house, the traffic back and forth was daily until Walter and Isabel changed ends with Bev and Norma in 1959/60 and got their own telephone. "It took us two weeks to move from one end of the house to the other," Norma recalled. "We often laughed about that. That's when [Isabel and Walter] put the wallboard on the dining room, and she said we wouldn't do any moving till they got that on." Thoughtful of others, Mom wanted to look after the resulting disorder, so that Norma wouldn't need to worry about the children getting into the construction dust and debris. After Bev and Norma moved into the larger part of the farmhouse, the carpenters put clothes closets in Isabel's bedrooms and built an enclosed front porch on the front of her and Walter's part—a place where Walter could have his couch and stretch out for a nap after dinner when he was working so hard during the summer. During the colder months, the unheated porch served as an extra refrigerator.

By 1958, Bev and Norma had provided Isabel and Walter with three grandchildren: Edward Wallace, born August 1953; Joanne Marie, born December 1955; and Marilyn Jean, born November 1957. "And she was a good baby-sitter," Norma declared. "We went off somewhere sometimes shopping… I can remember when Joanne was [small, Isabel] used to open the door so quietly and tip-toe in. She thought Joanne was sleeping, and there she'd be sitting playing. Joanne was the quiet one at that time. Marilyn was the noisy one. She had the loud cry. A couple of times, I think it upset your mother to hear her cry. The first time we left her with her, while we went shopping, she went into one of those crying spells. But [Isabel] says, 'I was kind of upset, but I know she does that. I've heard her before'." When the children got older, Norma told me, "She could speak to them very gentle-like, and get it across to them—what they'd done wrong." She did it in such a way that they maybe didn't realize they were getting counseled. Since she always had books available, the children would often go into her home to get something to read. She usually gave them a book for their birthday or Christmas gift. "She always made sure they tried to take care of books," Norma emphasized. "You weren't just to throw them around and tear them. She had the Thornton Burgess books. They…had to be very careful with them, because they were old books too, at that time."

In 2003, Joanne recalled for me how "She was always there for us every day, day in, day out." If their parents were busy, she and her siblings would just go into their Grandma's and get a snack. "Probably ninety percent of the people would say, 'Well, you're lucky'. But in another way, we took advantage of her. Looking back, you could probably think of a hundred memories, but because it was just part of your growing up [it's not as special]. You'd take a walk to the back forty [acres] to pick wild flowers. Some kids would think that's a special memory, where we might have done it every year. Or you'd go out to the garden and hoe weeds with her and talk." The grandchildren—and later the great-grandchildren—were always a significant part of my mother's life.

The fifties were important maturing years for me. Mom's guidance was discreet and supportive, but firm. One summer day in 1952, the year I was entering adolescence, she took the opportunity while washing my hair to tell me about menstruation. Well, sort of. I didn't really comprehend why I might suddenly start bleeding when I was away at camp the next month. But she had the foresight to warn me of the possibility. I can't recall her ever talking to me about anything related to sex prior to that—at least not directly. The aftermath of an incident at a winter house party earlier that year had come close. The older people were downstairs playing cards. The younger ones were upstairs. I don't know now what one of the boys had suggested we do, but I spoke up in disagreement. He told me I'd better comply or "I'll fuck you". I didn't have a clue what he meant. But the violence in his voice and manner petrified me. Mom knew by the time we got home that something was bothering me. When she tucked me into bed she asked what the trouble was. Through tears of terror, I told her what had been said. She must have known what the word meant, even though the f-word wasn't in common currency the way it is today. She gave no hint of its meaning to me. She just reassured and comforted me enough that I was able to sleep.

Such reticence about sex wasn't unusual then. When Wilf Wees presented me with a set of books on girls' health and personal development, which he'd got through the publishing company where he worked, Mom had seemed insulted and annoyed. At the time, I couldn't understand why. My guess is that she thought she was doing a good job and didn't need his or any book's advice. And she was. If she'd been worried about what the book was going to tell me about sex, she needn't have been. Amazingly enough, even the third in that series, called *Into Your Teens*, made only oblique references to the sexual aspect of growing up, with the briefest of nods to hormones and glands. Ten years later, when I was preparing to be married in June 1962, Mom and I were comfortable discussing birth control options together. She was pleased, I'm sure, that I had no desire to forfeit with an unwanted pregnancy the teaching position that was waiting for me in September.

As a teenager, I didn't have a strict curfew for dating. Sometimes a specific time was mentioned. Generally there was just an unspoken expectation that I'd get in at a reasonable hour. And usually I did. Thanksgiving weekend, 1958, was different. I'd gone to an all-night drive-in movie with my summer boyfriend. When we got back to the farm, we sat in the car talking for at least an hour, possibly more. I got into the house around 5:30 a.m. When I made my appearance in the kitchen much later that day, I got a stern lecture. Whatever did I think I was doing? I was a grade thirteen student planning to go to university. I needed my sleep and time to do homework. Underlying all of this, I'm sure, was a fear that I might never make it to university but be stuck as an unfulfilled unwed teen mother. Ever astute, Mom got me where it hurt the most. She stated that if I stayed out that late again, I needn't expect any support from her for university. She wasn't referring to financial support. She had no personal income. But since my dad wouldn't give me financial support because he was afraid of tax implications, and since I had my heart set on studying English at university, this announcement had the desired effect. That was my last all-nighter while I lived at home.

My first Christmas home from university, in 1959, Mom and Dad drove me to Orillia for the latter part of the holiday. I was to stay at the home of my new boyfriend's sister and return to university with him. A major ice storm had hit the day before, so the drive up was difficult. Since neither I nor my parents knew how to find the house, we went into a service station to phone for directions. Boyfriend Vern (later my husband) came to pick me up. Mom and Dad headed home. "And it was an awful storm," Mom told me years later. "It affected my eyes so they never were the same again—that ice and the glare, and it probably was bothering Walter. And I didn't have any sunglasses with me, not thinking about any sun on a night drive. But the car lights on the ice, it was awful. And I was positively ill when I got home. I remember that, because I couldn't eat a bite of supper." This cloud was a sad and tough one for an avid reader. She decided to read in smaller bites, with stronger light. She and Dad also had to deal with no telephone service for three months afterwards because the ice had broken down many wires south of the farm. Their phone was with the Stouffville-Bethesda Company, which Bell was trying to buy. Bell had bought out the Uxbridge Home Telephone Company years before. Early in 1960, Bell took over Stouffville-Bethesda, but it was spring before their telephone was back in service.

Isabel's father, the only grandparent I ever knew, died on February 24, 1961. Since the death of Kate in 1937, Will had lived in his parents' former house with his eldest child, Annie, keeping house for him. Badly crippled with arthritis, Annie went to live with her youngest sister Jessie soon after Will's death. The Wallace side had its difficult person, just as the Beach family did. Jessie was it. She seemed to spend most of her life playing one person off against another. After Will's death she claimed, to quote Mom, "Dad had no money until he came to live with Annie in the old house. Whatever money he had at the end was Annie's anyway. [Jessie] said it right out to me. Only I'm puttin' it into my own words. And Dad with a hundred acres over there, on the ranch, and a marvelous hardwood bush on it, and a creek going through for water for the animals and fifty acres where they were living…" Jessie persuaded Annie, who was by then totally dependent on her, to change her will and leave Jessie nearly all her money. This money had come to Annie from their father as payment for the years of looking after him and as security for her own future. The rest of Will's children came up short in the arrangement. More than once, when I visited her in subsequent years, Mom shared with me her anger over Jessie's behaviour. The rift between them never healed.

In 1962, I decided that Isabel's wedding veil would be the perfect accompaniment to the gown I was making for my marriage to Vern Ashton. She handed it over without any qualms. The orange blossom circle was carefully replaced with a circular form covered in some of the gown material. I sewed the veil on so that it reached just to the floor, with the remainder hanging down to the waist in a second tier, showing the beautiful embroidery at both levels—a unique and special way of wearing 'something old'. One week before the wedding ceremony, on June 22, all of my family, including Bev and Norma and their children, went to Trinity United Church in Uxbridge for the rehearsal. A community shower at the farm was to follow at about 8 p.m. Norma and Isabel left the rehearsal early to prepare for the shower. Walter and Edward (who was almost nine) went home together a little later. On the way, Walter decided to stop at an empty neighbour's house that he was looking after, to see what a truck and two men were doing there. He soon became suspicious and told Edward to get home as fast as possible. When the men trained a rifle on my dad, he figured they intended to rob the place. He jumped the man holding the gun, trying to wrestle it from him. Dad took a blow to his left temple, but got possession of the gun. Then he threw it with all the force he could muster. The men quickly left. With a gashed forehead and a broken little finger, Dad got into his car to drive home. Minutes later, several of us standing in the yard near the farmhouse were shocked to see his car come weaving down the hill, turn into the driveway, and barely miss the gatepost. He got the car to the garage, then staggered out. When questioned, he told his story. Someone got him into Bev and Norma's part of the house and called the family doctor. Fortunately, doctors still made house calls in rural areas.

Meanwhile all the shower guests were in Isabel and Walter's part of the house waiting for the party to begin. I was told to keep quiet, to act as if nothing had happened. After a short delay, my mother appeared and carried on—just as if nothing had happened. Most of the guests had no suspicion of what was going on in the other part of the house. By our wedding day the next Friday, Dad had the bandage off his forehead and just a small one on his broken finger. Some women would have collapsed or become hysterical, but, for the sake of her family, Mom's practical and stoical nature took over. She performed the mother of the bride role admirably.

Grandfather Wallace, Walter and Isabel joined Beverley and Norma for this photo in August 1952

Walter and Isabel with Catherine on her wedding day in 1962

In May 1964, Isabel went to Toronto General Hospital (the one from which her sister Chris was a proud graduate), for a hysterectomy. Following the surgery, she spent a few days with Chris before returning to the farm. When Vern and I went to visit her in Toronto, I got into the spot in our conversation of having to tell her that I'd resigned from my teaching position. She immediately knew that I was pregnant. Having a hysterectomy, as any woman who's had one can attest, is a big enough emotional trial. The cruel collision of these circumstances—her reproductive system savaged by surgery just as mine came into full bloom—must have increased that pain. She'd already thought I had married too young. Now I was going to have a baby at age twenty-four. She hadn't married until she was twenty-six, with almost five years' teaching experience behind her. I had taught for just two years. I could see by the expression on my mother's face how upset she was. She must have been so disappointed, even dismayed, that I hadn't planned my life as well as she had planned hers. But she was exceptionally wise. She communicated nothing more to me about these feelings—ever.

That August, my dad suffered a cerebral hemorrhage. A physically strong and determined man, he got home from Uxbridge Cottage Hospital after a two-month recuperation period. Mom's sister Chris helped with the continuing therapy process. Dad had to squeeze a ball to improve his hand and arm muscles, practise walking, and keep his mind actively engaged in life. His emotions were unpredictable, but Mom patiently helped and encouraged him to such a remarkable recovery that they were able to come to our house in Orillia for a few days over the Christmas season. In September 1966, they enjoyed a small quiet family celebration of their fortieth wedding anniversary in Bev and Norma's part of the farmhouse.

At the beginning of December 1967, Bev and Norma and their three growing children moved out of the double farmhouse 'a hop, skip and a jump' down the concession to a bungalow they'd built. A few days later, on his granddaughter Joanne's twelfth birthday, Walter died of a massive heart attack. Joanne remembered receiving her grandmother's birthday gift that week. She later commented, "I thought, 'Gee, you don't have to be thinkin' about that', but I imagine it was something she had bought weeks before anyway." Again, Isabel probably wanted life to go on as normally as possible, especially for the grandchildren.

Dealing with the great cloud of widowhood that had overshadowed her life must have been unbearable for my mother. Family and friends visited and called, and she went about her usual community activities, but she was unexpectedly—for the first time in her life—completely alone. In the spring of 1968, she gladly said 'Yes' when the Al Chapmans from Siloam and the Ted Chapmans from Uxbridge asked to stay in the south part of the farmhouse while the plaster dried on the new houses they had built. Their presence in the house helped her decide to go on a trip west with her sister Chris to attend the wedding of their niece Kathleen's youngest daughter. They left by car on March 29, arriving in New Westminster, British Columbia on April 2. They stayed until mid-April, then took the train to visit more relatives in the Cariboo area. On April 22, back in Vancouver, Isabel, Chris and Kathleen crossed the channel to Vancouver Island. While there, Isabel recorded in her travel notes that she had met a woman who was born in Orillia when Reverend Grant was the minister at St. Andrew's Presbyterian Church. Reverend Grant had performed the wedding ceremony for her parents, Will and Kate, at the manse in 1888. "A small world," she wrote. In a letter dated April 29, she said, "I fell in love with Victoria and could hardly leave it. The flowers were everywhere and the lovely old buildings and museums were most interesting." I wrote in return asking if she'd fallen in love so much that she planned to retire there. Her reply on May 8 soon set me straight: "You can rest your mind as far as coming to Victoria to retire. In the first place, I'm not retiring and in the second place it is too far from my family and friends *but* it is a beautiful place and maybe when I come to the point of sitting in an 'Old Folks Home' I may consider looking out at the blue Pacific, the mountains and the flowers." On May 3 she, Kathleen and Chris left Vancouver for Castlegar, where they briefly visited my in-laws, Dorothy and George Ashton. After a harrowing adventure going through the mountains (recounted in Chapter One), they arrived home safely in mid-May.

Through the summer, the south end of the Beach double house was empty. Then a Mr. and Mrs. Hudson rented it. In September that year, Mom answered my call for help and took our three and a half year old James to live with her for a couple of months until we could move into the house Vern was building for us. We'd been living on our property since June in a tent trailer and an eight by twelve foot uninsulated one-room structure. Cool damp weather had caused James to catch cold; we were concerned about his health. His grandmother soon nursed him back to good health, at the same time stirring in him depths of love and admiration to last a lifetime.

The deaths of her sister Annie in May 1969 and her brother-in-law John Owens in June 1970, which widowed her next youngest sibling Minnie (who'd retired with John from Los Angeles to the home farm), placed more clouds on Mom's horizon. Life was a see-saw for a few years, but she clung to it steadfastly. She had important things to do. The farm business, which she and Walter had developed to quite a successful level, and which was further enhanced when Beverley and then Ed joined it, was still a top priority with Mom. After my Dad's illness resulting from a cerebral hemorrhage in 1964, she devised agreements on paper to keep the arrangements clear and business-like. She also recorded various transactions. A receipt from 1969 reads, 'Received from Bev and Ted, for use of land and farm buildings'. Isabel had written these receipts into the 1970s. She always emphasized a strong business approach, knowing so well what tangles could result otherwise. In his 2003 interview with me, Ed gave his rather different perspective on the situation: "It got a little interesting until we got the farm straightened up. That was kind of—you could go along so far, but you didn't know what you should be doing. When we got it straightened up and it was go ahead from there, that was good. That took quite a bit of discussion. That took quite some time, and you had to be very tactful."

Isabel finally agreed to pass the ownership of the farm over to the men who were conducting the business, in November 1987. She sold it to Bev and Ed for one 'loonie' each, but not before agreeing on a market value for the property, then going to a lawyer with them plus Vern and me. In her strong sense of fairness, she was determined that I would get a share of what was, in effect, her estate. I certainly hadn't contributed much towards its development. Taking the cows to pasture on the Wees' property each morning and bringing them home for milking each evening during the summer, going to the fields with a cool drink and honey and peanut butter sandwiches for the men, and helping with the hay and potato harvests was about the extent of my involvement. Together, we agreed on a value for the farm. Bev received a half share, Ed a quarter. I received the remaining quarter, which Ed bought from me. With the exchange of the 'loonies', Ed and Bev each owned half of Echo Valley Farm. The arrangements also included a memorandum of agreement which stated that, "notwithstanding the conveyance by Isabella to Beverley and Edward of the property…Isabella shall be permitted to remain in possession of that portion of the house located on the property which she now occupies upon the following terms and conditions", which included "without any rent charge whatsoever" but responsibility for heat and telephone costs. It was also agreed that Beverley and Edward would pay for alternative accommodation, should Isabel desire it, "consistent with the lifestyle and the manner to which Isabella has been accustomed during her lifetime", if the cost exceeded her pension and other income. Isabel loved living at the farm and was remarkably healthy for most of her life. This part of the agreement was never invoked.

Through all these years, the grandchildren often dropped in to share with her their latest adventures. Joanne played hockey in her teens and twenties and, although Isabel never watched her play, she was always interested. Joanne told me in our interview: "No matter what you went in to talk about, she was always interested anyway. It usually ended up, you'd start talking about something and she'd have a story related to it from her days too." Joanne felt she was just interested in knowing what was going on and keeping up on everything. Girls playing on a hockey team, such a significant change in the sports scene, was of special interest to Isabel. She had played basketball when a progressive young high school physical education teacher made sure the girls had the opportunity, even if only boys were allowed to use the gym. Although she would never have called herself one, not wanting to be associated with the late twentieth century bra-burning radicals she had read about, my mother was a feminist.

Living a greater distance away in Orillia, our sons James and Bruce came for longer stays with their grandmother. Sometimes, especially at Christmas and in summer holidays, our whole family went for a few days. James told me about some of his summer holidays there on his own. "I spent a lot of time reading and wandering around," he said. "And I remember spending a lot of time playing in the junk cars [behind the barn]. And I loved that." When asked about memories of her, he said, "Most of it is about being at Grandma's, as opposed to Grandma *per se*. Actually, the only time I remember her getting mad at me (I don't know how old I was. Obviously I was old enough she thought I should have known better.), I was sick, and she specifically told me not to throw anything in the toilet except for toilet paper, and I absent-mindedly chucked in a Kleenex, and she had to fish it out."

Eventually James got interested in helping with the farm work. "The summer I was thirteen started as just a visit," he recalled, "and then I wanted to go back so badly that I spent a lot of the summer there and unofficially worked." Isabel provided free room and board—and more. "I remember her fixing me up with a lamp to read, too. She made my reading very comfortable. I just remember how cosy it felt." My guess is that she was more concerned about his eyesight than with atmosphere. He had worn glasses since he was six years old. "I guess a lot of my recollections put her in the background as the figure responsible for the things that I actually remember," James admitted. He remembered her as a support person, which was her role in much of her life. "A lot of it does connect with food—apples and cheese and—'If you're hungry, just have a soda cracker and some water. It'll swell up in your tummy'." This was the advice given close to mealtime. He also remembered going to the garage to get the ice cream from the freezer there. "She always made sure that she had some. She knew what I liked," he said. She did the same for everyone, considerate of others to a fine point.

When the house was to be renovated for her grandson Ed and his fiancée, Pam, before their October 1973 wedding, the Hudsons moved to Toronto. Vern had just gone into renovations, so he was hired to do the work. He put a bathroom in each part of the house, and converted part of the back porch into a small kitchen with plumbing for Isabel. At seventy-three years of age, she finally had running water and a full bathroom. Ed told me that after he and Pam moved into the south part of the house, "It was a little hard when we were first there, trying to start and do your own thing, but you always had to take into consideration what Grandmother wanted or what Grandmother would accept. So you always kept that in the back of your mind." Ed found, however, that "She was always supportive. If you had to borrow money or something like that, you could always borrow money. She didn't give it to you. You always made sure you paid it back, but not with interest. When we were first married, she gave us rent for the house that was border-line cheap. But I guess she knew that she needed us around there to help her as much as we needed her, so it kind of worked both ways—maybe not so much at first, but it did later on."

In these later years, family helped her out a little more. Norma and Isabel often went grocery shopping together. Only occasionally did she drive on her own. Isabel did all her own laundry until she was in her eighties. Then, Norma said, "I think it was one winter we started, and I was doing her sheets, and maybe just her heavy towels. For a while, I wanted her to give me more to do." But Isabel declined. As long as she could do it, she did. She always paid Norma for this work. In the summer, she liked to wash her own lightweight articles by hand, then hang the laundry on her clothesline. In fact, she looked after her own underwear and other hand washing until she was ninety-eight, one of several ways in which Mom looked after her body and kept it 'supple', as she said.

Isabel always kept up connections beyond her immediate family. Cousins on both sides issued shower and wedding invitations. She provided a gift in response to them all. Often, in the summer, she spent a few days visiting Minnie at the family farm. Her date-book from 1975 shows that she also attended euchre parties, Tupperware parties, wedding anniversary parties, bridal and baby showers, church services, suppers, and meetings, helped at a quilting, and chauffeured Dell Badgerow (the woman at whose home she had met Walter) to Uxbridge. The summer of 1983, she came to Orillia to house- and goat-sit while our family drove to Castlegar, British Columbia, to visit Vern's parents. Yes, she was eighty-two years old. We didn't ask her to feed and milk the half-dozen or so goats, just to keep an eye on them. James' friend, Tim, came to tend them each day. When the goats jumped the electric fence around noon one day, Isabel had to phone Tim. She was nimble for her age, but… She did prove her nimbleness in a different way, however, when she climbed in a basement window and managed a four-foot drop to a wooden box on the floor below the window. She'd gone shopping and forgotten the house key. We were so relieved to find her without a scratch. We never again asked her to take on these responsibilities.

Still going strong, she wrote a letter to me on April 16, 1989, telling how her busy week had caught up to her on that Sunday and caused her to sleep in until ten. "Monday was United Church Women at Goodwood, Wednesday was Women's Association at Siloam, and Thursday evening [great-granddaughter] Candice invited me to the school program at Goodwood. I couldn't refuse as I always enjoy it and this will be her last year at Goodwood. They put on "Robin Hood" as an operetta and did quite well too. The school has been doing this for a few years. Last year they did "Alice in Wonderland" and the year before it was "Sleeping Beauty" and [Candice's sister] Vanessa was the old witch. She certainly did her 'cackle' quite well. They go to a great deal of trouble on the costumes and the stage props which makes for a good show." Mom also wrote about her sister Chris, who'd been ill and had left her Toronto apartment to live in a seniors' apartment in Stouffville. "Chris continues to improve. We talked from 9 till 10 p.m. last evening and she really sounded as she used to from Toronto." From the youngest to the oldest, family was never far from my mother's thoughts.

As her own physical health deteriorated, Mom needed more help. But her mind was so healthy and active that she wanted to keep going as usual. And she didn't want to leave the farm. Ed saw this every spring. He told me, "You always had to make sure there was a garden planted for her. Her garden was important every spring, it didn't matter what. It was just her one row—always had to be there." Ed did many little jobs around her part of the house. "That was just part of it, you just did 'em. You didn't question it. You put some of it off sometimes, but eventually it was done. Lots of times you had to drop whatever you were doing and go and do it." However, if Isabel saw that Ed was especially busy with the farm or his own family, she'd often wait a few days before putting in her request. She tried to time it so that Ed wasn't too harried. Likewise, she tried not to inconvenience or call on Norma more than was necessary, in her view. She handled an amazing amount on her own, in her own way.

Grace (Beach) Thompson remarked how my mother never changed much. "To me," Grace said, "she wasn't a young person when she was married, and really, when she was fifty she didn't look much older than she did when she was married. She just seemed to stay the same. She always seemed as if she was an aunt that you go to and ask anything. You kinda' looked up to her, for some reason or other. Now some of them, I didn't feel that way. But with [Isabel], I did. It's strange, isn't it?"

Maybe not so strange for someone like Isabel, who treated almost everybody in the family—and many who were not—as one of her own.

CHAPTER NINE: Always Helping

Little Places

I'm glad I live in a little place.
It doesn't matter how small
A place may be, if friends are near
And sometimes come to call.

I feel at home in a little church.
The sermons are simple and clear,
And the hymns are sung to the grand old tunes
I'll always love to hear.

A country store is a wonderful place.
The shelves are all stacked high
With cans and boxes, bottles and bags
Of things that plain folk buy.

It's fine to go to a country school
To learn to read and spell.
Your school-mates will be life-long friends;
Few others you'll know as well.

News travels fast in a little place.
When a neighbour comes down with "flu"
This one and that stop by to ask,
"Is there anything I can do?"

Oh, let me die in a little place!
When I come to the journey's end
Let me lie in a country graveyard,
Where friend rests next to friend.

Pauline E. Gerber

Not only did my mother reach out to family; she was an involved community-minded person. Her granddaughter Marilyn put it this way: "She was always helping others and would jump at the chance to help anybody and everybody: the neighbours, the community people. She would send a pie, other baking, tea biscuits." Isabel's friend, Shirley Chapman, made a remarkably similar statement in a letter to me: "She was always helping with every community event, whether it was a shower, a church play or a dinner." Through these involvements, Isabel made a variety of friends in her eighty adult years. Some were relatives, some other community-minded people, some close neighbours, some members of the same organization. A few of these friendships developed into a deep and rich soul-mate communion; others demonstrated a cordial sharing of interests or social concerns. She was enthusiastic, interested, open and honest. She listened well and seldom complained. Her generous and caring heart combined with the 'turning clouds' spin she put on most situations to make her good company for people of all ages.

One of the first female Beach farm neighbours that Isabel got to know was Mary McGee. Apparently Mary didn't get along well with her family. She lived in a little one-storey house on property about half a mile out 'the sandy sideroad'. Possibly it had been Crown land granted to her father, Captain Collins, as a reward for service in the navy. Mary's husband Davey was of the mail order variety. "She hitched up the horse and buggy and went down to Goodwood to collect him off the train," chuckled Isabel. But "Mary and I got along fine because she read *The Globe and Mail* every morning and came over and talked politics or anything we wanted to talk about. It wasn't so many years until she died". A bit of an eccentric, it appears, but just as acceptable to my mother as anyone else in the community.

Neighbours and others were welcome in her and Walter's home any time of the day or night. Once, Shirley Chapman's father, Jack Wallace, came into the house when Isabel and Walter were in bed. When Walter called out to see who it was, Jack said, "It's only me. I've got to use your phone. The baby's coming." Shirley recalled (in her letter to me after my mother's death) an early visit to Walter and Isabel's that she and her sister Aileen made on their own, again to use the phone. "My earliest memory of [Isabel] is when Aileen and I, being the oldest, would be sent down to the Beaches to get a message through to the trucker or it could have been to a relative sometimes. Your parents had the closest phone in those days. Our phone came out in the depression days. Anyway, Bev had rubber building blocks and we would be allowed to stay and play for half an hour before trundling off home." A few years later, Shirley married Al Chapman on Isabel's birthday. Of this circumstance she said: "We also shared September 16 each year, her birthday and our anniversary, and we'll always remember her with love and affection and count ourselves lucky to be called friends." Shirley had often talked and worked with Isabel at church and other community events. She knew her well. Shirley noted: "[Isabel] was always a leader, one with firm Christian beliefs and she put that faith to action. Certainly we felt that was what she did for us when she opened her home to us for six to eight weeks when we needed it [in the spring of 1968]."

Bev and Norma had moved from the double farmhouse the first of December 1967 to their new house nearby. Shortly after, Walter died. So Mom spent her first winter as a widow alone, the larger south end of the house empty beside her living space. Shirley explained the 1968 situation: "We were getting our home plastered and had to move out. Not only did she share with us, but with Ted Chapman and his family, whom she didn't even know. And she expected and asked nothing in return. She even got a little annoyed with me for washing the kitchen ceiling. With a wood stove it's hard to keep them clean. Maybe annoyed isn't the right word; she just didn't think I should be doing it, and I thought it was the least I could do." Shirley gave Isabel a colonial style braid rug as an extra thank-you, but Mom never put it down on the floor. Nobody in the family could quite figure out why; Mom was never quite able to explain why. When I asked her she side-stepped the question with, "Oh, I wasn't ready to". Shirley made a larger punched rug for Isabel, to celebrate the Uxbridge town centennial in 1972. This one occupied a prominent spot in her living room as long as she lived at the farm. It reminded her of the town so dear to her heart—and of the circumstances in which her one decision in 1968 had turned three clouds inside out.

Another woman whom Isabel met early in her marriage became a companion much later in life. Lily Hope first saw Isabel at one of the house dances that continued to be popular during the 1930s depression, because they cost little and gave people a social outlet beyond church and neighbourly visits. Lily related in her interview how one particular family often had house dances in the winter, in the back kitchen. Square dancing was popular at these get-togethers. Lily's dad sometimes played the mouth organ for them. The fox trot, the waltz and the military schottische were also featured. Lily thought Isabel liked the schottische "'cause she sure could do it". Between thirty and fifty people attended one of these dances that were by invitation only. Lily went on. "It was just for the neighbours, and you'd take sandwiches or something for lunch. They had a stove out [in the summer kitchen]." The coffee often was boiled in the same copper boiler that was used for laundry, canning and other hot water household tasks. A crude kind of sanitation was applied. The person making coffee added an egg to gather the undesirable specks, flecks, and bits of this and that. These were, of course, all scooped out before serving the coffee.

Because Lily was about fifteen years younger than Isabel, they didn't become acquainted immediately. Eventually, they met through Lily's first cousin, Eleanor Hosie, who attended Siloam United Church with her husband George. When the Siloam church closed in 1966 because the congregation was deemed too small to support a minister, people were encouraged to transfer membership to Goodwood United, where Lily went to church. Not everyone from Siloam made this move, but Isabel did. So, Lily said, "We'd talk about different things that would happen around, here and there, and the church, and that." Lily recalled Isabel's participation in the maple syrup supper in Goodwood. "Her tea biscuits for the maple syrup supper—she wouldn't make 'em until they were about ready to go out the door. They had to be hot. But when they got down here, they weren't that hot, by the time they sat out. But they'd be fresh." When she was older, Lily knew, Isabel evened out the work of making tea biscuits by putting the dry ingredients together the night before. All she had to do on the day of the supper was add the milk, mix them up and bake them. Until she stopped making pies, her lemon sponge pie (made from 'scratch') was a popular menu item, too.

In January 1970, Lily was Mom's roommate on a bus trip vacation to Florida that included four of the Beach nieces, two of whom brought their husbands. In our interview, Lily recalled the conversation that led to this arrangement. One fall day after Sunday School at Goodwood United Church, Isabel had approached Lily and said, "I've got a chance to go to Florida. You know, I gotta' find somebody to go with me. You wouldn't like to go, would you? And I says, 'I sure would'." Lily went on: "So that's how I got more acquainted with [Isabel]. We had a good time." They left on Sunday, January 10, for a two-week trip. I was fortunate to find the notes my mother had jotted down about each day and its personal highlights. En route, the bus went through Washington past the well-known sights, including The Library of Congress, the National Museum and Arlington National Cemetery. Always abreast of current events, Mom wrote, "During ride saw signs of result of earlier riots, etc." She also made note of the cotton fields and how poor many areas looked. On day four they stopped at Marineland to view the "educated seals and whales" and the trained porpoises.

Lily described some of the expeditions they took from their motel: "They took us on a glass-bottomed boat and [we saw] the fish down under. Oh, [Isabel] got quite a kick out of that." Mom's notes suggest she also got a kick out of mailing her postcards under water. The day they went to the Busch Gardens, they also attended dog races in the evening. The notes on this expedition intrigued me. "Got there before they started and had a lot of fun *but* very late finishing. It was nearly 1 a.m. when we got home." My mother was out *that* late at dog races? Then, one Sunday she had to skip church because the cold she'd contracted was making her cough so much. However, in the afternoon she went to Sarasota to the Circus Hall of Fame and Ringling Museum, "which was quite interesting". She knew how to have a good time. The next

day she enjoyed the Cypress Gardens and "Orange trees and oranges as far as the eye could see." She noted countless oranges strewn on the ground for animals to eat. At some point, she and Lily encountered the long-horned fellow in the photo on the left. Isabel is standing on his left. These side trips took place during their five days at the Colonial Inn at St. Petersburg Beach.

Their housekeeping unit contained a table where they could eat lunch and breakfast, plus two double beds. Lily and Isabel slept in one bed, Isabel's two nieces in the other. Lily recalled one incident that brought her and Isabel together a little more. "This one morning somebody got some oranges for breakfast. And [Isabel] got up, and she says, 'I can't eat that orange. I can't peel it. I can't stand to peel it!' She says, 'It does something to me'. I peeled the orange for her. So every morning after that we had oranges, and I'd have her orange peeled before she'd get up."

When they headed home via Cape Kennedy, the temperature was only thirty-three degrees Fahrenheit. Smudge pots attempted to keep the fruit from freezing. As they traveled through Georgia and South Carolina, Isabel recorded "Many signs of frost. Ice on water and white frost heavy on grass and shrubs. But beautiful sunshine." The next day they encountered snow on the ground in Virginia. On the final day, snow slowed the driving. She must have wondered why she had left her cosy home, but disappointment was nowhere in her notes. Lily told me, "We all brought some orange honey home, and some oranges and some grapefruit. And of course when you're comin' across the border you're not supposed to bring that stuff into Canada. But the bus driver, he always stuck it underneath a certain part of the bus, and then when he opened it up for them to inspect, all they could see was the suitcases." Though Mom was a stickler for honesty, I seem to recall my family receiving some Florida grapefruit when she got back!

Three years later, Isabel, Lily, and Eleanor Hosie's two unmarried sisters-in-law took a one-week bus trip around the Great Lakes in the early fall. They went north to see Lake Superior, then into Michigan where they experienced Lake Huron and Lake St. Clair, then crossed the border back into Canada. Lily had one especially outstanding memory from this trip: "But when we got up north there, well we went to Sault Ste. Marie and you get the train and go up the Agawa Canyon. Of course we had a box lunch with us." At the Agawa Canyon "…there was a flight of steps, over a hundred, you can climb and see up over all the ravines and all over the top of the whole canyon." Isabel started up, Lily walking behind her. Isabel, in her early seventies but still full of energy and strength, made it to the top. Lily, at least fifteen years younger, didn't. Lily thought the reason was that "I was carryin' the lunches, and she didn't have nothin' to carry. She said, 'Oh Lily, you should come up and see how beautiful it is!' And I says, 'Well I cannot make it, Isabel. My legs won't let me'. She stood up there, and she looked and looked. 'Oh,' she says, 'it's so beautiful up here.' And it had snowed the night before…quite a big snowfall. But you know, that was the most beautiful-lookin' scenery—the snow on those colours. We had a good trip that time, too," Lily concluded.

Lily remarked to me in our interview how "[Isabel] would talk about a lot of things of bygone days". In fact, my mother remembered in such detail that nearly everybody was interested in her spellbinding stories. Lily "… often wondered if it was because she was a teacher that made her that way. Well, anyway, she was quite a knowledgeable lady, you know, and she seemed to mix with everybody." Isabel could converse with anyone. She also had a wonderful memory. "Oh, that's what kept her goin'," declared Lily. Isabel was always interested in the community, which included the church. "That's why, you know, I often thought that they could've done a little bit more for her at the church," Lily confessed. "But, anyway, anything that came up, why I would phone her and let her know. I phoned her lots of times to tell her what was goin' on down here, when she wasn't drivin' any more in the '90s." In those years Isabel herself felt a little neglected by the church to which she'd devoted so much of her life. The feeling had been somewhat soothed by the Goodwood United Church Board of Session's presentation, in January 1990, of a certificate of appreciation for her "...many years of faithful service and commitment rendered to our church and community".

The Wees family—Wilf, Frances, and Margeurita—came to Echo Valley in 1938 when Wilf purchased from Mary McGee's brother, Charlie Collins, the fifty acres that Mary had occupied on the north side of the sideroad that went east from the Beach farm's south property line. Frances Shelley Wees became a widely recognized writer; Wilfred Rusk Wees, who had a doctorate in psychology, worked in education publishing. In 1956 he became an associate professor at the Ontario Institute for Studies in Education in Toronto. At first the Wees family lived in Toronto and came to the country on weekends. They renovated Mary McGee's small home, which they called "Lost House", to use as a cottage. Occasionally they came to the Beach farm to use the telephone. On the way from Toronto to their property, they often stopped in for a chat and to buy fresh cream and milk. They enjoyed Isabel, Walter and the farm. On one visit, they said, 'Well, we came over to borrow a cow'. Mom giggled as she told me this story. "My ears picked up and I wondered what was goin' on. I expect Walter was the same way. And so, when we got talking to them, there were so many weeds and so much long grass and that kind of thing all around the place—and they were just there weekends mostly—", they wanted a cow to keep the grass and weeds down! Frances and Wilf also owned some property on the south side of the sideroad. "So it ended up," Mom recounted, "I think Walter said, well, he had some young cattle around here that he could just put them over and let them run around, you know, only that he'd have to have fences to keep them in a certain place." Before long, Walter pastured the cattle on the south Wees' property every summer. Then he worked some of the land, because grass or hay had to grow on the land to make pasture.

Wilf was in the personnel department of the army during WWII, helping to decide on recruit placement in various branches of the armed forces. He, Frances, and Margeurita lived in Ottawa then, so contacts were fewer. After the war, they bought another fifty acres on the same side of the sideroad as the cottage, but closer to the Beach farm. I was a little surprised to learn from my mother that "Walter used to say if he'd known it was going to be for sale, he would've bought it, but he didn't know it was for sale". She believed Wilf knew the right people to talk to in order to get it through the government as a veteran. In the 1950s, the Weeses hired a local builder to construct a large permanent home on the property. They sold their Toronto house to live there year-round. Gradually the contacts increased. They often got milk at the farm because, Isabel explained, "The milk you buy now, it won't curdle to make cottage cheese. And Frances always liked to make this cottage cheese with the separated milk. But we never charged for it. It was pig feed, as far as we were concerned... But then, they got whole milk too sometimes." A little later, they added manure to the farm products they wanted because Wilf had got interested in vegetable and flower gardening. It also was provided at no charge.

Tim, who was born in Ottawa in the mid-forties, was naturally interested in the farm and its owners—all so different from his own home and family. Sometimes, when Frances was busy with her writing, she would send him to the farm on a small errand so she'd have time to herself. Mom loved to tell of his showing up with an armful of coat hangers, offering them to her with small boy enthusiasm saying, "We've got 'sousands of 'em." Of course she accepted every one. Tim was always welcome at our home. He became a regular playmate for me. Not only did he live closer than any other neighbourhood children; our families had a closer relationship.

When Frances visited the USSR in a carefully guided group tour the summer of 1957 (one of the first to be admitted from the West) she wrote a letter to Isabel describing some of her adventures. The letter clearly indicates that Isabel had already booked Frances to speak at a church meeting after her trip. Frances wrote, "I have some wonderful material for the [Women's Association]. I have been thinking of you all at Siloam so much since I came, watching for things that you'd like to know about." A few lines later she wrote, "As Mona Clark said last night, 'I wouldn't make [the trip] again for a thousand dollars, but I would pay a thousand to see the farm if I had never seen it'. It is unlike anything we know at home… I'm not going to tell you too much because it will spoil my speech for you." Frances also wrote about shopping, education, and the spirit of the people she met. She closed on a personal note: "Thank you all again for being so good to my boy. He loves you, and I am so afraid he will impose on you, but I can see that the matter really is out of my hands and lies between those two boys, Walter and Tim, with their undying friendship. So I have sort of given up. Love to everyone, Frances."

The Echo Valley setting and lore often provided inspiration and detail for Frances' stories and novels. *Melody Unheard*, published in 1952, provides many examples. Most prominent is the heroine, Isabel Gay. Frances wrote in the copy she gave me for Christmas in 1955, "For Catherine—the story in which her mother's name, Isabel, was borrowed for the heroine—with love Frances Shelley Wees". Those who knew Mom and read the book would quickly realize that Frances borrowed more than the name. Several of Miss Gay's personality traits were also hers. In one example, Arthur says, "You've got a fine mind, Isabel. A fine straight realistic understanding" (105). Mom was angry that Frances got so little recognition in Canada for her writing that received awards in the United States. She pasted an article from the *Uxbridge Times-Journal* in her copy of Frances' mystery *Where is Jenny Now?*—an article that she often referred to in conversation. It stated, "Mrs. Wees has written about thirty novels, most of them mystery and suspense plus many magazine and newspaper articles" (Agatha Christie…). She also wrote stories for school readers. One of her books for young readers, *The Treasure of Echo Valley*, published in 1964, featured Walter and his "warm neighbourliness". Frances wrote in my copy, "I am sorry [Isabel] isn't in it—but Isabel is such a wonderful person the whole book would have had to be about her". In my opinion, that book was *Melody Unheard.*

The Weeses went to British Columbia in the early '80s to be near Tim. By 1985, both of them had died. A June 1983 letter to Isabel from Tim, referring to his parents' move from Echo Valley, elaborates on the neighbourly ties that he remembered:

"I want to thank you a lot for the time and energy and love you put into that final caring for Mom and Dad. You were always like that for us, and Walter is of course included there too. It was as though the valley worked because the Beaches were there and would always be there if they were needed. It could have been that there was an emergency or some work to be done or just some friendship. You were always there and willing to be there too. I have a million memories of my own of those years. Peanut butter and honey sandwiches are way up on top of the list. Jumping into the strawstack at threshing time, and driving the horses. Saying I would go and get the water for some very thirsty men and then not bothering to come back (sorry) and going fishing on the first of May with Walter, getting into a fight about something or other with him and both of us walking off in a huff and then out of not being willing not to be in relationship apologizing to each other… You were always so forgiving, you people. If the world would work like you do our problems would be solved." Mom must have treasured that letter and its sentiments. It was among her few personal effects when she died.

Another neighbour, also called Wilfred, had cause to feel the same sort of appreciation for my parents, but then he was an equally good neighbour, as demonstrated when Isabel and Walter were getting ready for the barn-building in 1946. This story of Mom's intrigued me, for Wilfred Mantle was a bachelor most of his life, a shy reclusive man who lived sparsely in his unpainted old frame farmhouse. Mom told me this about him: "He was just one of those persons that just never thought about himself. If his neighbour needed help, that's where he was. And he was here helping Walter when we put that stove in from the Weeses [in 1946]. Well, it was the devil to get the pipes to fit. To make the number of links of pipe that you needed wasn't quite the same as it was for the original stove. But we had pipes around that you could use. And he and Walter worked at that thing. And he had to go home and do his own chores (he had his supper here, of course)…and do you think you could get that man to go home and do his chores? 'Oh we'll fix it tonight,' says Wilfred. And they stuck with it, and I'm sure they were doing chores about ten and eleven o'clock that night."

Almost two decades later, Isabel found a way to return the favour. While visiting Walter in hospital in 1964 after his cerebral hemorrhage, she discovered that Wilfred was a patient there too. They had a student minister at Goodwood, Isabel said, "And he was a conscientious man, I don't mean he wasn't, but you see, we had students, and sometimes some of our people that were sick up here didn't get much attention, while around Goodwood where the manse was…there was something done, when we were left in the cold up here." Chances are that Wilfred had never set foot in Goodwood United Church. Certainly he hadn't on a regular basis. That was not the point. So she told the minister one Sunday morning, "I don't know who is responsible for the souls of the people around Siloam when they're sick, but one of my neighbours is in the hospital. He may be from the other side of the track, but he's been a mighty good neighbour." The minister did visit Wilfred and, when he died, led the service of remembrance for this man whose overalls weren't always clean, who often smelled too much like a stable, but whose heart, my mother knew, was in the right place.

In 1963, Hartley and Barbara Spinney bought and moved into a house about a quarter of a mile north of the Beach farm, across from Wilfred Mantle's property. They became fairly close neighbours to the Beach family, partly because their girls, Lorraine and Diane, liked to come to the farm to play with Bev and Norma's girls. Because Barbara got involved quickly in the United Church Women's group, the euchre nights, and whatever else was going on, she soon became part of the community and of Isabel's life. In her interview with me, Barbara had this to say about Isabel: "She was Grandma to Joanne and Marilyn, so we called her Grandma Beach, and she was always so cuddly to Dianne and Lorraine. She always remembered their birthdays and sent them a card. She was sometimes like a mother for me because if I didn't know for sure what to put in a recipe, I'd phone her up and ask her, you know—'Which was which?' and she'd tell me—just a wonderful neighbour." Barbara and her girls sometimes walked down 'the big hill' (as we all called it) for a visit. Isabel always had a cookie for the girls. "She used to come out with some good stories and jokes for us and some good laughs. If Diane was playing the piano, Isabel always told her, 'Well you're doin' a good job' and never said, 'Now, you can't play the piano'." For years, 'the Spinney girls' came around for Hallowe'en treats. They were never disappointed at my mother's house.

Our son James spent part of each summer with his grandmother, a period that got longer as he was old enough to help around the farm. "One time when I was down, and Jamie was there," Barbara recalled, "he said about playing games or something, and then playing cards. So Jamie said, well, he could play euchre. 'OK, we'll have a game,' [Isabel said]." So they played three-handed euchre. Barbara noted how much Isabel liked euchre. In fact, she went to euchre games at Siloam community hall every two weeks from Thanksgiving until sometime in May, whenever she had the energy. These euchre nights started when the school was closed and converted to the community hall. With both the church and the school closed at Siloam, the evening provided a rare community social event, an opportunity to see friends and neighbours. Isabel stopped going to the hall euchres sometime in the '96-'97 season. But she still played in a ladies' group (for which she was a spare) when the meeting was at Pam's place, right beside her in the farmhouse. If she got the booby prize, she wasn't concerned. It was all just for fun.

During the 1970s, Isabel sometimes went to Barbara's to have her hair set. She walked north from the farm gate up 'the big hill'. "Later on," Barbara said, "she used to take her cane with her—and swingin' the cane, she'd walk up. And she had a little bag with her clamps; she had the clamps for the waves, you know… And one time she came up with her apron on. 'Oh Barbara,' she says,' I've got my apron on. Well, I was doin' this, doin' that, you know. And I didn't take my apron off.' And I said, 'Well, that's all right'." I can well imagine how Mom laughed about that little oversight. After she had broken her hip she wasn't able to navigate the hill, so found a hairdresser that she drove to. Barbara noticed how "She would persevere and do what she was supposed to do, to get goin'. If she had a cold or anything, you know, she did what she was to do and looked after herself." Sometimes Mom picked up Barbara to go to United Church Women meetings. "Isabel would always say, 'Well, weather permitting, I'll be there'," Barbara noted. Mom was still driving in 1989 when Barbara moved away from the second concession of Uxbridge Township.

Eleanor and George Hosie were cherished friends who attended Siloam United Church. Mom and Dad visited back and forth with them; Eleanor and Mom worked together on many church and community projects. During WWII they and other women in the Women's Missionary Society (WMS) at Siloam made quilts to send through the Red Cross to the Russian people. When Russia turned against the wartime Allies later on, Mom was furious at the ingratitude she saw in this political move. Over the years, she brought this sore spot up in conversation several times. Fortunately, many of the times she spent with Eleanor created happy memories of music, accomplishment and fun—three aspects of life they both valued. As members of the Women's Association (WA), the other United Church women's organization until the two were combined as the United Church Women (UCW) in 1962, they worked together on a variety of fundraisers.

In 1954, Eleanor suggested a Conundrum Supper, which Isabel agreed to host at the farmhouse. These suppers were a challenge to those who put them on and a conundrum to those who attended. Eleanor had prepared the menu; the WA women made additions and changes until everyone was satisfied. Every menu item was a riddle. An order of broken glass, for example, was a serving of cubed jelly. Norma explained in her interview, "You could get a full-course meal if you ordered everything on the menu. And we had prices for each thing. I know some of it was only five cents or ten cents [which might have been an olive]." One man at this supper ordered just two items. He ended up with a toothpick and a pickled onion. He failed to see the humour in his situation, but with an entire evening of entertainment and laughter also on the menu, he probably recovered. This sort of fun was exactly what Mom enjoyed so much.

Particularly in the 1960s and 1970s, Isabel, Eleanor, and Florence Beach, wife of Walter's nephew Bruce, often teamed up to prepare and help present skits at Siloam church gatherings such as an ice cream social, Canada's centennial celebration in 1967, and that church's centennial in 1975. Eleanor provided jokes and ideas. She also played the organ or piano. Florence wrote scripts and sang. Isabel provided most of the costumes. Like Mr. Dressup, she had a 'Tickle Trunk', which was the steamer trunk her parents bought for her to take to Orillia in 1915. She also wrote her own 'Aunt Fanny' monologues. She'd shown an early talent for this sort of entertainment. When Isabel was eleven, one evening Eva Luke, the teacher boarding at her family's home, "...came up the back stairs and had to pass our bedroom door to get to her bedroom. As she was going by, I wasn't paying any attention to her." Isabel had a Mother Goose storybook, "...and I was going over these rigmaroles, you know. And Eva looks in the door and says, 'Did you ever think of being an elocutionist?'" At that time, elocution was popular. Isabel knew of a local girl who had gone to Toronto to study the art. She told Miss Luke that she hadn't thought of it. But, she told me in one of our interviews, "I know, because it stayed in my head, that it did have an impact on what I might be able to do, but I didn't do it that way."

Mom certainly did her share of amateur theatre as Aunt Fanny, prompted by her fun-loving friend Eleanor. The real Aunt Fanny, who was born Frances (Fran) Allison in Iowa in November 1907, also had a teaching career. However, Fran soon moved with her considerable musical and theatrical talent to radio, stage and television work. She appeared on Don McNeill's "The Breakfast Club" for over twenty-five years, where Isabel and Eleanor encountered her as Aunt Fanny, a gossipy spinster who loved to chat about fictitious characters (Don McNeill, February 20, 2000). In my mother's version, she was also known for her outrageous hats. Norma explained what Isabel did: "Her monologue would consist of people's names from around the community, a funny saying or something about them...not really jokes, but she'd bring it in on a story line, a story that had been told somewhere else before—or maybe something that had happened in the community. [Her monologues] were quite famous."

Probably a good part of the monologue was based on something Isabel had heard on "The Breakfast Club". In one of her notebooks that I found she had scribbled down her ideas for monologues. One began with "Good morning, Mr. McNeil. How are you? Had a good trip to New York, didn't we? Oh, yes, I had a wonderful time, etc. etc. Caution what you see "On the Sidewalks of New York"... But it is a grand place to go shopping. Oh yes, I was shopping several times, and I ordered a few clothes and some other things. They are sending them out today. And so, I'm going to clean out a lot of things I've been carting around from pillar to post for years. Now, if you would like some of them, Mr. McNeil, I'm sure you're welcome to them. It's as I've often said: anything that I have got that I can spare that you and Mrs. McNeil could do with you are certainly welcome to them." The script went on to describe various items that Aunt Fanny would sell if Mr. and Mrs. McNeil didn't want them. The whole rough script, some parts a little racier than one might expect from Isabel, is reproduced in Appendix R.

Much of my mother's social and volunteer life revolved around the church community. She used her teaching skills generously there. She taught Sunday School at Siloam church for many years, often the adult class that no one else wanted to tackle. Florence (Harrison) Kemp, a mother's helper for Isabel the summers of 1945 and 1946, went with our family to Sunday School every Sunday. "I had Mrs. Alice Alcock [another of Isabel's friends] for Sunday School. I think [Isabel taught] boys. But I can't remember just who she had in her group... Seemed to me as if they were boys about my age and Beverley's age." That would make sense. Like smart mothers today, Mom would be sure she contributed to the religious education of her children by helping to provide it.

Isabel served on the Manse/Parsonage Committee for the Siloam and Goodwood United Churches for several years. One of her little notebooks shows that she was the secretary from the summer of 1949 to the summer of 1954. While the committee met only intermittently, it was responsible for ensuring the manse was cleaned and ready for each new student minister. Often the committee arranged for painting and repairs. These excerpts from her rough copy minutes demonstrate in more detail the committee's and her responsibilities:

"Goodwood Parsonage Committee met in the basement of Goodwood United Church Thurs. eve. July 2, 1953. Decided to build garage using what material was suitable from old barn torn down in June. Mr. Watson consented to finding a carpenter to undertake the job of overseeing the laying out of material etc. When such a person was available the men of each congregation to be notified and any who could come and help would be invited to do so. Mr. Watson reported bought [curtains] for south bedroom and the study, and new drapes for dining room. 4 new blinds also to be bought."

1954: "Parsonage Committee held pot luck supper at the annual meeting Jan. in Goodwood United Church basement. Proceeds to be used towards paying for garage remodeling. Each W.A. (Goodwood, Fifth Line and Siloam) assumed the responsibility of remaining sum to be paid."

She used her considerable talent in other areas too. As Norma noted, "She was always great for getting up programs and devotions at the UCW [meetings]. If you wanted a special one, she was quite a bit for doing special ones—put a lot of work into them." For a layperson, Isabel had an extensive collection of devotional books. She also had her clippings collection. Usually those that would serve for devotionals or programs at UCW meetings were in a different place from her other famous (to the family) box of clippings of editorials, articles, poems, jokes, inspirational sayings and essays. Norma had often observed that "You'd see them tucked under this and that, ones she was saving, wanting to put her hands on them in a hurry." Often they were in a book.

A glance through minutes of the Goodwood UCW meetings testifies to Isabel's interests and involvement in just the last decade of her life.

Minutes, January 1991: "Isabel Beach had the *Observer* list today. Price is up to $8.50 per *Observer*. She is to see Bill Williamson about names to be removed, and new ones to be added." She also led the programme for which she read "The Old Model T" and "A Chuckle for the Day".

On the schedule for the meetings for the rest of the year, she was slated to prepare the devotional for June and program for October.

January 13, 1992: "Moved by Isabel Beach and seconded by Mary Mitchell that we give the Mission and Service fund $200. As we are short of funds, we will not be making other donations at this time. Hope to make them in early fall."

The United Church's Mission and Service Fund was a cause dear to Isabel's heart. At one time both she and her sister Minnie had wanted to be missionaries.

November 2, 1992: "A letter from Fred Victor Mission was read re: donation. As we sent a donation in summer, this one was declined. Isabel moved and Mary Mitchell seconded that we send a donation of $25 to each of the following: John Milton Society, St. Christopher House, Ina Grafton Home, Massey Centre."

Profits from three weddings in June and July of 1993 netted a $2,519.07 profit. As part of that meeting, "It was moved by Norma, seconded by Isabel, we give the manse committee $1000. The new minister has already done a lot of decorating, and there has to be work done in the bathroom."

March 13, 1995: "Isabel Beach had devotions. Read a poem, "Spring Awakening", then read a history of the men who wrote the hymns "What a Friend We Have in Jesus", and "Amazing Grace".

She was ninety-four years old.

Isabel had used her administrative and leadership skills with the UCW for many years. "She was president of both the general and the Siloam [UCW] for quite some time," Norma stated. " I think she was the first president when we started UCW [in 1962]—for general: Goodwood, Fifth Line and Siloam. If not the first, she was the second." Siloam United Church was closed, i.e. had no minister, in 1966. However, it was still maintained. The Siloam UCW cleaned it each year, held events there, had two annual services, and sometimes an extra Easter service that the UCW members arranged.

For Siloam church's centennial celebration in 1975, prepared and presented by the UCW, Mom wore her 1967 Canadian Centennial dress and bonnet. In one of the skits, she portrayed an 1875 mother with her children at breakfast. Celebrations also included a service at the church and a potluck supper at the community hall. With her keen memory and interest in history, Mom retained some of the Siloam community information she'd gleaned in her early years there, and she probably contributed it to the church's centennial program. She told me in the mid-nineties that "Siloam was originally Dykeville, and the Widdifield's place was called Slabtown. The Uxbridge road originally went right past Widdifield's house and across somewhere in the area of [what is now] Matthews' place. There used to be a house across from the church…on the third [concession]. That's where Sam Widdifield lived, that donated the land for the church. He was the first postmaster. They brought the mail into his living room, dumped it on the table and sorted it." (See 1877 map of Uxbridge Township.) When some of the Siloam Church members researched its history for the centennial, they discovered the Siloam village name was chosen around that time.

Norma, a friend of Mom's in a different sense, shared with me her own knowledge and experience of the depth of Isabel's church involvement: "She was always interested beyond the UCW, the next step up. She always went to the Presbyterial meetings to keep her more informed while she was on the Presbytery for the church." As a member of the Presbytery Book Club for three or four years, she went to Toronto to get books for display at the semi-annual meetings. She had to know what would be interesting to people. She always gave a book review on two or three of the books the day of the meeting, hoping to encourage people to buy United Church resources for programs, devotionals and their own reading.

Being a highly efficient and practical person, she went to Toronto for two additional purposes: shopping and a visit. Norma said, "She always went down to Aunt Chris' place, had a visit, and went to the United Church bookstore, picked up the books and brought them out." Sometimes she got a 'perm' in her hair. Her shopping often included buying her special shoes, the 'duty shoes' she always wore working around the house and outside, with a dressier pair for social occasions. Florence Kemp remembered meeting Isabel at York University in 1972 when Florence was studying for her teaching degree. Isabel was a delegate to the Toronto Conference of the United Church of Canada that was meeting there at the time. Mom attended Toronto Conference at least two other times, in 1964 and 1974 in Orillia, when she stayed with me and my family.

Norma spoke of the personal effect Isabel's church activities had on her. "And that kept me interested in it, too, as long as I was taking her to all those [presbytery] meetings. We were pretty good up at Siloam to go to those meetings. That's one thing I did miss when we went to Goodwood. They never promoted that nearly as much. And we don't even go to them any more." This was a sore point with Isabel, who missed the Siloam UCW Unit, its energy and its friends. Some of the members had died, however, while others had moved to another community. A separate Siloam Unit was no longer feasible. The last few years Norma and Isabel went to those presbyterial meetings, they were the only ones from the Goodwood church. Isabel made it her mission to rectify another irritation. While several members who'd been involved with the UCW for just a few years had received a life membership, Norma—who'd been involved since 1952—had not. With pride and satisfaction, she presented Norma with her life membership in 1990.

Regardless of the frustrations, Mom kept involved. The church and its work was an integral part of her life. She could not possibly leave. She attended fewer UCW and congregational meetings in the last few years of her life, but before that, if she felt well enough and Norma was driving, she went. At Goodwood United Church, she looked after the *Observer* magazine subscriptions for many years. She recorded the names of all subscribers, then sent the list to United Church headquarters in Toronto. The UCW paid for these subscriptions—one of the group's projects. Isabel resigned from her *Observer* job on September 11, 1995, five days before her ninety-fifth birthday. Norma had special recollections of attending UCW meetings in those later years. Mom was getting hard of hearing. She never did get a hearing aid—possibly thinking she couldn't afford one or really didn't need one that much. "If she happened to be sitting in a room that was kind of long," Norma explained, "[Isabel] couldn't seem to hear what the person down here was saying, especially if there was talk going on in between." So when they were driving home, she'd always ask Norma what was said, and what other people said about topics of discussion. Norma laughed, saying, "We would spend about as long after we got home, sitting in the car going over the meetings, so she'd really know what was going on." With her active mind, interested in family and community doings, Isabel naturally wanted to be up-to-date.

The records show that she didn't miss a single UCW meeting in 1994. She missed two winter months in 1995. She got there only in May 1996, not at all in 1997. By 1998 she was not on the membership list. That May, because the meeting was held at Norma's house closeby, Mom did attend. The minutes mention Camp Big Canoe, of which she was a keen supporter. That interest probably stemmed from the time she went to CGIT camp at Geneva Park on Lake Couchiching, and from her recognition of how valuable camp experience often is for young people. She had, after all, arranged for me to attend Camp Big Canoe in 1952. In addition, "She was a great one to push a lot of the donations to all United Church facilities, like Fred Victor Mission, Ina Grafton Gage Home and the Victor Centre," Norma said. "She did her best to make sure the UCW gave to them each year and to the manse committee."

I know she personally made a difference for one family much closer to home, on the fringes of the Siloam community. She decided that a particular woman with several children who smelled unwashed and wore poorly fitting outdated clothes needed to be more accepted in the community. She encouraged the children to come to Siloam church Sunday School, made sure they received presents at the Christmas concert, and gave their mother good clothing that I'd outgrown or that had been passed on to us. This quiet lesson in compassion and inclusion, in offering a friendship that probably couldn't be reciprocrated, I now recognize as one of the best my mother taught me.

In her eighties, she expressed dismay that the UCW was concentrating solely on raising funds, to their own detriment and that of the church. She put her opinion this way: " 'Had I two loaves of bread, the one would I sell, aye, aye,/ And buy a hyacinth to feed my soul, or I would die'. They're not feeding your soul when they're concentrating so much on money-making. And no wonder the church is behind." She observed that Goodwood church members were using the UCW as a crutch, rather than getting all members involved in supporting it. By the nineties, fortunately, she felt the situation was improving.

These rough drafts of two letters my mother wrote to the Treasurer of Goodwood United Church demonstrate that she 'walked the talk' and—with the slightest touch of sarcasm—she wanted the church officers to know it.

Exact Date Unknown: *To the Treasurer for the Goodwood United Church. Enclosed please find a cheque for two hundred dollars (200.00), $50 for Mission and Service Fund and $150.00 for general expenses. This will complete my 1994 church commitment.*

You won't need to send me a "Thank You" card from the members of the congregation because I am also a member of the congregation and as such it is my duty and privilege to contribute towards the 'running' of my church. That is the way I was raised. As a matter of fact, when I married and came to live in this area I had hardly got settled when my father reminded me that I should be transferring my membership from my home church to Siloam Church (which was my church until it closed in 1966 and our records sent to Goodwood). My membership should be recorded in the records of Goodwood United Church since that time.

In a seasonal spirit she wrote to the treasurer in 1995: *Here it is December and I haven't got a cheque mailed away to you in 1995, which may appear to need an apology but to be quite honest an explanation is what it needs. For the past six months my health has 'decided' what I do rather than what I want to do. I simply do not have the energy (when I do what I must do each day) to carry on any further. However, I am glad and grateful to be able to say that there has been improvement lately, which looks encouraging for the future. Season's Greetings and may the work at Goodwood United Church continue to prosper.*

Sincerely...

Sincerely indeed.

CHAPTER TEN: It Was to Be

Leisure

What is this life if, full of care,
We have no time to stand and stare.

No time to stand beneath the boughs
And stare as long as sheep or cows.

No time to see, when woods we pass,
Where squirrels hide their nuts in grass.

No time to see, in broad daylight,
Streams full of stars, like skies at night.

No time to turn at Beauty's glance,
And watch her feet, my how they can dance.

No time to wait till her mouth can
Enrich that smile her eyes began.

A poor life this if, full of care,
We have no time to stand and stare.

William Henry Davies (1871-1940)

After almost one hundred years of rich and intelligent living, Isabel had accumulated an impressive collection of principles that guided her life and often those of family, neighbours and friends. The poem by Davies, referred to as the poet of the tramps, reflects at least two of my mother's principles of living. One was to keep in touch with nature. She once told me of an experience during World War I when she was going to high school and boarding in Orillia. She was 'in her time of the month' and feeling a little blue, so decided to walk west into the country. It was a glorious day. By the time she got back to her boarding house, the fresh air and sights and sounds of nature had turned her attitude around. She was able to get on with the schoolwork she needed to do. Well into her nineties, a country walk remained one of her favourite occupations. The second is a principle that many people of the late twentieth and early twenty-first centuries have discovered the hard way: a person can't physically, emotionally, or psychologically endure a constant frenetic pace. Something will go wrong somewhere in the body's system. Everyone needs 'down time'. She seemed to know instinctively when to do this, although her doctor did have to nag her for several years before she made herself stop to rest after two or three hours of work.

When her life ended, Mom had few material possessions. Over the years, she had culled and culled, down to those most precious and necessary items. Chief among the precious were her books and her collection of newspaper and magazine clippings. 'Instructional and inspirational' best describes this collection—and the principles she taught and followed all her life. She shared many of these principles so incidentally that her companions often didn't know what was happening. Her granddaughter Joanne had regularly experienced how Isabel "would have a personal story to tell us that always seemed to fit in with what we were doing or talking about at the time". Grandson James marveled at how "...she could always go off on all these tangents and then thread all these things back together again and actually get back to where she started". This gift never ceased to amaze him. Many times, he wouldn't remember where the story had started. But Isabel always ended it back at the beginning. Not only that; he had learned or been reminded of an important life principle, using 'good common sense' being a popular one. Granddaughter Marilyn added, "She enjoyed company. She enjoyed to sit down and chit-chat with everybody. She didn't sit there as if she was bored. She always had time for you." Through these natural methods, the grandchildren and others learned what counted in Isabel's approach to life. Marilyn, for example, had noticed that her grandmother often said, 'You make do with what you've got'. Like her grandmother, Marilyn doesn't need a particular gadget to do a particular task—objects with which the North American consumer society is glutted and which I know my mother would speak of sardonically. She preferred to use her problem-solving skills to find another, more economical, way to do the job.

Mom knew plenty about household economy. The tricks she passed on to me are a rich part of my inheritance. She had lived through the penny-pinching years of starting her career, beginning her marriage and business partnership with Walter, surviving the Great Depression of the Dirty Thirties, and dealing with the Second World War food rations regime. That's three decades of 'making do'—more than enough, added to her pioneer/farm upbringing, to produce a lifetime habit. Her television sets are a perfect example. The first set, which Walter had purchased, was black and white because that's what was available. She used it mainly to watch "Front Page Challenge", the CBC farm show, and Sunday morning church services. A slave to the set she was not.

When that set quit working around 1980, only a black and white TV would do as a replacement. I found her a cabinet model for eight dollars at an auction sale. Its size presented a little problem. Her previous set was portable. Her living/dining room was not large, and other pieces of furniture—the overstuffed chair and chesterfield, the bookcase, the china cabinet, the compact folding dining table, Walter's black leather rocking chair, and the piano she'd bought with her teaching money—were far more important to her than a TV. She solved the problem by putting a small armchair upstairs and the cabinet TV beside the piano. But she was never totally happy with this arrangement. The look was too heavy for that side of the room. A few years later, when she fell heir to a cabinet from Chris' apartment, she decided she'd pass the piano on to me. Soon after, the cabinet TV died. Edward was recruited to buy her a portable to place on the cabinet from Chris. By then, finding a black and white TV was virtually impossible, but he located one. When it stopped working, the replacement had to be a colour set. Ed said she seldom watched it, and since it wasn't attached to the aerial, the picture often came out black and white anyway. She did enjoy joining Pam and Ed to watch such specials as Toronto's Santa Claus Parade on their colour TV.

Mom was an ardent saver of things that were too good to throw out, that might be useful to her or someone else at some time. Almost everyone who'd lived through those tough years of the early twentieth century had developed this habit. Thus she had a collection of elastics, string, used wrapping paper and bows, jars, screws, paper bags, boxes... She'd often ask family members whether they had any use for a particular item or knew someone else who did. Antiques we weren't interested in went to museums or church sales. Less valuable items traveled to the second-hand store run by a religious organization in Stouffville or to the Uxbridge Cottage Hospital Auxiliary shop. When it came to clothing, she seldom had anything to pass on. By the time she was through with it, it was ready for 'the rag bag', a noble destination despite the name. These rags became dust cloths, scrub cloths (how she would scoff at the Swiffer concept), oil rags for the farm's repair shop, parts for mending clothing still in use, or soft cloths in which to wrap glass-framed photos and pictures. Recently I came across a small package containing a photo of Westminster Abbey and a painting of an English cottage surrounded by thriving flower gardens. Each was individually wrapped in parts of light cotton denim overalls she'd made for me when I was a pre-schooler.

Mom once told me in an informal way how little material possessions meant to her and how out of step with the world she knew she was. "Of course, I'm queer, I know I am, and different. Because I never can understand people that can't let somebody else have something that they haven't got. Now, there are some people, supposing they were here, instead of me, and somebody drove in here with a Cadillac car, 'Well, next week, [I'm] gonna' have to have a Cadillac car, no use talkin'. If that guy can afford it, I can too. I'll just go to the bank and get the money'. That's what they do. That's why they get in such a mess with their finances sometimes." It wouldn't take her long to figure out how Canadians got into the deep collective personal debt they have today.

While careful with her spending, she was generous in her giving. Every family birthday and anniversary card included a bill or two. As the cost of living increased and taxes were added, she often would write, "As we all know $20 is not worth $20 when we go to purchase with it so I often add another bill (as I do today) for the GST." The note with my birthday card in 1997 continued, "The extra $20 I am now adding as a result of our talk on the phone when I kept you so long and then allowed myself to let you take on the job of phoning Ted Wallace. (And it would cost you to get his phone number.) Of course I really was relieved to be relieved of the job at the time. So accept the extra as a plus for your birthday…and…and…Love, Mom."

Blessed with a healthy mind, she knew instinctively when and how to keep it that way. She also knew the connection between a healthy mind and a healthy body. As she aged, Mom was deeply aware of the need to keep her body in shape if she were to continue living, virtually independently, in the usual way. She regularly exercised many parts of her body, often while lying in bed. To the woman in her forties who recently told me she didn't make fudge the old-fashioned way (stirring it madly with a wooden spoon until it lost its gloss) because her shoulders weren't strong enough, I can hear Mom say, 'Well, sister, if you don't make use of them they're never going to get any stronger'. Marilyn observed some of the other habits her grandmother practised to maintain her health: "She went for a walk every day, it seemed. She was determined. She'd take her cane and she'd walk out the sideroad and back, and it didn't matter the weather. You'd just dress for it. She very rarely went to the doctor. She always cured herself—mostly I think just common sense, rest. If she felt the need to sit on the couch with her shawl around her, she would do that and put her feet up." Mom always evaluated the way her body felt, then chose her activities and food accordingly. Sometimes in her later years when I visited her she'd tell me that I could get my own supper, with precise instruction on where to find each suggested menu item. She was having just a poached egg and maybe a piece of dry toast or some cream of wheat cereal. Whenever she felt a little 'off' she didn't force-feed herself with food she was sure her stomach would rebel against.

One method of keeping her body healthy was used, and worked, only once and entirely by accident. As background to the incident, she recounted a story from her Thorah Township days. "It got it into my young brain…I didn't have much use for these chiropractors/bone-crackers. They didn't know what was the matter with Nellie [a neighbour woman] and they took her to Orillia to see what was the matter. Someone said to try the chiropractor." The result was galling to Isabel, who declared, "I don't see how anybody that was in a position that that doctor was couldn't have known, should have known, her history a little bit, and should have detected a little bit what was the matter." Nellie had paid to go on the train to Orillia. Then the chiropractor charged her for tuberculosis (TB) treatments. "What did he know about lungs and TB? Not a damn thing, or he'd have had her up in Gravenhurst." (When my mother swore, she was incensed.) The sanatorium was in Gravenhurst, she said, and any doctor in Orillia should've been aware of the 'san'. "I never could get that out of my system," she confessed; therefore, she never did consult a chiropractor.

One day when I was an impatient five-year-old and she in her mid-forties, I functioned briefly in that role. Mom had been working in the garden. Her back muscles knew it. In our interview, she reminded me, "I couldn't get off the couch. You came to me and just pulled my leg, and that was all there was to it." Her back felt fine again. She got up and went on with her work. As someone who has relied on a chiropractor to keep me going for almost thirty-five years, I wish she had agreed to see a professional chiropractor when she was older. Arthritis probably wouldn't have taken such a deep hold on her body if she had. At the age of ninety-three she admitted, "I know it's quite a different story now, and…[chiropractors] have a different procedure for their work. But in my heart, I can't put myself under their hands. But then, if it came a certain thing I might have to, I'd probably change my mind, I don't know. I'm not looking for them, anyway, and certainly not when I've got just a headache or something like that, like some people do."

Isabel and alcohol never did mix. She came by this principle of living early and honestly. Liquor wasn't part of her birth family's lifestyle. Likely her Grandpa Wallace's use of liquor contributed to this attitude. Her grandmother Wallace's views had been shaped by Grandpa Wallace's habits, as well. Mom recounted how she was put in charge of getting Grandma Wallace to the polling station for the 1924 Prohibition vote in Ontario: "The women were allowed to vote. I went down to help Grandma Wallace get ready, for she'd never been dressed to go out anyplace for long enough, you know." But she was strong on voting, particularly in this case, Mom thought, because "I gathered that Grandfather was a little fond of his bottle when he was young. And she'd had her session of dealing with that. And so she knew…when she had the opportunity to stop it, why she'd do her share. And she did." *The Canadian Encyclopedia* notes that, "It had been thought that the extension of the franchise to women would sustain prohibition since it was commonly believed that women were sympathetic to it. However, referenda of the 1920s, in which women had the vote, showed a consistent decline of support" (Decarie, 1801). So Grandma Wallace's outing was just that.

While the vote on prohibition of liquor had little significance for Isabel's immediate family, the topic "…made a lot of fun/jokes over the people that had stills, the bootleggers. And you see, Eldon Township was just over the town line from our place, from Thorah, and then the next township in Victoria County was Carden. And I guess Carden Township was…just lousy with bootlegging. And you know it was always a joke about the Carden bootleggers." Neighbours Jack Westcott and his son, who played the fiddle for dances, contributed to the joking. "The old gentleman, he had quite a sense of humour. He'd say, 'Well now, we'll give ya' a new tune. This is "Up and Down the Portage Road and In and Out o' Carden". (A provincial historical plaque in Eldon Township, Victoria County, at the intersection of Highways 46 and 48, just east of Bolsover where Isabel's family attended church, provides the following information on the Portage Road: *This road follows the general route of the Indian portage from Lake Simcoe to Balsam Lake. The portage was first mapped by the Honourable John Collins, Deputy Surveyor of Canada, when he surveyed the Trent Route from the head of the Bay of Quinte to Balsam Lake and thence by way of Lake Simcoe to Georgian Bay in 1785. The Trent route was used by Champlain and his Huron allies in their expedition against the Iroquois in 1615. Subsequently, at the time of settlement the portage was surveyed (1834-1835) by John Smith and a large portion of the old trail was incorporated in what became known as the Portage Road.*) "Well, that was where everybody was going. It'd be some old tune, but he'd put a new name to it. And they'd put these jokes in the concerts sometimes. It didn't seem to fizz very much, because I never remember [liquor] being sold in Beaverton." Brechin, she noted, was always a 'watering hole' and it still is. It voted to stay 'wet'.

When Isabel attended high school in Orillia, her landlady, Mrs. Glover, kept her up-to-date regarding the local option for alcoholic beverages in that town. "Well, she'd always come out with some joke or another about it. To tell the truth, you didn't take it too seriously, because it didn't affect us to the same extent as some places, you know. But Mrs. Glover, she was against this alcohol business too, of course. Well, I guess most women were," Isabel continued, "because they had the hardest part of it to put up with. And now, you see, oh it makes me feel so sad when I stop and think about it, and then I won't let myself think too long—how the women fought to be equal with the men. They've gotta' be equal with the men, and they've gotta' drink with the men, and they've gotta' get drunk with the men, and they've gotta' act like fools with the men." As she told me this, her voice rose in frustration, then dropped in disappointment. "Oh, isn't it sad? These foolish women! They want to be like the men. Good heavens, why did they want to take the rotten spots on the men? It's an awful shame, that that's the extent of their brainpower. And then they think they should have work positions with the men, and everything. Well, maybe they should. And I don't know; I just know what I read—that women cannot carry the amount of alcohol that the majority of men can carry. They don't have the same body to carry it." In her own home and family, alcohol was never part of the scene. I wonder if she ever knew that my dad kept a bottle of whiskey in his workshop behind the barn, or that he cheerfully joined Wilf Wees in a bottle of beer while visiting the Wees' home?

When it came to voting, Isabel herself seldom, if ever, missed the opportunity to cast her vote. She took her responsibility and privilege seriously. Although she generally voted Liberal, this was not always the case. She weighed the candidates and the party platforms carefully. For the June third, 1998, election, she instructed her grandson Edward to register her proxy vote as Liberal, although she had given the NDP serious consideration. She had ruled out the Conservatives fairly early in her life. Three key incidents sealed that party's fate.

The first took place over several months leading up to the first election in which she was eligible to vote. She was teaching in the Roseville school and had turned twenty-one the previous September. Leading up to that 1922 election, a certain Mr. S. in the community had badgered and badgered her to support the Conservative party. She declined. He snubbed her, refused to look or speak whenever she met him in Uxbridge. Shortly before election day, she found out she would be asked to swear her eligibility to vote. She figured Mr. S. was behind this request. Isabel decided to be ready for him. She sent to Bolsover Presbyterian Church for her baptismal certificate. She appeared at the polling station on election day, the evidence in her purse. Mr. S. was working there, but another gentlemen asked her to swear that she was of age to vote. He was so nice about it, she said, that she didn't pull out the ultimate ammunition. She just stepped into the voting booth to cast her vote for the United Farmers of Ontario (UFO).

The second incident occurred while she was teaching at Riverview School close to her birth home in Thorah Township. A dirt-poor farm family that had trouble getting food on the table and clothes on the backs of their children lived near the school. Again, Isabel wanted to support the UFO. As she said, she was born and raised on a farm; farm people were paying her salary. She discussed the UFO party with the father of the poor family. He couldn't get beyond, 'My father voted Conservative and so did my grandfather. If it was good enough for them, it's good enough for me'. She was thoroughly disgusted with this method of deciding which party and candidate to support.

Several years later, (now Mrs. Walter Beach) she attended an official function at Uxbridge High School with Walter, who was an invited guest. At the door, they were met by the chair of the school board and the local Member of the Ontario Legislature. The latter "practically hugged me", she said, when he heard that she was Mrs. Beach. When he learned that she was the aunt, not the mother, of a certain Beach family Conservative supporter, the Member turned "as cold as stone". She became a nobody. And the final nail hit the Conservative coffin.

Her interest in politics and other current issues led Isabel to spend countless hours listening to the radio, especially when she lived by herself. She could work or rest her eyes at the same time. But her mind didn't rest. She regularly argued with the broadcasters and commentators. Norma recalled how "She talked back to Gord Sinclair on the radio an awful lot. We could hear her in there sometimes having some great conversations." She liked Gord Sinclair, probably admired his 'self-made man' stance "but it was just that sometimes he'd get ranting on about something, and she'd be in there ranting back: 'You don't know what you're talking about'. The only [swear word] she'd say once in a while would be 'damn'. That would be about the strongest you'd ever hear. You could tell she just hated saying it."

Mom also listened to Earl Warren, even though she didn't like him much as a broadcaster. She phoned him two or three times. Once she had a lengthy discussion with him about Daylight Saving Time. Norma explained the background: "He'd had an article on it, and she said it started in the First World War, and he said it was only the Second World War. But she said she could remember having it [earlier]." Of course she was right. An article in a broadsheet published in 1935 confirms the time period: "In Canada, the Daylight Saving cause was taken up in the House of Commons by Mr. Lewis, and was favourably reported upon. But opposition developed from the farmers, and no action was taken until the war, when Canada went on daylight saving, as a measure of economy, along with the other Allied nations" (*A Short History*). M. Downing confirmed that the practice ended with the First World War when he wrote, "In 1919, Canada rescinded its Daylight Saving law" (46). Although Isabel phoned CFRB several times, she was never on air. In those days, listeners were seldom invited to phone with their opinions. If Mom felt strongly enough, or knew information that needed to be corrected, she'd call anyway.

Marilyn had noticed her grandmother's relationship with the media too. "She would sit and talk to the radio and to Pierre Berton on TV and tell them that they'd better change things. The radio was always on to keep her well informed, and that she was." Wanting to be well-informed just came naturally to Isabel. She had to satisfy her curious and active mind. I wouldn't be surprised if she even felt obliged to be informed, so that she could intelligently perform her duties as a Canadian citizen. A related issue that bothered her, and that no doubt provoked some ranting, involved comparisons of Canada's progress with that of the United States. She knew that the area was far from settled when Walter's parents first came to the Uxbridge Township property in 1876, and that her own parents were still in the pioneer era when they started out on their farm in 1888. "That's where I keep saying we're a pioneer people," she emphatically told me. "And it makes me so mad when they get talking about comparing us with the USA. Why the USA was a country, with their own *everything* before we were born. But they won't consider that, a lot of people. Well, they don't know, and they won't learn." Yet ultimately she held no rancourous feelings. "I just laugh about it," she concluded.

In addition to the radio, newspapers and magazines kept her up-to-date. One local issue that she followed tirelessly absolutely infuriated her. In the late 1970s, a new director of environmental health in Durham Region (of which Uxbridge Township was then a part), Dr. T.E. Watt, decided to interpret the Public Health Act to the letter. As reported in a *Globe & Mail* article, this strict adherence meant that "Churches, fraternal and service organizations, and community centres were advised that food cannot be cooked in private homes and transported to public premises for consumption" (Holbrook, n.p.), a decision that Holbrook declared "ridiculous". And so did my mother. Such a rule was especially disastrous for a rural community, she knew. Church suppers and other events where local people prepared and ate the food were important social events and fundraisers. What galled her most was that Dr. Watt's degree was in veterinary medicine. The issue was a hot topic of conversation for months with everyone she met. On many of my visits to her home during that period, she provided an up-to-the-minute report on the situation. Fortunately, after many protest meetings and letters, reason prevailed. Church and community suppers continued in Durham Region as they always had.

Mom had a saying—sometimes funny, sometimes commonly used, sometimes unique to her, always memorable—for most situations. If she didn't know a suitable saying, she created it. One that she must have created 'on the spot' stemmed from an incident when I was in grade eight. Everyone from our one-room rural school at Siloam had gone to the Santa Claus parade in Uxbridge. It was a cold day, so Isabel had insisted I wear the two-piece snowsuit, the boots, the hat, the mitts—what any sensible Canadian would wear on a cold December day. Being a teenager about to go to high school, I was far from sensible. And I wasn't at all impressed that the grade eights who went to school in the town of Uxbridge had made fun of us bundled-up 'country kids'. When I got home, I told Mom about their mean comments, how they pointed and jeered at those (to my sensitive mind and feelings) inferior 'country kids'. Isabel thought about my concerns for a minute then told me, 'It's better to be a country kid than a town goat', with just the right tone of derisiveness in her own voice. Many years passed before I fully absorbed the lesson in that unique saying: you must value yourself for what and who you are. These days, I hear the principle in different terms: you must love yourself before you can love others. Of course I'm now incredibly proud of those rural roots, deeply grateful for the experiences that lent strength to my character.

The sayings she habitually used reflected her values. The principle of honouring perseverance and the value of work appeared in her saying, "Can't is a sluggard, too lazy to try". When she could barely move because of osteoarthritis, she carried on, determined to stay in her own home. Sometimes she needed half an hour just to get out of bed. Occasionally she had trouble getting to her bathroom in time. She had surprisingly few accidents, considering how crippled she became. As for her grandmother and work, Marilyn observed, "She didn't know the meaning of boredom. There was always something to do. She was brought up in a generation that wasn't lazy like ours, a lazy society expecting everything to be done for you. She was always so strong and determined, and she didn't need a man in her life. She got along for forty years without a man and never complained about everything. My Grandmother never complained about work, never complained…" Isabel had a sanguine attitude to life's vicissitudes. Whether the suddenly changing circumstance was good or bad, she would often say, "It was to be". While this attitude may seem fatalistic, I don't believe it was. She had an underlying faith that her life was guided by a power vastly bigger than hers—and that whatever happened did so for a good reason. She just needed to wait, watch, and figure out the reason behind the circumstance. Then, if appropriate, she took charge and turned a cloud inside out.

Ed told me how he took on some of his grandmother's principles as his own: "I learn things from observing and paying attention." Gleaning the messages from stories his grandmother told and actions she took, Ed soon figured out that "You knew Grandma had certain rules and regulations and that's what you adhered to, and you'd better not cross it—like no playing cards on Sunday, maybe not even on Christmas Day, but it was all right to play games." Christmas Day 2005, almost six years after her death, he reminded us all that Grandma wouldn't have approved of the euchre games played that day (which was also a Sunday). Out of respect for her, he didn't approve and he didn't play.

In Ed's experience, if his grandmother asked a person to do something, "Well, you'd better figure out how to do it and get it done or she'd get upset with you maybe. You knew if she started sayin' 'Damn', you'd better run the other way because she was mad." But she wasn't so rigid that she wouldn't make exceptions or be a little lenient, depending on the circumstances. "She was always fair." As he grew up, Ed came to appreciate "…the sense of morals and values and standards" that his grandmother incorporated into his family's everyday life. Above all, he stated, "I think the thing that I admired most about grandmother is the fact that her friends and neighbours held her in great admiration and esteem for her judgment and her sense of what [is] right and the proper way things should be done."

What greater tribute to Isabel's character and principles could there be?

On her ninetieth birthday, September 16, 1990, Isabel was photographed with the children and grandchildren to whom she passed on many of her principles of daily living. In the back row, left to right, are Vern Ashton, Bruce Ashton, James Ashton, Edward Beach, Norma Beach, Beverley Beach, and Marilyn Burch. Front, left to right, are Catherine Ashton, Isabel Beach, and Joanne Burnett.

CHAPTER ELEVEN: I Love You

Folks Need a Lot of Loving

Folks need a lot of loving in the morning.
The day is all before with cares beset,
The cares we know and they that give no warning,
For love is God's own antidote for fret.

Folks need a heap of loving at the noontime,
In the battle-lull, the moment snatched from strife,
Half between the waking and the croon-time,
While bickering and worrying are rife.

Folks hunger so for loving at the night-time
When wearily they take them home to rest,
At slumber-song and turning-out-the-light time—
Of all the time for loving, that's the best.

Folks want a lot of loving every minute,
The sympathy of others and their smile
Till life's end; from the minute they begin it,
Folks need a lot of loving all the while.

Gillian Strickland

"Ah uhf ooh," my mother said to me one October day in 1999 from her bed in Soldiers' Memorial Hospital in Orillia, eyes brimming with emotion. I had just hung up the phone. In panic I'd called our minister, Karen, to come to the hospital right away. "I think she's dying," I'd said. Certainly Isabel had had a severe stroke, although the medical experts hadn't yet seen her to give that diagnosis. Her tongue moved helplessly as she tried to tell me what had happened. Her right side was paralysed. Within minutes Karen was at the bedside leading us through the twenty-third Psalm and a short prayer for Isabel's peace. Though my panicked prediction had been incorrect, this visit meant a great deal to Mom. She was no longer in her own community, and even there it seemed as if the church she was associated with had abandoned her. She hadn't had a pastoral visit for many months. Karen's brief visit meant comfort and reassurance to this woman who had had a rock-solid faith ever since her brother Willy had been cured of peritonitis. So, for the first time in her life—or at least in my memory—she told me, in deep gratitude, "Ah uhf ooh", a message that I understood immediately and that brought tears to my eyes: "I love you".

These days it's common to hear people say "Love ya'" as they hang up the phone from a conversation with a spouse or send their children out the door to school. Things were different in Isabel and Walter's family. In people's way at the time, those words were never spoken. But love was unquestionably there. When Walter's voice softened and his hazel eyes misted over as he said, "Ain't that right Momma?"; when Mom bought me a set of top-notch Samsonite luggage to take to university; when she sent a jar of farm cream to her niece Kathleen in Toronto; when she mailed home-made tea biscuits and cookies to me at my university residence during final exams; when she gave family members interest-free loans to pay back as they were able, a little at a time—the love was there. Love was there for her oldest sister Annie, the one who read to her and the other younger children on many Sunday afternoons, the one she welcomed to her Uxbridge Township home and urged to stay for a good rest. It was there for her next youngest sister Minnie, the one with whom she'd slept during their growing up years, the vulnerable one whom she protected and defended in many sisterly squabbles. It was there when she spoke over the phone in November 1996 to the Orillia *Packet & Times* reporter and read in a voice breaking with emotion Captain McKinley's letter that described her brother Willy's bravery and enthusiasm for service in the army (Size, 3).

Love was there for all her family, as remarked on by her granddaughter Marilyn: "The one thing that stands out in my mind is how she was very loving, but never had to show it. We never expected a kiss and a hug or whatever, and she didn't give one in return, which isn't saying she wasn't loving. You just knew. You automatically felt it as soon as you went [into her home]." And, I might add, you only had to look at her eyes, softly shining in their task as the windows of her soul, to fathom the depth of her love. Isabel's love for family, friends, and neighbours near and far manifested in thousands of gestures over her century of life. The neighbour children could depend on getting homemade cookies at Hallowe'en and Christmas. In the worst of the Depression years, a tramp wandering in off the road could split wood for an hour or so to earn himself a hearty hot farm meal. Neighbours in need could borrow the telephone or get a ride to town. During the Second World War, Isabel joined other local women to make quilts that the Canadian Red Cross delivered to the desperate Russian people.

My mother's personality and the respect others had for her solicited the love in return. Those closer to home took many opportunities to reflect back the love she gave. Nephews and nieces dropped in for a visit or invited her to join them for a special outing. Her ninetieth birthday celebration on September 16, 1990, attracted two hundred and fifty family, friends and neighbours to the Siloam Community Hall that had been School Section #8, the school where her husband, children and grandchildren had received their elementary school education and where she had done supply teaching. Marilyn expressed her love for her grandmother in this way: "And when you did go into Grandma's part [of the farmhouse], you always had to make sure you had lots of time on your hands, because she always had many stories to tell, and they weren't just 'this is it, cut and dried'. There was always a wealth of information in it. But you never got tired of listening to her stories. I know I always did make time. If I was going [to visit], I would say, 'Well I'm going to be half an hour—not fifteen minutes but half an hour'." That way, Marilyn knew she could stay to enjoy the story unhurried, to absorb the life lessons woven through. "She was good at [storytelling]. And the things that she enjoyed and that I enjoyed hearing stories about were things like the strawberry socials at the church, where she would do a reading or be in a skit. Her readings I treasure deeply. And another thing I really treasure is her sense of humour." Marilyn often thought of her Grandma doing a jig in the kitchen when there was fiddle music on the radio. For Christmas 2003, Marilyn received a CD with "Christmas in Killarney" on it. "I put that on, and I thought, 'Grandma, this is you'. I could just picture Grandma doin' the jig."

In the closing years, Mom needed that love returned. During the 1980s, she broke both her hips, fortunately not at the same time. Retaining calcium had always been a problem for her. When she was pregnant, the babies used all the calcium that she took in. She lost half of her teeth to decay with Bev, the remainder when pregnant with me. To my knowledge, her doctor never did a bone scan to measure her bone density. He never advised her to take calcium supplements. Her bones must have been light as a bird's.

Since he lived in the same double house as his grandmother, Ed was a participant in both hip-breaking occasions. He told me in our interview, "The first time she broke her hip, she was in the living-room and she did a pirouette and caught her toe and down she went." Isabel had answered the phone and was turning quickly (It was her way to move at high speed) to go and give a business-related message to either Ed or Bev. Ed described how "She lay on the couch for five or six hours, saying, 'Oh, there's nothing wrong with me, nothing wrong with me'. Finally, we got her convinced that the ambulance should come." This was in the spring of 1984. She went to Scarborough Centenary Hospital for surgery and stayed about ten days before being transferred to Uxbridge Cottage Hospital. Her healing and recovery went well. That September, she attended granddaughter Joanne's wedding to Joe Burnett, on the lawn of Bev and Norma's home. If she'd had to go in a wheelchair, she would've been there. Mom wasn't one to miss a special family occasion.

The other hip met its fate in late spring 1987. Ed described how "She'd come down off the bank from the rhubarb patch, and I was in the garden, and she just went, 'Oh no, Edward, I've done it again'. And I looked around and she was flat out on the driveway. So I just picked her up and took her in to the chesterfield and laid her down and I said, 'Well, let's call the ambulance'. And she didn't fight that time. She just said, 'OK'. She knew what she'd done." Repair for this second break was less successful. First, there was a delay of a day or two in getting the surgery done in a Toronto hospital. Just two or three days later, she was transferred to the Uxbridge Cottage Hospital. Spending the first few days in the maternity ward with another older woman provided many laughs for Isabel, her roommate, and their visitors. She felt she got good physiotherapy at the Uxbridge hospital, but not quickly enough. As she had done with the first hip, she followed instructions and did her exercises faithfully. When she got home again, Mom easily remembered how to go up and down stairs, using the formula provided by a therapist and described this way by Norma: "When you were going down, you were going down into hell, so you put the bad leg first. If you're going up the stairs, you always thought you were going up to heaven, so you put your good leg up first. And she would often say, 'Well, I gotta' remember, when I'm goin' up, I'm goin' to heaven'." Mom likely got some humorous satisfaction from saying that her other leg was going to hell!

Although recovery was less than one hundred percent, Isabel wasn't prepared to spend life in a rocking chair. She kept in circulation with her usual activities, using a cane when necessary. Not only did she like her independence; she often said she didn't want to be a burden to others. Keeping active was important, she knew. Her niece Florence Kemp recalled meeting her at a grocery store in Stouffville. "And she'd driven to town to do some shopping in that old car that she had. I had a little visit with her in the IGA. And I was so surprised that she had driven herself to town. She said she didn't drive anywhere much. I was surprised she still had her driver's licence, quite frankly." Mom was sharp. She knew what she needed to do in order to keep her licence. She was prepared when she went for testing. She managed to pass her driving test until she was ninety-one.

She also continued making her famous tea biscuits, which she shared lovingly with many people, well into her nineties. "Grandmother and her tea biscuits," Ed said. "In later years, she'd have them ready, and I'd go in and make sure she was ready, to take her to Christmas dinner or whatever." He knew the routine by heart: "The biscuits had to come out of the oven hot. Then you put the tea towel over them. Then you had to wait. Then you put them in the container.

Sometimes I'd put them in the container for her. She'd say, 'Well there's always the curly one at the end. You can have that one now'. I always ended up getting the curly one, the leftover…" What a tremendous amount of love and patience in this interaction.

During the 1990s, Mom continued to attend the special family occasions, such as her sister Minnie's ninetieth birthday celebration in 1992, Jessie's ninetieth in 1994 and Chris' hundredth in 1996. But these times soon turned to sadness. By the fall of 1997, all three sisters had died and Isabel had become the last living member of her birth family. Other trying times tested her strength and patience. The summer of 1995, she battled a pulled ligament in her leg, then an attack of arthritis. I spent many days with her that summer—cooking, keeping the house in order, and working with other family members to get bi-weekly home care set up for the fall. Combined with various supports from the family, this arrangement allowed her to continue living in her part of the farmhouse. Her letter to Vern and me, near the end of February 1996, expressed her love in return this way: "It is a great big thank you to a couple who did so much for me when I really needed somebody. Catherine, you came so faithfully so many weeks; and Vern, you 'held the Fort' while she was away. It certainly made a big difference to my life then *and also now*. It is hard to explain, but *I* realize it. Of course Norma was also a big part of it all and Edward with his helpfulness and straightforwardness. (How is that for putting it all in one word?) My gratitude to you both. Looking forward to seeing you both next week. Love from Mom Beach."

Mom was tremendously conscientious about doing the recommended thing or figuring out what worked best for her. Using this approach, she recovered from many setbacks. In June 1996 she pulled something in her rib area while stretching to open a kitchen window as she leaned over the counter. Her doctor couldn't really say what the problem was or give her anything to make her better. She just had to wait it out. The wait turned out to be a long one. She was in agony. Her whole body felt as if it had been run over by a bulldozer. All summer, she shuffled around the house, seldom going outside. By mid-fall, she was getting out for little walks in the driveway. She looked after herself as well as she could, with Norma's help.

She never asked Norma to do much, especially in the area of personal care. Somehow she managed to keep herself clean through 'sponge baths', an operation that she described with a twinkle in her eye as, "You wash up as far as possible. You wash down as far as possible. And then you wash possible". She had home care, but either didn't feel comfortable with the caregiver or just wasn't physically able to do the full tub bath. During my visit in late February 1997, she was ready to tackle a tub bath. At one point, she asked me to use the shower hose to spray her genital area, smiling at the pleasure of feeling thoroughly clean then saying, "She'll think it's Christmas". "Or her birthday," I replied. And together we laughed softly in the joy of this resurrection.

But another difficulty appeared later that year. The skin on her legs broke down; her legs were 'weeping'. Norma recalled this circumstance in vivid detail. "It was in the fall when I took her to the doctor. And he called it kind of like an ulcer. And he was bound and determined I could look after it. And so he showed me how to dress it and what to put on it and everything. It had to be done, to start with, every second or third day. And after we took the bandage off, we had to wash her leg with soap and water and then with clear water, let the clear all run down through it, then put Ozonol on it, bandage it all up again, and then put a tensor bandage on it. When it wasn't healing up properly and she was getting more swelling, he brought me into the office and showed me how to put this tensor bandage on it. He didn't think we needed a nurse to come to the house and do it." Just before Christmas, Bev and Norma moved from their second concession house to their retirement home in the town of Uxbridge. Looking after the leg got more demanding for Norma, but she wouldn't abandon Isabel. For a few weeks, she went to the farm nearly every afternoon. The battle seemed to be a losing one. "One time, [the leg] got breaking out in other places. Then we got it pretty well healed up, it was pretty good for a while and then it started up again. I guess she never really was free of it... We kept washing them about every second or third day and rubbing the cream on to moisten them. The skin got so dry and scaly, it just scaled right off. That went right up to her knees, pretty near. Any little scratch would kinda' break it, and then you'd have to get that healed." Another labour of love.

On a beautiful cloudless September day, Isabel was able to enjoy a quiet ninety-eighth birthday celebration with her niece Kathleen (in photo at right with Isabel) and me at the farm where Isabel had lived for sixty-two years. But soon the clouds of her life became darker and thicker. In February 1999, osteoarthritis put a tremendous grip on her. She could barely move. She continued to struggle up and down the stairs every day, including going to the bathroom when necessary. Her saving graces were the hand-rail which had been installed when Walter came home from hospital after his cerebral hemorrhage in 1964, and her steely determination. She could not get to a doctor and didn't think one could do much for her anyway. Again, she decided she just had to persevere. By the end of February, she was exhausted. Even with her home help, two hours weekdays and one hour on weekends, plus considerable support from Norma, she could not go on. Ed and I talked it over with her and she agreed to go to the hospital. On March 1, the ambulance came to transport her to Uxbridge Cottage Hospital where she was admitted through the emergency department, assisted by her doctor's recommendation.

After plenty of rest, good food and good care, she was ready to return home on March seventeenth, with maximum home care support still in place. My journal entry from a day or two before speaks volumes about her personality. "I have just spent a good part of the weekend transforming my mother's home into 'her new apartment', so she can live fairly comfortably on one level. On my way home, I stop to see her in hospital and describe what I've done. She'll be going home soon. Her brown eyes sparkle, she smiles, laughs, makes little jokes. What a reward! As I prepare to leave, she says, 'Thanks a million' in an offhandish way so she won't get too emotional. I simply say, 'You're welcome.' Moments later, driving out of the parking lot, I know what I wish I'd added—'a hundred thousand million'. Her joy has made mine." Ed had helped move a bed from upstairs into the living room. We put a commode in the corner of the living room, so that she wouldn't have to climb the stairs to the bathroom. She was using a walker most of the time. Her legs still needed daily attention. A nurse came to apply the saline solution and pads. The skin was so fragile that when her legs swelled up with fluid retention the skin burst, unable to hold the excess fluid. It was a vicious cycle. Amid all this discouragement, my mother made one of the best and dearest friends of her life.

Cheryl Haines arrived as her new Home Care worker. They were in tune from day one. Isabel admired Cheryl's practical approach. She didn't need to be asked to do every little thing; she just knew. Cheryl also knew how essential it is for older folk to have items put back exactly where they were found. Ed had often seen how important this factor was to his grandmother who "…always had everything organized. It was always in the same place, and she always knew where it was. That's the schoolteacher; that's the training. In later years, she was always chewing about the nurses' helpers—that one girl'd come and never put the stuff back where she got it." Because Cheryl had that understanding, and for other reasons, Mom trusted her implicitly. She had no trouble giving over to Cheryl her personal care, bathing included. Every week, Cheryl brought fresh flowers from her garden. They had chats about their common interests, including the writer of the *Anne of Green Gables* series, Lucy Maude Montgomery, who had lived for several years with her minister husband in the Presbyterian manse in Leaskdale, just north of Uxbridge. Cheryl sometimes stayed beyond her designated time, so pleasurable was the conversation between them.

Far too soon, this mutually valued relationship ended. In June, Cheryl left her job to move with her husband to their retirement property in Nova Scotia. Mom couldn't thank her enough for being the wonderfully sensitive person that she was. She and I decided to give Cheryl a water jug from an antique washstand set. Cheryl was reluctant to accept, fearing that taking it would break up a set or that the jug should stay in the family. But it wasn't part of a set or a valuable family treasure, just a lovely vessel in which to display flowers—a tangible reminder of their beautiful friendship. When this was explained, Cheryl accepted the gift. Not that she needed a reminder of their close relationship. Cheryl kept in contact through the summer. When she got to Nova Scotia she regularly wrote beautifully scripted letters telling how she missed their chats, what adventures she had had while driving to her new home, and how life was for her there. Appendix S contains the letter of remembrance that this dear friend wrote to me early in 2000.

In late June, Mom had a spot on her leg that swelled almost overnight and burst the next day, letting loose what seemed like a huge amount of fluid. Ed and Pam bandaged her leg, but so much fluid was escaping that the bandage needed to be changed twice daily. Ed and Pam did this in the morning and Norma took care of it in the afternoons. I was on holiday and able to be with her some of the time. Her optimistic attitude still shone, on the good days. On June 27 she had told me how she moved around her downstairs with the walker she was using: "I've got it all mapped out. In a place like this, you've gotta." Feeling hopeful, I went home to pack for a scheduled bus trip to the Maritimes. In the back of my mind was the knowledge that Mom had other problems. Afraid to lose control of her urine, she didn't want to get up to use the toilet, and so would sometimes refuse to move for any reason or anyone. On June 28, Ed called me to say that something seemed to have happened to her mind. She was no longer rational. Early the next morning, I met the other bus tour passengers just before the tour left Orillia to explain why I wasn't going with them to the Maritimes, then drove to the farm. I planned to get Mom back into the Uxbridge hospital, to see if she could be stabilized. Her doctor had already agreed over the phone to have her admitted. When I arrived at her house, I found her curled up on the floor beside her bed. She would not move. Ed and I tried to convince her, but she refused. This was not the Isabel we knew. Finally, Ed decided there was no choice. He told her that he was going to pick her up and get her back into bed. The experience was physically painful for her, but it did cause her mind to snap back to be with us. We told her that her doctor had agreed she should go to hospital again, and she agreed that plan was best for her.

So Mom spent the month of July in Uxbridge Cottage Hospital. Her care there was wonderful. Once stabilized, she enjoyed visits from family and friends. With other patients, she attended the hospital's activation program where she especially enjoyed 'Current Events' and contests, soon demonstrating that her mind was among the sharpest in the group. When she was ready for release, we did not see how she could possibly look after herself, even with maximum home care. Without Cheryl, home care held no appeal anyway. She agreed to live in Orillia with Vern and me. We had two downstairs rooms, both close to the bathroom, that she could use. We could get home care in Simcoe County, although not as many hours a week as in Durham Region. August went well. I was home from work to look after her and make arrangements for extra help. As Ed commented when he and Pam came to visit her, "She thinks she's on vacation".

September brought shocking changes. I was back at work. Each day, I prepared her breakfast before leaving. Vern helped her get some lunch, but she felt she was putting us out. She had always told Ed and me (We both had power of attorney for her personal care), "Now I don't want either of you to jeopardize your careers for me". I was managing all right, but one morning she got upset to the point that I couldn't reason with her. Something was terribly wrong. Probably she'd experienced a minor stroke. We later decided she'd had several of these 'events' (often referred to as TIAs) over the previous few months. The morning of Saturday, September fourth, I found her on the floor beside her bed. She was lucid and able to tell me that she had fallen while returning from the bathroom. Vern and I got her into bed and called for an ambulance.

The diagnosis was a fractured pelvis. She was admitted from emergency to a room in Soldiers' Memorial Hospital. My workplace responded immediately to my request for a part-time workload for three weeks, so that I could give her the extra bits of special care that the nurses didn't have time for. She had her ninety-ninth birthday in hospital, and was delighted that her nieces Kathleen and Winnifred and grand-niece Frances came to share it with her. Winnifred stayed on with us a few days so that she could go to visit Isabel every day. That was wonderful therapy. One of the birthday cards Isabel received—from someone she would probably call a casual friend—included a note that captured how the love Isabel radiated to others was returned. "Happy Birthday to a Truly Lovely 99 year Old Lady. I can't recall knowing anyone that has reached this age. What a pleasure meeting you and having the occasion of being in your company. You bring joy to all who meet you."

Many visitors arrived to see Isabel during her hospital stay. Former neighbour Barbara Spinney came with her friend, John, and Barbara reported that, "She had a real good conversation with John because he used to live in Orillia. So they were talkin' about roads up there. When we went to see her that day, she was really good." Mom did especially well, I noticed, when people from her earlier life came to visit. She perked up and reverted to the Isabel we knew—animated and chatty, wanting to know what was happening with the visitor and his or her community. Marilyn remarked on this transformation too. "One of the things she said to me, I remember, seeing her in the hospital was, 'Now you make sure that young man of yours gets into his uniform all right'." She and her husband, Roger, puzzled over this comment for a while until they recalled that their son, Darren, had said that he wanted to be a policeman. "Forty-eight hours later, we decided, 'That's what she meant'. Here she was, on her death bed basically, and she said, 'You make sure that man gets into his uniform'," Marilyn marveled.

In October, Mom experienced the stroke that left her speech garbled and her right side paralysed. Fortunately the speech returned within a few days. She did therapy for the limbs, but they remained almost useless. She never walked again. But within a week she was learning to eat with her left hand and soon became quite adept. A measure of peace came, too. She never shared with me her feelings but I know mine were running over on November 11 when I represented my workplace and placed a wreath at Orillia's war memorial in front of the hospital as my mother, who had lost two brothers to the First World War, watched from a window in the second-floor solarium. Within a few days, she had to leave the hospital to go to a nursing home, since she needed so much help with all aspects of living. I wasn't able to keep working and look after her at our home, and she wouldn't have wanted me to try. We had to take the first nursing home that had an opening. It was not my first choice of Orillia facilities. I tried to compensate by spending time with her every day on my way home from work and on weekends. She enjoyed having the *Uxbridge Times-Journal* read to her, and then the cards of best wishes and the Christmas greetings that flowed in, once people knew where she was located.

Family and friends continued to visit. Lily Hope had her son bring her from Goodwood to see Isabel shortly after Christmas, and she later told me, "I was awful glad I got up to see her before she died". Knowing how much Isabel liked oatmeal, Lily brought some homemade oatmeal cookies. She thought that Isabel's mind was good—and it *was* for people and events from the past. The strokes, however, had taken their toll. To make conversation, Lily had asked, "Where did you spend Christmas? Did you have a nice Christmas?" Lily recalled Isabel's reply: "And she says, 'Yes. There was a party here; we had it here. And there were all the family here'. And she says, 'Somethin' happened to me. I don't know what happened to me'. She says, 'We were havin' such a nice time, and somethin' hit me, I don't know what it was, but they had to bring me back in here, and I spoiled the party'." In truth, only Vern and I were there on Christmas Eve. We took a tablecloth, juice, chicken dinner and homemade Christmas cake to have dinner in the nursing home sitting room. Mom said her stomach felt upset; she didn't finish her meal. She had wanted to be at the family gathering the next day. We didn't see how she could take the hour's trip to Uxbridge or the chaos of the day. She was disappointed, and so were we all. Christmas without her with the family was unheard-of. It was a subdued celebration.

Our family realized that Mom would never be back at the farmhouse. So on December 28 and 29, Bev, Norma and I, with help from Marilyn and Joanne, cleaned out all the drawers, cupboards and closets in her part of the farmhouse. After we had laid out on tables all the things that we thought family members might like, everyone came to make their choices of special objects to complement their special memories of her. On December thirtieth, I visited Mom at the nursing home and sat with her for part of the afternoon and through supper, leaving at about 6:30 p.m. When I returned the next day to visit, a sign on the door informed me that everyone was under quarantine because some of the residents had the influenza A virus. I could not go in. I called the next morning to get details. The Director of Care explained that each floor was isolated. Family members were discouraged from coming in, but could if the family in residence were very ill. The quarantine sign had gone up at 9 p.m. the night before. By 11 p.m., all the residents were on amantadine, a drug designed to ward off influenza A. The Director said I could phone at any time. Someone would bring my mother in her wheelchair to the phone at the desk.

So that is what I did. In our December thirty-first telephone conversation, I reminded Mom that Vern and I had decided to spend New Year's Eve in Uxbridge. Many cities and towns were having extra-special celebrations to welcome the new millennium, the year 2000. The Uxbridge celebration would be extra- extra-special, particularly to my mother. For their millennium project the town had installed electronic chimes in the library tower. She had loved the original bell that rang out the hour while she waited below in the library reading room for her train home to Gamebridge or her ride to Roseville during her first teaching years, 1920 to 1923. One of Isabel's newspaper clippings from the *Uxbridge Times-Journal* must have warmed her heart with its content. "At one time there was a reading room on the main floor of the Gould Institute. This room was open to the public even when the rest of the library was closed. Townspeople were welcome to come in and read the Toronto newspapers while they waited for friends or relatives with errands in town or just to relax with their choice of reading material. With the purchase of comfortable wing chairs, this use of the room, now called the Gould Room, has been re-established.... The trustees and staff of the library hope that the community will use and enjoy the Gould Room as it was used in the past" (McLean, n.p.). The room my mother had loved was re-established in 1986 (McGillivray, 126).

I knew that Mom was deeply disappointed when the bell was removed from the library tower in 1954 in response to complaints of nearby residents. Peter Hvidsten, whose parents owned and published the *Uxbridge Times-Journal* from 1953 to 1976, wrote: "The old bell was removed from the tower and the library clock became silent after ringing out the hours for over 67 years" (32). He went on to say that the bell tower was constructed in 1884 to act as a firehouse with an alarm bell. The library (first called a Mechanic's Institute) was built in 1887 to house the bell but it was too heavy to be rung by hand, so was connected to the library clock by a cable, to "sound the hours" (33). Vern's and my 1999 Christmas gift to Mom was a donation towards the cost of the electronic chimes. On New Year's Eve, he and I took two tape recorders to Uxbridge, determined that she would get to hear those bells. The night was clear and cold—perfect for recording the chimes as they rang out the beautiful and familiar songs of the season. New Year's Day, I phoned and told her of the successful taping. I spoke to her on the phone each subsequent day. And I waited for the quarantine to be lifted.

When I called her on January fifth, Mom's voice was hoarse but her mind had been at work. She wondered if Ed could make a temporary arrangement with the Bell Telephone Company so that she could have a phone in her own room for a month "while this is on". I told her it was okay to use the nursing home's phone and that I'd been reassured of this by the Director of Care, whom I knew on a casual basis. Mom, however, felt the phone was needed for business purposes and shouldn't be used to call her. How I wish I were good at lying. How I wish I'd told her I'd see to it. She must have worried and stewed about that phone. Around seven that evening a nurse called me. Mom had had a massive stroke.

Though the nursing home was still under quarantine, of course I could now go in. What an irony. I notified my boss that I had to take some time off. Each day, I spent several hours at my mother's bedside. Though she soon lost consciousness, I couldn't accept the inevitable. Finally, on January 8, I realized if she were ever going to hear those bells, I had to bring in the tape and play it. As the melodies rang out from the tape player, she didn't stir. But I have read that people who are unconscious can hear what's going on around them. And so I believe she heard and rejoiced at the sound of bells ringing again from the Uxbridge Library tower.

Just after seven the next morning, a nurse held Isabel's hand to take her pulse. Then it stopped. She had conquered the last and darkest cloud. It was Sunday, the day of the week on which she was born, the day that was always so special for her, the day she entreated the rest of us to honour as she did. You'd almost think she'd planned her bookend exit.

This beautiful spirit and the shell that held it have vanished like a winsome breeze. Reminders survive, of course—in her taped voice, stories, values and traditions, photos, poems and other clippings, and the spirits of those whose lives were enlarged and enlightened by hers. Somewhere in this measureless universe, I am sure, a brilliant force once known as Margaret Isabella still exists. As I think of my mother, the familiar WWII song, "We'll meet again/Don't know where/Don't know when/But I know we'll meet again some sunny day", echoes through my mind.

How I hope that we do.

EPILOGUE

The reader may notice some discrepancies of fact in the following eulogies as compared to the text of the biography. Family members, not blessed with Isabel's unbelievably long and accurate memory, made some errors in their recollections, and the tapes recorded with Isabel in earlier years had not yet been transcribed in 2000, to provide the corrections. Every effort has been made to provide correct dates and information in the main text of *Turning Clouds Inside Out*.

Despite the errors, these eulogies portray clearly and lovingly the woman my mother was.

EULOGY
for Isabella Margaret (Wallace) Beach
delivered by Edith Ann Shantze
January 12, 2000

This afternoon we have the honour to entrust back to the Good Shepherd's keeping our sister in faith, Isabelle Beach.

I was privileged, in my pastorate here at Goodwood/Epsom/Utica, to have such a lively, engaging, intelligent, spunky, parishioner who in 1981, when I arrived, already would have been in her early 80's. Hard to believe!

I always looked forward to seeing Isabelle in the pew, in her home, or at a UCW meeting. For years Isabelle was committed to helping keep Siloam going...and yet she was, along with Norma, an important bridge with the Goodwood UCW. It seemed, almost whatever Isabelle was involved in, there was an important part linked to the past, and an equally important part linked to the future. This was Isabelle, a woman who offered those closest to her... ROOTS and WINGS.

I remember, after one of my first sermons here, Isabelle pulling me over on a Sunday morning, and offering me, a young newly arrived overly conscientious minister, a wonderful piece of sermon advice that I never forgot: "Edith Anne (said Isabelle) I know you are trying to do it right—but those of us in the pew do not care *which* author said *what*, in whatever quotation. Just present an idea, and we'll enjoy it a whole lot more."

Interestingly enough, just this past Sunday we had a guest speaker at our church, quoting from some author or another, and without knowing of Isabelle's death, I once again sat there thinking about Isabelle's advice—We really don't need the bibliography!

I've sidetracked from my point that Isabelle was a woman of strong faith and deep love for her Lord. It isn't hard to imagine Isabelle as one of the Good Shepherd's fold. It isn't hard to imagine Isabelle walking through the valley of the shadow of death protected by God's rod and staff, and coming out on the other side, to a banqueting table where her loved ones await her in the presence of God.

Isabelle loved poetry. Psalm 23 is not only an affirmation of faith, but also poetry. When the Psalmist writes of death, he writes of it as a valley through which we walk. Death is *not* an abiding place but a thoroughfare, a small portion of the journey.

Likewise, the Psalmist speaks of "the valley of the shadow of death". Shadows may scare us, but a mere shadow cannot hurt us. We walk through the shadows to the Light of a brand new day. And so, as we repeat this Psalm together, a psalm that has offered comfort to Christians of so many generations, let us think of Isabelle seated at the Heavenly Table, already dwelling in "the House of the Lord" FOREVER.

Isabelle came into the world September 16, 1900—the seventh child in a family of nine. Isabelle was born at home to William E. Wallace and Catherine McFadyen. Her early years were enlivened by the company of three brothers and five sisters, and enriched by growing up on a farm.

At an early age, Isabelle learned the value of hard work, family ties, and being content with what you have. Her parents were Scottish Presbyterian, which speaks for itself, and Isabelle was proud of her Scottish roots.

Not many people are lucky enough to have their life span an entire century, but Isabelle was. So perhaps it wasn't by coincidence that Isabelle became quite the local historian. For simply by daily happenings and observance Isabelle noted many changes throughout her lifetime.

Already by age 10 (to name only one example) Isabelle experienced, right on their own family farm near Gamebridge, the coming of the new Grand Trunk Railway. And Isabelle had great childhood memories of the men who were working on the railway coming into their home to be fed the huge hearty meals prepared by the women. In fact, the Wallace women prepared such good food that even as the men moved down the line, they would try and come back to the Wallace's to eat!

One of the pay-offs in those simpler days was the privilege of just walking out to the rail line to flag the train down, instead of having to travel into town to the proper station. Unfortunately, while Isabelle got to see the introduction of the railroad at the beginning of the century, she also got to witness towards the end of the century its struggle for survival, and for many little lines…their last breath.

Isabelle was always a bright, sharp student, with an inquisitive mind, and an eagerness to learn. She had a fantastic, in fact a phenomenal, memory that lasted her a lifetime!

Isabelle was the youngest in her family to pass grade 8 and went on to Orillia for high school. From Orillia Isabelle went on to Peterborough for Normal School, but because her mother fell out of the family buggy, it was Isabelle's turn, as a daughter, to stay home and help her mother around the house.

In those years churches and schools had more than their fair share of fires, and Isabelle's two teaching posts were no exception. Isabelle came to Roseville to teach and the Roseville school burnt. She went to Riverview School, and it burned! But it was when Isabelle returned to Roseville that she met Walter Beach.

Like many young couples, Isabelle and Walter met dancing at a home party, this one at Garnett Smalley's. Walter, a farmer, proudly married his young teacher bride Isabelle on September 22, 1926.

In 1932, along came Beverly, and in 1940 their family was completed by the arrival of Catherine. Since then, Isabelle's family has grown to include five grandchildren—Edward, Joanne, Marilyn, James and Bruce—and five great- grandchildren—Vanessa, Candice, Darren, Daniel and Kelly. And with Isabelle's great love of children, these additions were considered the ICING on the CAKE OF LIFE. She loved each and every one of her grandchildren and great-grandchildren very much.

Isabelle was a proud, responsible, and committed wife and mother. She was energetic by nature and could go out to help with the cows, cook fantastic meals, care for the house and children, serve her church and community, and make it all look so easy.

In 1946, when all the men came to help build a new barn, Isabelle proved herself her mother's daughter by getting some of her sisters and nieces together and putting up unforgettable meals for the men. She could cook, bake, and preserve to perfection.

Isabelle not only had a great memory, but she had a good sense of humour, a creative writing streak, and an ability to put any kind of program together—whether it be for her UCW Unit, a community event, or whatever else. Of course her training as a teacher helped, as well as the mountain of resources she collected and saved over the years from books, newspaper clippings, poems and articles, Not to mention a trunk full of old clothes to liven up any occasion of old-fashioned homemade entertainment. When Isabelle did something, she put *everything* into it!

One thing Isabelle was consistent about was her encouragement to her family, the grandchildren, and great-grandchildren, to continue their education. Avid reader that she was, Isabelle wanted her family to experience the joys of learning. This was WINGS to their future.

Isabelle and Walter enjoyed a good marriage together, but unfortunately Walter died in December 1967.

Fortunately, Isabelle was a strong woman, independent, and enjoyed a close relationship with her family. For many years she shared the house with Bev and Norma, and later with Ed and Pam, and although she respected their privacy, they had the comfort of knowing "she was always there". Visits to Catherine and her family were also highlights of Isabelle's later years.

Although Isabelle did a little supply teaching in the 50s and 60s, she never really *had* to work outside her home, and this left Isabelle the precious time to write her reams and reams of notes—and be a resource for everybody else! Not one to enjoy TV, she kept her ear to radio CFRB—Gord Sinclair, Andy Barrie, Jack Dennett.

Over the years, Isabelle's body may have aged but her spirit always remained open to the new. If her grandchildren presented a challenge, Isabelle was ready. She tried 16 year-old Ed's new motorcycle and his first snowmobile while she was already in her mid-60s! Yet adventuresome as she could be, Isabelle encouraged strict adherence to life's sensible rules: respect, honesty, fairness, schooling, no cards on Sunday!

Although Isabelle thoroughly enjoyed her "home in the country" she also enjoyed some traveling…to California, B. C., Newfoundland, Florida, Expo in Montreal. If Isabelle wanted to go somewhere, she got there. Driving her car right up till she was 90, she was determined to get herself out to her church and to her hairdresser's!!

Isabelle was practical, clever, very kind, very helpful, generally very easy- going…but NO pushover! If she ever did get angry, you'd better be a long way away. Isabelle knew her own mind, and it was this strong inner spirit that helped her beat whatever disappointments came in her life—two broken hips in the 1980s and her physical problems for the last few years.

In a nutshell, some of her most common expressions demonstrate Isabelle's inner self: her love and appreciation of humour, integrity, and realism. "That's the pot calling the kettle black," she'd say, or "I see, said the blind man, as he picked up his hammer and saw" or "Holy smoke, the preacher cried, the church is on fire" or "If wishes were horses, beggars would ride".

The very last book Isabelle received was about the Queen Mother. Isabelle was just a month and 12 days younger than the Queen Mother, and she really admired her. Today, those of us gathered here, who knew Isabelle, really admired her, and to her own family Isabelle is really their Queen Mother, their "Queen Mum". And why not? Isabelle, in her love of children, gave unselfishly to her children, her grandchildren and her great-grandchildren, and she has reaped the rewards of giving and receiving a hundred fold in return.

Although Isabelle made it to the millennium, the last year has not been easy. And so it is we entrust Isabelle's soul back to the Arms of God, holding fast to the words of St. Paul, to "Be brave, keep hold of all that is good, knowing nothing can separate us from the love of God which is in Christ Jesus."

****

Below is part of my son James Ashton's tribute to his grandmother at her funeral service.

My Grandmother taught me the meaning of Remembrance Day. This was fairly recently, and I, who like the vast majority of my generation of North Americans have no first-hand experience of war, was skeptical regarding a holiday which seemed to have been created to glorify its memory. I thought there must be more to it, and if I wanted to find out I should ask the only person I knew who had been around, who had actually lived through both wars.

"Grandma," I said, "What is the point of this holiday? Why do we take a day to celebrate something as useless and futile and ugly as war? And these wars weren't just last week. This is a lot of years ago. Shouldn't we just drop it and move on?"

A great many people, not just from her generation but those considerably younger as well, would get their hackles up at a question like this. Never in my life do I recall my grandmother taking exception to one of my questions.

Here is what she told me. She said the wars themselves weren't really so much what we were intended to remember. The remembrance is for the people – the thousands upon thousands of very ordinary people – who suffered and sacrificed for something they believed was right and necessary. We don't need to remember them because we believe they were right – whether they were or not isn't the point. We need to remember them, to be reminded of them, simply because of what they had to endure. It isn't the wars we're remembering – it's the people.

Throughout her whole life, Isabel Beach remembered about people. She remembered each person, each family member, each neighbour, each friend and schoolmate and stranger.

Today, Grandma, today is your Remembrance Day. I want to remember you.

I remember your home. Your home was always my second home, and a number of times during my life it was even more home to me than my real home. You always made your home available to me when I needed somewhere else to go. No pressure, no obligation, just come and go. Take a walk for a while. Amble around the farmyard or in those hills, those beautiful hills.

I remember your house on Christmas Eve. I was four and I couldn't go to sleep. You gave me a farm set, big steel barn, sheds and tractors and animals. We still played with it when I was fourteen.

I remember reading as a child in the summer. I remember early mornings, creeping up to your bookcase by the bed. You always kept peppermints under the pillow. You always remembered there was an extra one. They were Scotch mints and I still like them.

I remember sitting in your gold-coloured armchair on a cold winter night. Sitting reading, brief respite from the raging storm of adolescence. You fixed the lamp up so the light was better. Indians and generals leapt off the pages. Charlie Farquharson gave me sore sides. Go west, young man, go west/ To prairie lands Sunkist and bless'd…

I remember how you told stories. You always had so much to tell, and you could never just tell the story you started out with. You began with one, then branched out to another, then veered off to yet another, until I was almost dizzy. But you always remembered. And back you would come, through one conclusion and another, until you reached the end of the story you began with. And you never forgot.

I remember how you took your first motorcycle ride when you were seventy-two. Edward took you out to the end of the sideroad and back, I think. I told my friends at school, "My grandma rides a motorcycle!" I still tell people that story. It's so you.

I remember you were married in 1926, seventy years before Crystal and I. You gave us the glass candlesticks you were given at your own wedding, and on our first anniversary you gave us the bowl that went with them. You never forgot about our anniversary, never forgot a Christmas, a birthday. For how many of us did you remember all these things?

I remember you this fall, at Mom and Dad's house. Coming in the mudroom door and seeing you there, reading under the lamp in Grandad's old rocker. Or sitting at the table at breakfast, listening to all the goofy conversation, throwing something in where no one expected it. I remember how it was just having you there.

I remember a thousand things. I remember you.

****

Isabel's funeral procession exited Low's Funeral Home in Uxbridge that January day to an old Scottish air played by a kilted bagpiper. The more traditional "Amazing Grace" was not for her. She had told me, regarding the lines 'Amazing grace, how sweet the sound/ That saved a wretch like me'—"I'm not a wretch!"

How right she was.

GLOSSARY

BINDER: an implement used to harvest grains in the fields

BOOBY PRIZE: a token prize given to the person with the lowest score at the end of the evening of playing euchre. Booby is a slang term for a stupid person, a fool.

BOX STOVE: a large rectangular wood-burning stove

CHARIVAREE (SHIVAREE): a surprise party for a newly married couple, generally starting after the couple was in bed with a 'serenade' using homemade instruments such as a cowbell, pots and pans, a washboard, or a washtub. The couple was obliged to invite the serenaders in and give them something to eat and drink. Often they were presented with a gift from the neighbours who instigated this party.

CUTTER: a sleigh made for carrying people over snow or ice, usually drawn by one horse, and made by putting a light carriage on runners (*Gage Canadian Dictionary*, 1997 edition)

DIRTY THIRTIES: the decade (1930 to 1939) when an economic depression impoverished many Canadians

THE "ELSIE" BOOKS: a series of "One-and-Sixpenny Juvenile Books" published in London, England, around the start of the twentieth century, and written by Martha Finley. In the final volume, *Elsie's Children*, the author wrote of the characters, "…may their society prove sweet, comforting and helpful to many readers and friends both old and new". Such books were written partly for moral instruction.

EUCHRE: a card game played with part of the deck (usually excluding all cards below nine), in which one suit of cards is called the 'trump'. The partners who determine the trump try to capture the most tricks. If they don't win that round of play, they are 'euchred'.

FLAPPER: the hair, clothing, and behaviour style of progressive young women in the 1920s—the "Roaring Twenties"

FLAT IRON: a clothes iron made of iron, used prior to hydro electricity and the electric iron. In shape it's similar to today's iron. Early versions had a handle made of the same material. Later ones had a detachable wooden handle. This handle was put on after the iron had been heated on the surface of a hot wood-burning stove.

FRENCH SAFE: condom

'H': the letter that was formed when moving a gearshift in a standard shift car from first to second to third to reverse gear.

MANSE or PARSONAGE: the home for a church congregation's minister, provided and maintained by the congregation.

GLOSSARY (Cont'd)

MILITARY SCHOTTISCHE: a dance in 2/4 time, popular in the 1800s and early 1900s. Literally means Scottish (*Gage Canadian Dictionary*, 1997 edition)

MR. DRESSUP: Ernie Coombs, the only visible human being on the Canadian children's TV show, "Mr. Dressup", which ran from 1967 to 1996. Ernie's assistants were puppets Casey and Finnegan and his "Tickle Trunk" filled with wild and wacky costumes. (www.canadianaconnection.com)

OBSERVER: newsmagazine produced by the United Church of Canada

PARSONAGE: See Manse

PITCHFORK: a three-tined fork used to put hay into the mangers/feed boxes for horses and cattle

SCOURS: diarrhea in cattle

SHIVAREE: See Charivaree

SMOOTHING IRON: See Flat Iron

SNAPSHOT: photo

STOOK, STOOKING: (oo sound as in boot) before the invention of grain harvesters pulled by tractors, cut grain lying in a field was tied into sheaves by a binder pulled by a team of horses. These sheaves were stooked by the farm help—stood up against each other in groups of five or so, in order to dry before being threshed.

THRESHING: a process in which the grain is removed from the stalk on which it grew and the stalk is cut up for straw to be used as bedding for animals.

MAP OF THORAH TOWNSHIP, 1895

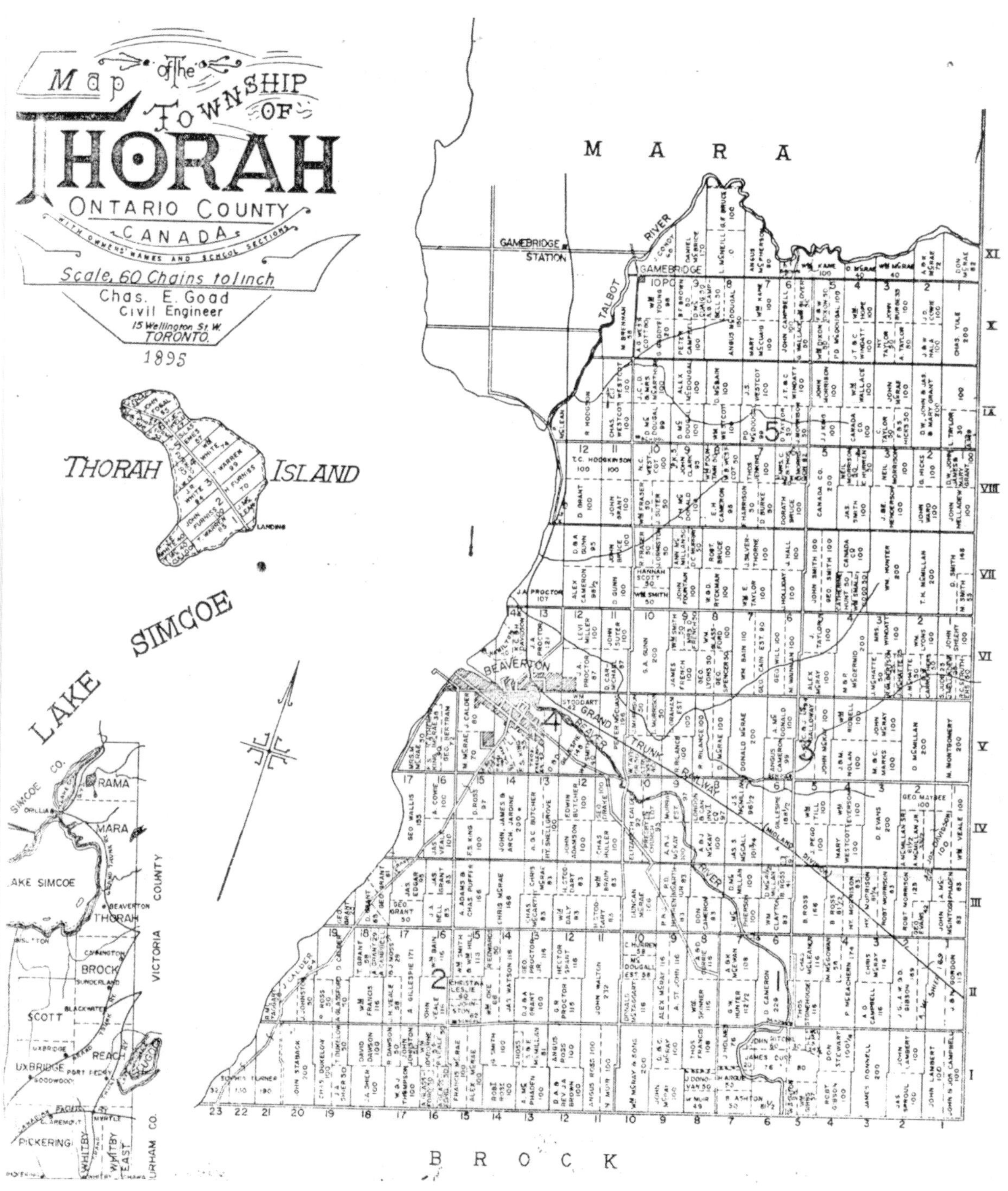

MAP OF UXBRIDGE TOWNSHIP, Northwest Part, 1877

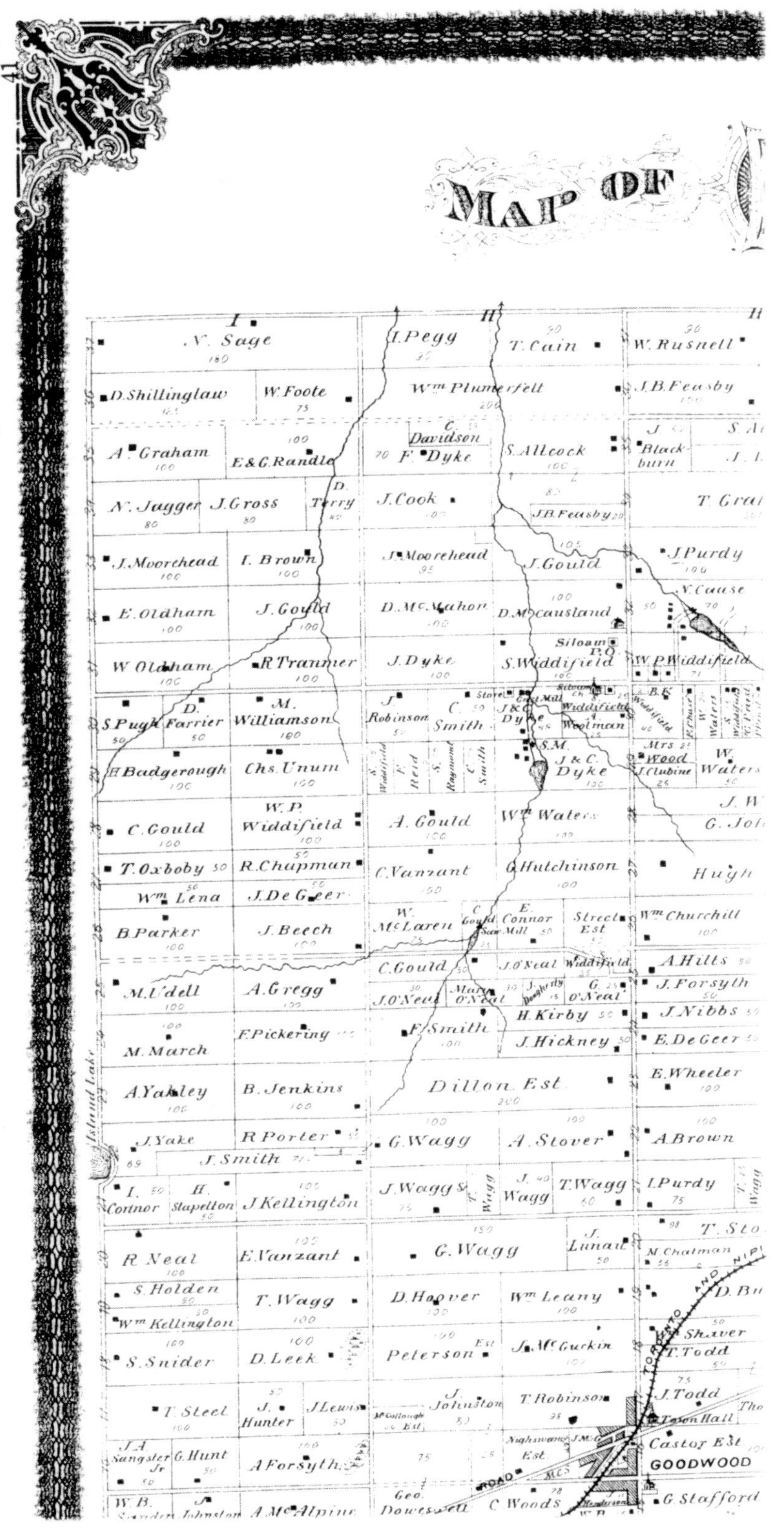

MAP OF UXBRIDGE TOWNSHIP, Northwest Part, 1895

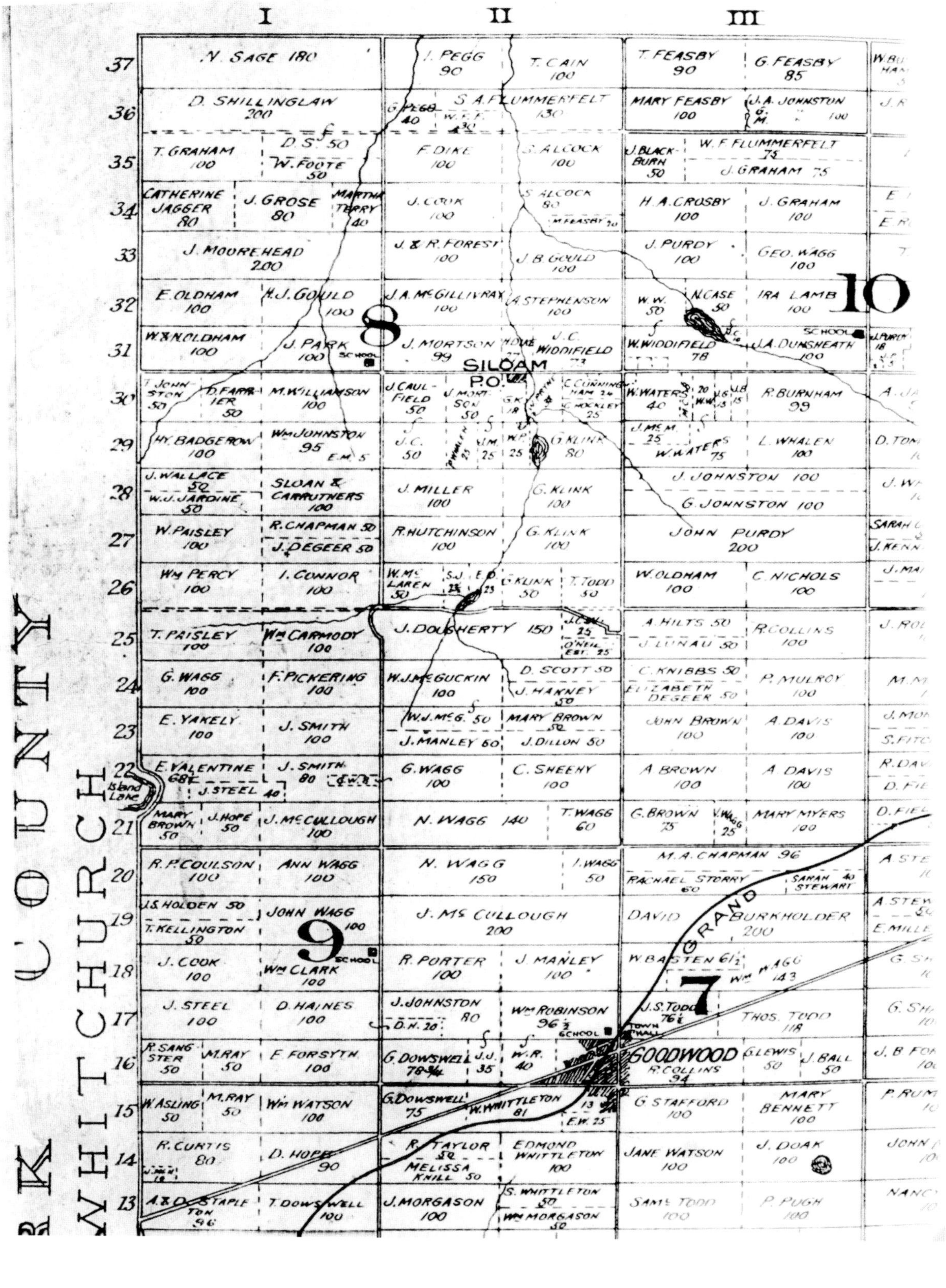

MAP OF UXBRIDGE TOWNSHIP, Northwest Part, 1915

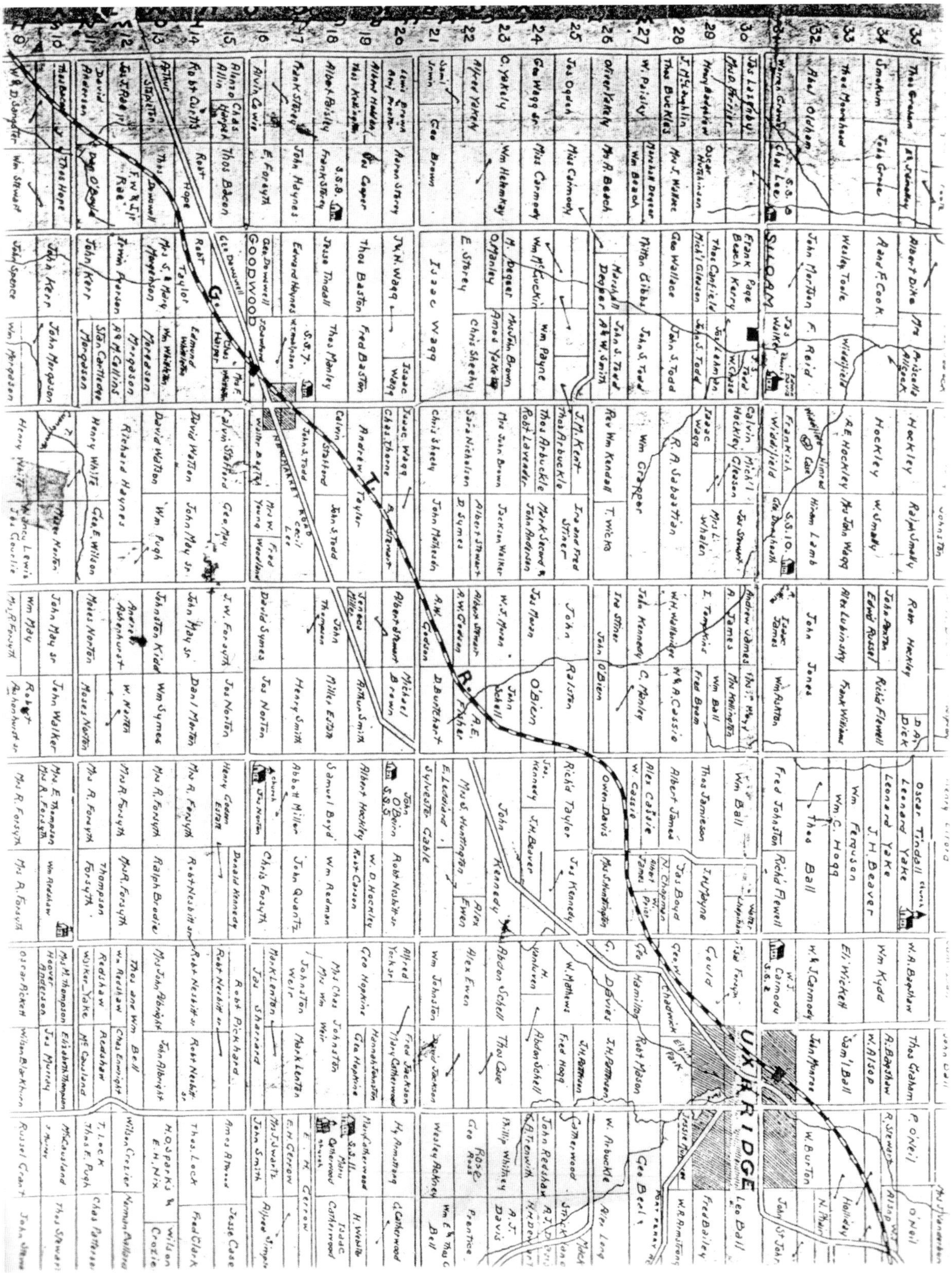

MAP OF UXBRIDGE TOWNSHIP, 2003

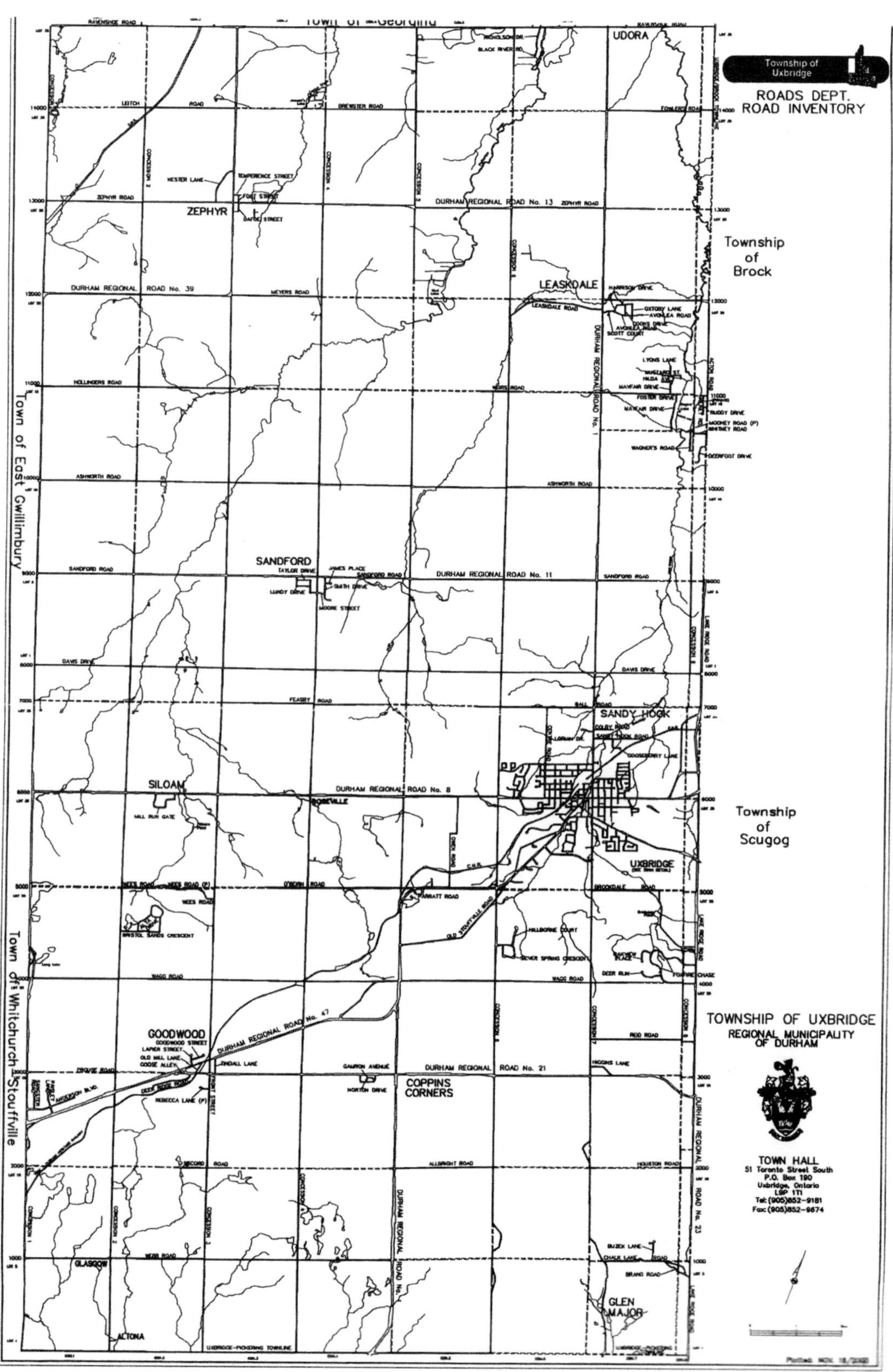

LIST OF APPENDIXES

APPENDIX A: Wallace Descendants

A-1

Generation One

1. John Wallace, b. March 8, 1803, d. February 16, 1892. He married Catherine Reid, married June 4, 1838, b. January 14, 1817, d. December 29, 1895.
Children:
2. i. George Wallace b. July 10, 1840.

Generation Two

2. George Wallace, b. July 10, 1840 in Upper Canada, d. February 15, 1927 in Thorah Township, Ontario, Canada. He married Catherine McBain, married March 17, 1863 in York, Canada West, b. April 11, 1843 in Mara Township, Canada West, d. March 24, 1928.
Children:
3. i. William (Will) Wallace b. December 12, 1863.
ii. John Wallace, b. November 19, 1865 in Upper Canada, d. June 21, 1934.
iii. Catherine Wallace, b. August 23, 1867 in Province of Ontario, Canada, d. June 6, 1957.
iv. Jennette Wallace, b. August 23, 1867 in Province of Ontario, Canada, d. February 11, 1868 in Province of Ontario, Canada.
v. Margaret Wallace, b. July 30, 1870 in Province of Ontario, Canada, d. June 27, 1942.
vi. George Hamilton Wallace, b. October 31, 1873 in Province of Ontario, Canada, d. April 10, 1967 in Toronto, Ontario, Canada.

Generation Three

3. William (Will) Wallace, b. December 12, 1863 in Canada West, d. February 24, 1961 in Thorah Township, Ontario, Canada. He married Catherine (Kate) Anne McFadyen, married September 18, 1888 in manse of St. Andrew's Presbyterian Church, Orillia, Ontario, Canada, b. February 19, 1863 in Hartley, Canada West, d. May 4, 1937 in Toronto, Ontario, Canada.
Children:
i. Annie Laurie Wallace, b. July 5, 1889 in Thorah Township, Ontario, Canada, d. May 28, 1969 in Beaverton, Ontario, Canada.
4. ii. Duncan George Wallace b. February 24, 1891.
iii. John Reid Wallace, b. March 1, 1893 in Thorah Township, Ontario, Canada, d. August 23, 1918 in battle at the Hindenburg Line in France, World War I.
iv. Viola Catherine Wallace, b. February 21, 1895 in Thorah Township, Ontario, Canada, d. March 29, 1929 in Saskatoon, Saskatchewan, Canada, of acute appendicitis.
v. Christena May Wallace, b. November 24, 1896 in Thorah Township, Ontario, Canada, d. April 17, 1997 in Stouffville, Ontario, Canada.
vi. William (Willy) Alexander Wallace, b. January 24, 1899 in Thorah Township, Ontario, Canada, d. October 8, 1916 in France serving as a runner, World War I.
5. vii. Margaret Isabella Wallace b. September 16, 1900.
6. viii. Minnie Elsie Wallace b. May 14, 1902.
ix. Jessie Agnes Wallace, b. August 11, 1904 in Thorah Township, Ontario, Canada, d. November, 1997 in Stouffville, Ontario, Canada. She married Samuel Stanley, married October 6, 1951 in St. Andrew's Presbyterian Church, Bolsover, Ontario, Canada.

Wallace Descendants

A-2

Generation Four

4. Duncan George Wallace, b. February 24, 1891 in Thorah Township, Ontario, Canada, d. November 8, 1985 in Aurora, Ontario, Canada. He married Bertha Winters Switzer, married December 23, 1916 in Wingham, Ontario, Canada, b. November 29, 1895 in Province of Manitoba, Canada, d. April 16, 1987 in Aurora, Ontario, Canada.
Children:
i. Kathleen Margaret Wallace, b. October 7, 1917 in Thorah Township, Ontario, Canada. She married David Cecil Jones.
ii. William (Billy) Reid Wallace, b. January 25, 1919 in Thorah Township, Ontario, Canada, d. November 20, 1942 in Sudbury, Ontario, Canada. He married Mary Lillian Carr.
iii. Mary Winnifred Wallace, b. May 24, 1920 in Thorah Township, Ontario, Canada.
iv. Victoria Elsie Wallace, b. May 24, 1920 in Thorah Township, Ontario, Canada, d. May 24, 1920 in Thorah Township, Ontario, Canada.
v. Donald John Wallace, b. May 30, 1926 in Thorah Township, Ontario, Canada, d. May 21, 1999 in Victoria, British Columbia, Canada. He married (1) Myra Elaine Ross, married September 10, 1946, b. June 6, 1924. He married (2) Margaret Boyce.

5. Margaret Isabella Wallace, b. September 16, 1900 in Thorah Township, Ontario, Canada, d. January 9, 2000 in Orillia, Ontario, Canada. She married Walter Thomas Beach, married September 22, 1926 in Thorah Township, Ontario, Canada, b. December 24, 1897 in Uxbridge Township, Ontario, Canada, d. December 5, 1967 in Uxbridge Township, Ontario, Canada.
Children:
i. Beverley Wallace Beach b. January 31, 1932.
ii. Catherine Rose Beach b. April 20, 1940.

6. Minnie Elsie Wallace, b. May 14, 1902 in Thorah Township, Ontario, Canada, d. October 31, 1996 in Orillia, Ontario, Canada. She married John Owens, married December 31, 1930, b. 1901 in Scotland, d. June 6, 1970.
Children:
i. Marjorie Elizabeth Dowsley Owens, b. October 23, 1931 in Thorah Township, Ontario, Canada. She married Clifford Thompson, married April10, 1953 in Los Angeles, CA, United States of America, b. June 23, 1930.
ii. Wallace Gardiner Owens, b. August 15, 1933 in Thorah Township, Ontario, Canada, d. February 23, 2003 in Los Angeles, CA, United States of America. He married Karen Margaret Kelsen, married September 29, 1962 in Los Angeles, CA, United States of America.

NOTE: Information on Generations Five, Six and Seven, descendants of Margaret Isabella Beach, is listed in Appendix M, Beach Descendants.

APPENDIX B: McFadyen Descendants B-1

Generation One

1. Donald McFadyen, b. 1791 in Losset, Kilchomen, Argyleshire, Scotland, d. date unknown in Scotland. He married Mary McDougall, married May 1813 in Scotland, b. circa 1796 in Kildalton, Argylshire, Scotland, d. date unknown in Scotland.
Children:
2. i. Duncan McFadyen b. July 1, 1830.

Generation Two

2. Duncan McFadyen, b. July 1, 1830 in Scotland, d. March 31, 1911 in Bolsover, Eldon Township, Victoria County, Ontario, Canada. He married Christena MacLean, married April 3, 1862 at the manse, Knox Presbyterian Church, in Woodville, Victoria County, Upper Canada, by Reverend John McTavish, b. August 12, 1842 in Scotland, d. April 20, 1927 in Eldon Township, Victoria County, Ontario, Canada.
Children:
3. i. Catherine Anne McFadyen b. February 19, 1863.
4. ii. Gilbert McFadyen b. October 18, 1864.
iii. Donald McFadyen, b. December 23, 1866 in Balsam Lake, Canada West, d. August 25,1930.
iv. John McFadyen, b. August 12, 1869 in Balsam Lake, Bexley Township, Ontario, Canada, d. April 5, 1934.
5. v. Hector McFadyen b. October 22, 1870.
6. vi. Mary Ella McFadyen b. February 18, 1873.
7. vii. Christena (Tene) Janet McFadyen b. September 2, 1876.
viii. Isabelle (Belle) Elizabeth McFadyen, b. September 7, 1878 in Bolsover, Eldon Township, Ontario, Canada, d. 1962.
8. ix. Margaret (Maggie) Jane McFadyen b. October 20, 1880.
x. Andrew James McFadyen, b. September 15, 1882 in Bolsover, Eldon Township, Ontario, Canada, d. 1957.
xi. Duncan Alexander McFadyen, b. June 9, 1884 in Bolsover, Eldon Township, Ontario, Canada, d. April 4, 1924 in Eldon Township, Ontario, Canada.
9. xii. Minnie Elsie McFadyen b. August 26, 1886.

Generation Three

3. Catherine Anne McFadyen, b. February 19, 1863 in Hartley, Township of Eldon, Canada West, d. May 4, 1937 in Toronto, Ontario, Canada. She married William (E.) Wallace, married September 18, 1888 in the manse of St. Andrew's Presbyterian Church, Orillia, Simcoe County, Ontario, Canada, b. December 12, 1863 in Canada West, d. February 24, 1961 in Township of Thorah, Ontario County, Ontario, Canada.
Children:
i Annie Laurie Wallace, b. July 5, 1889 in Thorah Township, Ontario, Canada, d. May 28, 1969 in Beaverton, Ontario, Canada.
10. ii. Duncan George Wallace b. February 24,1891.
iii. John Reid Wallace, b. March 1, 1893 in Thorah Township, Ontario, Canada, d. August 23, 1918 in battle at the Hindenburg Line, France, World War I.

McFadyen Descendants **B-2**

iv. Viola Catherine Wallace, b. February 21, 1895 in Thorah Township, Ontario, Canada, d. March 29, 1929 in Saskatoon, Saskatchewan, Canada, of acute appendicitis.
v. Christena May Wallace, b. November 24, 1896 in Thorah Township, Ontario, Canada, d. April 17, 1997 in Stouffville, Ontario, Canada.
vi. William (Willy) Alexander Wallace, b. January 24, 1899 in Thorah Township, Ontario, Canada, d. October 8, 1916 in France, serving as a runner in World War I.
11. vii. Margaret Isabella Wallace b. September 16, 1900.
12. viii. Minnie Elsie Wallace b. May 14, 1902.
ix. Jessie Agnes Wallace, b. August 11, 1904 in Thorah Township, Ontario, Canada, d. November, 1997 in Stouffville, Ontario, Canada. She married Samuel Benjamin Stanley, married October 6, 1951, in St. Andrew's Presbyterian Church, Bolsover, Ontario, Canada, b. December 26, 1892, d. August 31, 1967.

4. Gilbert McFadyen, b. October 18, 1864 in Hartley, Eldon Township, Victoria County, Canada West, d. May 2, 1904. He married Florence McFadyen.
Children:
i. Gilberta McFadyen.

5. Hector McFadyen, b. October 22, 1870 in Glenarm, Eldon Township, Victoria County, Ontario, Canada, d. March 16, 1956. He married Isabella (Belle) Mackenzie, married 1906 in Uptergrove Presbyterian Church, Simcoe County, Ontario, b. October 4, 1878, d. September 23, 1973.
Children:
i. Florence McFadyen.
ii. Jessie McFadyen.
iii. Mary McFadyen.
iv. John McFadyen.

6. Mary Ella McFadyen, b. February 18, 1873 in Eldon Station, Eldon Township, Victoria County, Ontario, Canada, d. June 16, 1916 in Omaha, Nebraska, United States of America. She married Dr. Fred Edwards.
Children:
i. Gilbert Edwards.
ii. Mary Edwards.

7. Christena (Tene) Janet McFadyen, b. September 2, 1876 in Bolsover, Eldon Township,Victoria County, Ontario, Canada, d. January 7, 1946. She married John (Jack) McEachern, married circa 1909.
Children:
i. Farquar McEachern.
ii. Duncan McEachern.
iii. Alexander (Alec) McEachern.
iv. Christena McEachern.
v. Hector McEachern.

McFadyen Descendants **B-3**

8. Margaret (Maggie) Jane McFadyen, b. October 20, 1880 in Bolsover, Eldon Township, Victoria County, Ontario, d. date unknown. She married Frank Shaw, married date unknown in Province of Saskatchewan, Canada.
Children:
i. Boyd Shaw
ii. Helen Shaw.

9. Minnie Elsie McFadyen, b. August 26, 1886 in Bolsover, Eldon Township, Victoria County, Ontario, Canada, d. December 27, 1961. She married Hugh McIntyre, married August 3, 1921 in Presbyterian Manse, Kirkfield, Ontario, Canada, b. October 1, 1886, d. October 9, 1960.
Children:
i. Margaret Lois McIntyre.
ii. Anna Isabel McIntyre.
iii. John (Jack) Andrew McIntyre.

Generation Four

10. Duncan George Wallace, b. February 24, 1891 in Thorah Township, Ontario, Canada, d. November 8, 1985 in Aurora, Ontario, Canada. He married Bertha Winters Switzer, married December 23, 1916 in Wingham, Ontario, Canada, b. November 29, 1895 in Manitoba, Canada, d. April 16, 1987 in Aurora, Ontario, Canada.
Children:
i. Kathleen Margaret Wallace, b. October 7, 1917.
ii. William (Billy) Reid Wallace, b. January 25, 1919, d. November 20, 1942.
iii. Mary Winnifred Wallace, b. May 24, 1920.
iv. Victoria Elsie Wallace, b. May 24, 1920, d. May 24, 1920.
v. Donald John Wallace, b. May 30, 1926, d. May 21, 1999.

11. Margaret Isabella Wallace, b. September 16, 1900 in Thorah Township, Ontario, Canada, d. January 9, 2000 in Orillia, Ontario, Canada. She married Walter Thomas Beach, married September 22, 1926 in Thorah Township, Ontario, Canada, b. December 24, 1897 in Uxbridge Township, Ontario, Canada, d. December 5, 1967 in Uxbridge Township, Ontario, Canada.
Children:
i. Beverley Wallace Beach, b. January 31, 1932 in Uxbridge Township, Ontario, Canada. He married Norma Jean Jordan, married August 23, 1952 in the United Church manse, Stouffville, Ontario, Canada, b. April 2, 1934 .
ii. Catherine Rose Beach, b. April 20, 1940 in Uxbridge Township, Ontario, Canada. She married Vernon Edward Ashton, married June 29, 1962 in Trinity United Church, Uxbridge, Ontario, Canada, b. February 8, 1935.

NOTE: Appendix M, Beach Descendants, shows Generations Six and Seven for Margaret Isabella

McFadyen Descendants **B-4**

12. Minnie Elsie Wallace, b. May 14, 1902 in Thorah Township, Ontario, Canada, d. October 31, 1996 in Orillia, Ontario, Canada. She married John Owens, married December 31, 1930, b. 1901 in Scotland, d. June 6, 1970.
    Children:
    i. Marjorie Elizabeth Dowsley Owens, b. October 23, 1931.
    ii. Wallace Gardiner Owens, b. August 15, 1933, d. February 23, 2003.

APPENDIX C: Private Tom C. Kennard's October 1916 Letter

France Oct 31, 1916

Mr William Wallace
Gamebridge
Ontario Canada

Dear Mr Wallace:—

Owing to the fact that I am ~~so~~ well acquainted with you and your son Willie I think I am justified in telling you the facts about Willie's death.

We had made an attack and at the last moment Willie and another chum were made runners, that is, they were to carry messages to and from the company and Battalion headquarters

Willie and his chum had just carried a message when a big shell burst pretty close to him and a piece struck him just above the heart.

"I'm hit" said Willie.

His chum started to unbutton his coat when Will said; "I'm afraid its no use, I'm hit pretty bad," and he died almost immediately.

I had the above from the chum who was with him when he died.

Please accept this letter as a tribute to a dead comrade

With my heartfelt sympathy and deepest consolation I am

Yours truly
Pte Tom C. Kennard

APPENDIX D: Captain McKinley's November 1916 Letter

West Sandling
Nov. 20th, 1916

My dear Mr Wallace:–

I am afraid you will think that I am very thoughtless or careless since you have not heard from me sooner. I have intended writing you for some days now but I have been kept very busy lately and have little time left me for private affairs.

It was with deepest sorrow I learned of your son's death and I assure you we who knew him sympathize with you and your family in your great loss. Every one who knew him loved him and he is a great loss to us.

I have had several letters from the boys at the front and they all spoke most highly of him. Although he was one of the last to join our battalion he made wonderful progress and was one of the very first to be ready to take his place in the field. You knew him as a loving son and boy. I knew him as a faithful soldier and a man anxious to take his place among men.

In your great loss I too feel a personal loss as I was very fond of him and the great consolation to me is, that he had performed real service for the great Cause and he is the richer and greater for his work and his last sacrifice.

I may tell you that my greatest regret at this time is that I was not permitted to go to France with the brave fellows who left Orillia with me. A large number of them have made the supreme sacrifice and others have been severaly wounded but I have yet to hear of one who did not do it nobly. It was a privilege to know and associate with such men.

If there is anything I can do for you let me know and I shall be glad to do it.

Yours with deepest sympathy
J. M. McKinlay
Major.

APPENDIX E: Orilla Collegiate Institute Invitation to "At Home" Dance

Programme

1. One Step "Swanee"
2. Waltz "Land of Lullaby"
3. Fox Trot "When My Baby Smiles at Me"
4. One Step "Strawberry Glide"
5. Waltz "Alice Blue Gown"
6. Fox Trot "Down in Chinatown"
7. One Step "Land of Old Black Joe"
8. Waltz "One Loving Caress"

Intermission

9. Fox Trot "Feather Your Nest"
10. One Step "I Never Knew"
11. Waltz "Love and Roses"
12. Fox Trot "Whispering"
13. One Step "Why Don't You"
14. Fox Trot "Japanese Sand Man"
15. Waltz "Home Sweet Home"

Engagements

1. ....
2. ....
3. ....
4. ....
5. ....
6. ....
7. ....
8. ....

Intermission

9. ....
10. ....
11. ....
12. ....
13. ....
14. ....
15. ....

Refreshments between Nos. 6 and 11 inclusive.

Inside: The Dance Card

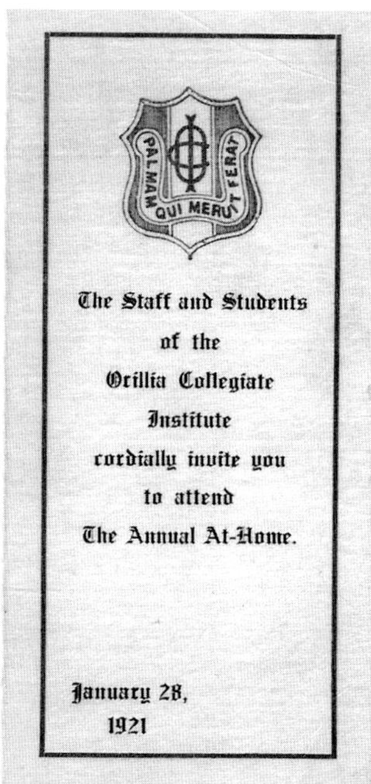

The Staff and Students
of the
Orillia Collegiate
Institute
cordially invite you
to attend
The Annual At-Home.

January 28,
1921

Cover

Conveners of Committees

Miss Mary Curran
Miss Gladys Grey
Miss Lesley Tudhope
H. Janes
K. Bernhardt.
C. Taylor.
J. Thomson.
N. McPhail.

Back

APPENDIX F: School Management Exam for Normal School Students

F-1

Department of Education, Ontario

APRIL, 1920

SECOND CLASS PROFESSIONAL EXAMINATION

NORMAL SCHOOLS

SCHOOL MANAGEMENT

1. (*a*) Taking into account distance from school, and home conditions, state how you would deal with (i) irregularity of attendance, (ii) truancy.

(*b*) State the School Law in regard to the appointment and duties of School Attendance Officers.

2. (*a*) You are asked to give suggestions for the seating of a rural school. What considerations would guide you in your recommendation as to the kind of seats to be used, their suitability to the pupils, and their arrangement in the class room?

(*b*) Specify the minimum equipment required by the Regulations for a rural school.

(*c*) Give suggestions for the proper care of such equipment.

3. (*a*) Discuss the advantages and disadvantages in the organization where only one grade is found in a class room.

(*b*) Contrast with it the advantages and disadvantages of the ungraded rural school.

(*c*) Show how the disadvantages of both plans may be obviated.

4. State how you would deal with the following problems in the management of your school:—

(*a*) One or two pupils exercise an influence over their fellows in opposition to the teacher's authority.

(*b*) Pupils indulge in rough play in the school grounds, or on the way to and from school.

(*c*) Pupils in their seats are disorderly while the teacher is giving class instruction.

[OVER]

APPENDIX F: School Management Exam for Normal School Students F-2

5. (*a*) Criticise the following time-table which shows the morning work for a Third Form with two divisions. Note that (S) means seat work, and (C) means class recitation.

Hour	Juniors		Seniors	
9.00- 9.30	Arithmetic	(C)	Geography	(S)
9.30- 9.50	Literature	(S)	Writing	(C)
9.50-10.15	Reading	(C)	Reading	(C)
10.15-10.30	Recess		Recess	
10.30-11.00	Art	(C)	Literature	(S)
11.00-11.20	Arithmetic	(S)	Composition	(C)
11.20-11.40	Spelling	(C)	Arithmetic	(S)
11.40-12.00	Spelling	(S)	Arithmetic	(C)

(*b*) Amend this time-table in accordance with the principles on which your criticism is based.

APPENDIX G: July First 1920 Programme at Beaverton

PROGRAMME

of Entertainment to be held in Town Hall on evening of

Thursday, July 1st

Toronto Police Pipe Band

Will Present the Following Selections :

1	Scottish Selection (Direction of Pipe Major Thos. Ross)		Toronto Police Pipe Band
2	Song	Lochnagar R. F. DAVIE	Byron
3	Sword Dance		JOHN REID
4	Reading	Selected WM BUCHANAN	
5	Echoes From Scotland		Toronto Police Pipe Band
6	Song	"The Rowan Tree" R. F. DAVIE	By Baroness Nairne
7	Reading	Selected	WM. BUCHANAN
8	Dance	Scotch Reel Messrs. REID, BUCHANAN, FLEMING AND DAVIE	Police Pipe Band

"Auld Lang Syne" "God Save The King"

Rose Stahl's Greatest Dramatic Production

"Maggie Pepper"

Will be shown on the screen

A picturization of the play starring Ethel Clayton, will be displayed at the Town Hall. Thursday, July 1st. There has probably been no play of recent years in which the element of heart interest has been so compelling as in this romance of a department store employe, for Maggie Pepper, head of the silk department, for fifteen years has had nothing but commonplaces of business in her thoughts until suddenly she becomes obsessed with the desire to enter society. This she does with complete success and wins the admiration of a man who turns out to be the head of the firm, recenty returned from a long sojourn in Europe. He makes Maggie manager of the business but the scandal spectre stalks about and to save the situation she resigns. Through many trying situations Maggie's love remains steadfast and ultimately triumphs

Doors open at 7.45 Curtain up at 8.30

APPENDIX H: December 1920 Edition of *The School* Newsmagazine, page 264

Agriculture for December

GEO. W. HOFFERD, M.A.
Normal School, London.

The Principle of Correlation

The public school course in agriculture for this month stresses the correlation of this subject with arithmetic, constructive work and a little simple accountancy. The problems set forth in the Manual, pp. 37-41 and pp. 109-113, and others which the teacher may make to suit the class, ought to be of real value as a means of securing more interest, and consequently better mental effort in school exercises. Such problems are not abstract and meaningless to the intelligent pupil from the farm. They make school work practical to him, because he can see the relation of the various subjects to the life outside of school.

A London Normal School Class Studying Poultry

The principle of correlation, in its various phases, is too little applied in much of our teaching. We desire interest and self-activity from pupils. To this end, what better can be done to arouse interest, to enlarge the range of a pupil's thoughtfulness, and to draw his feelings and will together, than to apply the principle of correlation among the different school subjects? It will often help to overcome the abstractness, unconnectedness and shallowness of some studies. Through its carefully planned use we can secure double economy of time, and a simplification of the course of studies. It is sure to make pupils more alert, open-eyed, clear-headed, and self-reliant.

[264]

APPENDIX I: Letter of Permission from J. B. MacDougall, Provincial School Attendance Officer for Ontario

ONTARIO
DEPARTMENT OF EDUCATION

Toronto, February 9th, 1931.

Dear Madam:-

I beg to acknowledge your letter of the 26th ult. addressed to the Deputy Minister of Education and transferred to this office for reply.

It is customary in such cases to refer the matter to the local Inspector, who investigates the conditions and reports on the situation. Your letter does not indicate what school section you reside in, and therefore we are unable to determine which Inspector has charge of the schools. Would you be good enough to give us this information? Meantime the arrangement you have made is satisfactory. An early reply will be appreciated.

A copy of the Public School Course of Study is being sent to you under separate cover.

Yours faithfully,

J. B. MacDougall.
Provincial School Attendance Officer.

Mrs. Walter T. Beach,
R. R. # 3,
Stouffville, Ontario.

APPENDIX J: Program from 1955 Performance of *The Merchant of Venice* at The Shakespearian Festival, Stratford, Ontario

STRATFORD SHAKESPEAREAN FESTIVAL
FOUNDATION OF CANADA

presents

The Merchant of Venice

(Characters in order of speaking)

ANTONIO .... Robert Goodier
SALARINO .... Edward Holmes
SALANIO .... Lloyd Bochner
ANTONIO'S SERVANT .... Peter Haworth
BASSANIO .... Donald Harron
LORENZO .... Neil Vipond
GRATIANO .... William Shatner
PORTIA .... Frances Hyland
NERISSA .... Helen Burns
BALTHASAR .... Bruce Swerdfager
STEPHANO .... Roland Bull
SHYLOCK .... Frederick Valk
THE PRINCE OF MOROCCO .... Lorne Greene
LAUNCELOT GOBBO .... Ted Follows
OLD GOBBO .... William Hutt
LEONARDO .... Grant Reddick
JESSICA .... Charlotte Schrager
THE PRINCE OF ARRAGON .... Eric House
TUTORS .... John Hayes, Roland Hewgill, Russell Waller
MAIDS —
Gold .... Pauline Galbraith
Silver .... Lynn Wilson
Lead .... Joan Watts
TUBAL .... Bruno Gerussi
THE DUKE OF VENICE .... Robert Christie

SERVANTS, MASQUERS, MEN-AT-ARMS, MAGNIFICOES — Guy Belanger, Tony van Bridge, Nomi Cameron, William Cole, Julian Flett, Barbara Franklin, Robin Gammell, John Gardiner, David Gardner, Robert Gibson, Margaret Griffin, Peter Henderson, Richard Howard, Charles Jolliffe, Jim Manser, Harry McGirt, Alex de Naszody, Louis Negin, Peter Perehinczuk, Thurston Smith, Orest Ulan, Beverley Wilson, Alan Wilkinson, Allan Zielonka.

CHORISTERS — Helen Baumbach, Audrey Conroy, Ilene Hunter, Jean Moorehead, Miriam Root, Velda Scott, John Boyden, Lloyd Bradshaw, Keith Elliott, Gordon Scott.

The action takes place in Venice and at Belmont.

DIRECTED BY TYRONE GUTHRIE
DESIGNED BY TANYA MOISEIWITSCH
MUSIC BY JOHN COOK

FOR THE STRATFORD SHAKESPEAREAN FESTIVAL
FOUNDATION OF CANADA

ARTISTIC DIRECTOR .... Tyrone Guthrie
DIRECTOR OF PLANNING .... Tom Patterson
MANAGING DIRECTOR .... Peter H. Bennett
PRODUCTION MANAGER .... Tom Brown
THEATRE MANAGER .... Richard Butterfield
PUBLICITY MANAGER .... Mary Jolliffe

For the Third Annual Season, 1955:

STAGE DIRECTOR .... Joanna Gibson
STAGE MANAGERS .... Jack Merigold, Donal S. Wilson
ASSISTANT STAGE MANAGER .... Jack Hutt

There will be one intermission of twenty minutes.

ACKNOWLEDGMENTS

Costumes made in the Festival Workrooms by Ray Diffen, assisted by Annette Geber, Judy Peyton-Ward and Ivan Alderman.

Properties and Jewellery made in the Festival Workshops by Brian Jackson, assisted by Martha Jamieson, Marie Day, Ann Drury.

Hand painting of costumes by Noreen Mallory; Hats by El Jamon, 30 Avenue Road, Toronto; Shoes by Snug-Fit Shoe Company, 144 Augusta Avenue, Toronto; Wigs by Nathanwigs, Panton Street, Haymarket, London, England and dressed by Nina Lawson; Wardrobe Mistress, Mary Shaw.

Woodwork properties by Preston-Noelting Ltd., 163 King Street, Stratford, John Gaffney Construction Company Limited, 29 Downie Street, Stratford, and Rodwell Manufacturing Company, Erie Street, Stratford; Metalwork by Kinkade's Stratford Sheet Metal Works, 20 Corcoran Street, Stratford; Plastics by Naugatuck Chemicals, Elmira, Ontario; stage painted by Harry Tribick, 296 Erie Street, Stratford; Electrical equipment by Strand Electrical and Engineering Company Limited, London, England.

THERE MUST BE NO SMOKING IN THE THEATRE

APPENDIX K: Program from Reunion at Siloam School

K-1

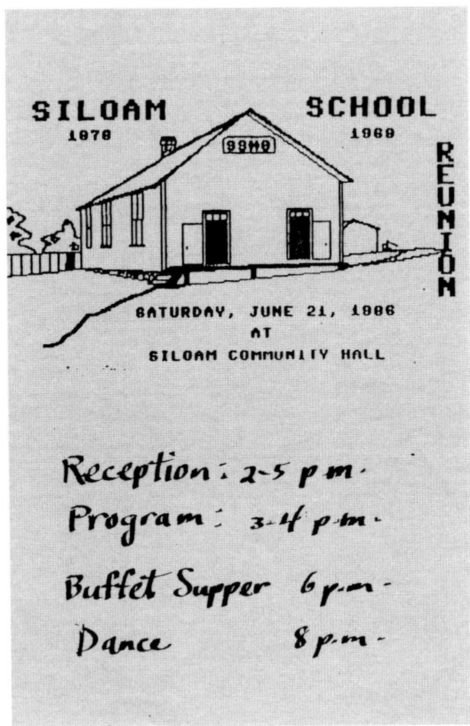

Front of Program

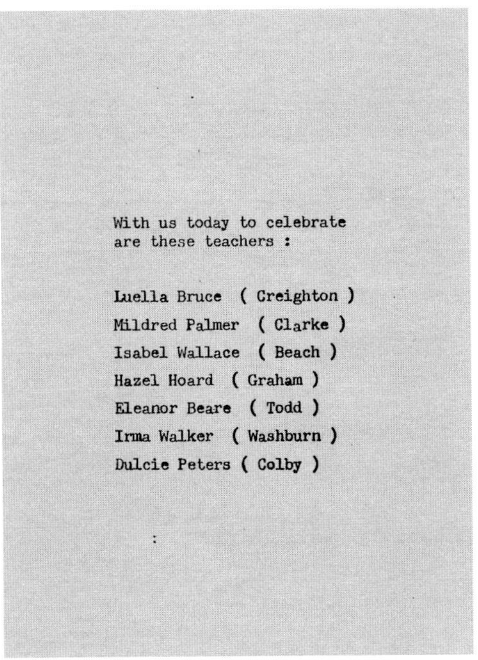

Back of Program

APPENDIX K: Program from Reunion at Siloam School

K-2

PROGRAM

1. Chairman's remarks and opening.
   Allan McGillivray
2. Introduction of Reunion Committee Members.
3. Introduction of former teachers.
4. Presentation to eldest lady and eldest man who were former students.
5. Reminiscences of S.S. No. 8 by Catherine (Beach) Ashton.
6. Singalong.
7. Closing remarks.

SILOAM SCHOOL

S.S. No. 8, 1878-1969

This building is the second known school in this corner of Uxbridge Township. An earlier school, probably log, was situated on the south-east corner of Lot 32, Concession 2, on the Third.

In February of 1878 the following notice appeared in the Uxbridge Journal: " Tenders Wanted - The undersigned will receive tenders up to the 11th day of March, 1878, for the erection of two Frame School Houses in School Section No. 8, Township of Uxbridge. For further particulars, plans and specifications, apply to Thomas Graham, Lot 34, in the 3rd Conc., on Tuesday, the 26th Feb., 1878, and up to the above date". The other School Board members were John Dike and James Smalley.

The new school erected on the Second was 28 feet by 42 feet. The other school mentioned was north of Roseville. Section 8 was later split with the Roseville area becomming Section No. 10.

The outdoor privies were at the north end of the yard, and were separated by a board fence. Later, chemical toilets were installed in the building.

At one time, concerts were put on in the Siloam Church in connection with Roseville School. When concerts were held at the Siloam School, they took place in the afternoon until the installation of hydro allowed for evening performances.

The lowest Teacher's salary was in 1886 and in the early 1890's when the annual amount was $250. The annual pay did not reach $1000 until 1920. It dropped below $1000 in 1930 and returned to that amount in 1943. The salary in 1955 was $2,600.

S.S. No. 8 closed in June of 1969, and the local students were then bussed to larger central schools. After more than 90 years the building took on a new life as the Siloam Community Centre.

Some former students of S.S. No. 8 who served with the armed forces are: May Oldham, Chesley Oldham, Cecil Graham, Olive Elliott, Gordon Matthews and Cecil Elliott.

The "Little Red School House" at Siloam evokes all the typical memories of the country school from playing hooky to being at the top of the class.

Inside of Program

APPENDIX L: Program from a Women's Institute Fundraiser

TOWN HALL, MARKHAM
SATURDAY EVE'G, OCT. 8, 1921

Concert and Drama

Under the auspices of the Markham
Branch East York Women's Institute

THE DRAMA

"What Happened to Braggs"

Will be given by friends of the Institute

CHARACTERS

Lilian Blight—Blight's daughter........Miss L. Matchett
Tom Scott—of the "Independent"........Mr. Elmer Heisey
Dan—Martha Murphy's man servant........Mr. D. Roberts
Martha Murphy—Tom's aunt........Miss C. Johnson
Mrs. Susanna Bird—a widow and Miss Murphy's intimate friend........Miss Beierl
William Blight—editor and proprietor of the "Independent"........Mr. G. Patterson
Arthur St. John—his chum while at college........Mr. Riley
Kitty Braggs—Bragg's daughter........Miss M. White
Hon. Alexander Braggs—candidate for Judge........Mr. H. Rolph
Aaron Cutter—a costumer........Mr. H. Ainsworth

PROGRAMME

1 Instrumental Music........Mr. G. Patterson
2 DRAMA—Act I
3 Solo........Mr. A. Empringham
4 DRAMA—Act II
5 Community Singing........Led by Mr. Geo. Crosby
6 DRAMA—Act III

"GOD SAVE THE KING!"

Doors open at 7. Concert to commence at 8

ADMISSION: 50 Cents, including War Tax

Proceeds in Aid of Public Library

Furniture kindly loaned by Messrs. A. & H. Wideman

MRS. R. D. CLARK, Pres. W. I.
MISS E. THOMAS, Sec'y W. I.

APPENDIX M: Beach Descendants

M-1

Generation One

1. William Beech, b. June, 1785 in England, d. date unknown. He married Elizabeth English?, married date unknown, b. January, 1805 in England, d. date unknown.

Children:

2. i. John Thomas Beech b. March 17, 1832.

Generation Two

2. John Thomas Beech, b. March 17, 1832 in Barton on Humber, Lines, England, d. August 5, 1912 at Lot 12, Concession 5, Somerville, Ontario, Canada. Partner Elizabeth DeGeer, b. 1832 in Uxbridge Township, Upper Canada, d. May 13, 1892 in Uxbridge Township, Ontario, Canada.

Children:

3. i. John (Thomas) (Beech) Beach b. May 23, 1851.

Generation Three

3. John (Thomas) (Beech) Beach, b. May 23, 1851 in Uxbridge Township, Canada West, d. March, 1901 in Uxbridge Township, Ontario, Canada. He married Roseanne Rusnell, married 1873, b. 1857 at Lincolnville, Canada West, d. June 24, 1927 in Uxbridge Township, Ontario, Canada.

Children:

4. i. John (Jack) Beach b. 1876.
ii. Angus Beach, b. 1877, d. 1900.
5. iii. Frank Beach b. 1879.
iv. Edlin Beach, b. 1880, d. 1917.
6. v. William (Bill) Beach b. 1881.
7. vi. Elizabeth Beach (Lizzie) b. 1884.
8. vii. Laura Beach b. 1886.
viii. Edith Beach, b. 1888, d. 1892.
9. ix. Arletta Beach (Lettie) b. 1889.
10. x. Oliver Beach b. 1892.
11. xi. Warren Beach b. 1896.
12. xii. Walter Beach b. December 24, 1897.

Generation Four

4. John (Jack) Beach, b. 1876 in Uxbridge Township, Ontario, Canada, d. 1929. He married Violet DeGeer.

Children:

i. Ida Mae Beach, b. 1907, d. 1984.
ii. Ethel Beach, b. 1915, d. 1989.
iii. John Thomas Beach, b. 1918, d. date unknown.
iv. Angus Beach, b. 1922, d. date unknown.

5. Frank Beach, b. 1879, d. 1945. He married Letta Tipp.

Beach Descendants **M-2**

Children:
i. Edith Beach, b. 1909, d. 1988.
ii. Douglas Beach, b. 1910, d. circa 1990.
iii. Bruce Beach, b. 1911, d. 1955.

6. William (Bill) Beach, b. 1881, d. 1949. He married (1) Edrie Rose Risebrough. He married (2) Elizabeth Beebe.
Children:
i. Clarence Beach, b. 1908, d. 1974.
ii. Rolla Beach, b. 1910, d. 1977.
iii. Edrie Beach, b. 1912, d. 2003.
iv. John (Jack) Beach, b. 1914, d. 1973.
v. Grace Beach, b. 1916, d. 2006.
vi. Ivy Beach, b. 1918, d. 2004.
vii. David Beach, b. 1920, d. 1994.
viii. Marion Beach, b. 1923, d. 2002.
ix. Herbert Beach, b. 1925, d. 1992.
x. Evelyn Beach, b. 1927, d. 2004.
xi. Howard Beach, b. 1929, d. 1998.
xii Laura Beach, b. 1932.
xiii. Dorothy Beach, b. 1934, d. 2004.

7. Elizabeth Beach (Lizzie), b. 1884, d. 1935. She married George Harrison.
Children:
i. John O. Harrison, b. 1906, d. 1991.
ii. Verna Harrison, b. 1909, d. 1989.
iii. Myrtle Harrison, b. 1911, d. 1973.
iv. Ross Harrison, b. 1914, d. 1978.
v. Edith Harrison, b. 1916, d. 2003.
vi. Tom Harrison, b. 1918.
vii. Elsie Harrison, b. 1924, d. 1925.

8. Laura Beach, b. 1886, d. 1930. She married Joseph Harrison.
Children:
i. Angus Harrison, b. 1907, d. 1985.
ii. Frank Harrison, b. 1909, d. 1978.
iii. Earl Harrison, b. 1913, d. 1980.
iv. Russell Harrison, b. 1913, d. 1984.
v. Willis Harrison, b. 1915, d. 1993.
vi. Morris Harrison, b. 1920, d. 1993.
vii. Cecil Harrison, b. 1923.
viii. Murray Harrison, b. 1927.

9. Arletta Beach (Lettie), b. 1889, d. 1951. She married Wilfred Lazenby.
Children:
i. Leone Lazenby, b. 1917, d. 1997.

Beach Descendants **M-3**

10. Oliver Beach, b. 1892, d. 1975. He married (1) Edith Beebe. He married (2) Lillian Forsythe.
Children:
i. Roy Beach, b. 1917, d. 1995.
ii. Dora Beach, b. 1918.
iii. Stanley Beach, b. 1920, d. 1992.
iv. Vera Beach, b. 1921.
v. Ivan (Jim) Beach, b. 1923.
vi. Norman Beach, b. 1925.
vii. Harold Beach, b. 1926, d. 1948.
viii. Leonard Beach, b. 1928, d. 1995.
ix. Lauraine Beach, b. 1930.
x. Lorne Beach, b. 1932.
xi. Lloyd Beach, b. 1935, d. 1991.
xii. Ruth Beach, b. 1937.
xiii. Myrna Beach, b. 1939.

11. Warren Beach, b. 1896, d. 1972. He married Donalda Wilson.
Children:
i. Frank Beach, b. 1946.

12. Walter Beach, b. December 24, 1897 in Uxbridge Township, Ontario, Canada, d. December 5, 1967 in Uxbridge Township, Ontario, Canada. He married Isabella Margaret Wallace, September 22, 1926 in Thorah Township, Ontario, Canada, b. September 16, 1900 in Thorah Township, Ontario, Canada, d. January 9, 2000 in Orillia, Ontario, Canada.
Children:
13. i. Beverley Wallace Beach b. January 31, 1932.
14. ii. Catherine Rose Beach b. April 20, 1940.

Generation Five

13. Beverley Wallace Beach, b. January 31, 1932 in Uxbridge Township, Ontario, Canada. He married Norma Jean Jordan, married August 23, 1952 in parsonage, Stouffville United Church, Whitchurch Township, Ontario, Canada, b. April 2, 1934 in Georgina Township, York County, Ontario, Canada.
Children:
15. i. Edward Wallace Beach b. August 6, 1953
16. ii. Joanne Marie Beach b. December 5,1955.
17 iii. Marilyn Jean Beach b. November 8, 1957.

14. Catherine Rose Beach, b. April 20, 1940 in Uxbridge Township, Ontario, Canada. She married Vernon Edward Ashton, married June 29, 1962 in Trinity United Church, Uxbridge, Ontario, Canada, b. February 8, 1935 in Flin Flon, Manitoba, Canada.
Children:
18. i. James Edward Ashton b. January 8, 1965.
ii. Bruce Walter Ashton, b. May 14, 1972 in Royal Victoria Hospital, Barrie, Ontario, Canada.

Beach Descendants **M-4**

Generation Six

15. Edward Wallace Beach, b. August 6, 1953 in Brierbush Hospital, Stouffville, Ontario, Canada. He married Pamela Glendean Forsythe, married October 27, 1973 in Siloam United Church, Ontario, Canada, b. May 20, 1955 in Mrs. Sopher's House, Uxbridge, Ontario, Canada.

Children:

i. Vanessa Amber Beach, b. September 22, 1975 in Uxbridge Cottage Hospital, Uxbridge, Ontario, Canada. She married Matthew Allen Jessop, married May 14, 2005 in Uxbridge Township, Ontario, Canada, b. October 18, 1970 in Scarborough General Hospital, Scarborough, Ontario, Canada.

ii. Candice Valerie Beach, b. January 27, 1978 in Uxbridge Cottage Hospital, Uxbridge, Ontario, Canada.

16. Joanne Marie Beach, b. December 5, 1955 in Brierbush Hospital, Stouffville, Ontario, Canada. She married Robert Joseph Burnett, married September 15, 1984 in Uxbridge Township, Ontario, Canada, b. April 11, 1945 in Brierbush Hospital, Stouffville, Ontario, Canada.

Children:

i. Daniel Walter Burnett, b. May 21, 1986 in Scarborough Centenary Hospital, Scarborough, Ontario, Canada.

ii. Kelly Elizabeth Burnett, b. October 26, 1991 in Markham-Stouffville Hospital, Markham, Ontario, Canada.

17. Marilyn Jean Beach, b. November 8, 1957 in Brierbush Hospital, Stouffville, Ontario, Canada. She married Roger Guy Burch, married May 27, 1978 in Goodwood United Church, Goodwood, Ontario, Canada, b. July 4, 1956 in York County Hospital, Newmarket, Ontario, Canada.

Children:

i. Darren Scott Burch, b. December 11, 1981 in Scarborough Centenary Hospital, Scarborough, Ontario, Canada. He married Jacqueline Suzanne Rodd, married October 15, 2005 in Trinity United Church, Uxbridge, Ontario, Canada, b. April 21, 1982 in Uxbridge Cottage Hospital.

18. James Edward Ashton, b. January 8, 1965 in Soldiers' Memorial Hospital, Orillia, Ontario, Canada. He married Marie Crystal Dolliver, married August 3, 1996 at Grave's Island Provincial Park, Nova Scotia, Canada, b. January 15, 1969 in Halifax, Nova Scotia, Canada.

Children:

i. Sierra Nicole Ashton, b. March 20, 2004 in Soldiers' Memorial Hospital, Orillia, Ontario, Canada.

APPENDIX N: Newspaper Account of Isabel and Walter's Wedding

Beach—Wallace

The home of Mr. and Mrs. Wm. Wallace, Gamebridge, was the scene of a very pretty wedding on Wednesday afternoon, September the twenty-second, when their fourth daughter, Isabel Margaret, was united in marriage with Walter, son of Mrs. Rose Beach, of Stouffville. The Rev. J. Burkholder, of Morrisburg, assisted by the Rev. A. J. McMullen, of Kirkfield, performed the ceremony, which took place under an arch of autumn leaves, asters and gladioli. The bride, who was given away by her father, was attired in white satin-faced crepe and veil, which was carried by the bride's little niece, Winnifred Wallace, and carried butterfly roses. Miss Minnie, sister of the bride, was bridesmaid, wearing peach georgette, with large black hat and carried sunset roses. The groom was supported by Mr. Angus Harrison, of Mount Albert. Miss Jessie, sister of the bride, wearing mauve georgette, played the wedding march, and Mrs. W. K. Blakey, of Toronto, sang "All Joy be Thine." About seventy-five guests were served at a buffet luncheon. The bride and groom, amidst confetti and rice, left by motor for a trip along the St. Lawrence, the bride travelling in a channel red costume, blonde shoes and hat to match. Present at the ceremony were the bride's three grandparents, the grandfather and grandmother Wallace having been married sixty-three years.

APPENDIX O: Envelope from Uxbridge Creamery, 1956

PHONE 186 **UXBRIDGE CREAMERY** UXBRIDGE, ONT.

Mr. Walt Brack Date Oct 10 1956

DATE	Lbs. Cream	TEST	Lbs. Butterfat: Special	Lbs. Butterfat: 1st	Lbs. Butterfat: 2nd	Price Fat	AMOUNT
	26	33		85		59	5 01

Less 3 lbs. Butter at 59 per lb. Dep.

REMARKS .... Producers' License Fee 1 77

.... 1/10c. Per Lb. Butter Fat.....

Please Return if Incorrect BALANCE 3.24

APPENDIX P: Rusnell Descendants

P-1

Generation One

1. Guillaume Rossignol, b. 1738 in Malbo, Diocese of St. Flour, Auvergne, France, d. November 26, 1798. He married Genevieve Gilbault, married April 11, 1768 in St. Laurent, Montreal, Quebec, Canada.
Children:
2. i. Antoine Rossignol b. April 13, 1770.
ii. Marie Joseph Rossignol, b. February 26, 1794.

Generation Two

2. Antoine Rossignol, b. April 13, 1770 in St. Laurent, Montreal, Quebec, Canada, d. October 31, 1811 in Bay of Quinte off Belleville, Canada; drowned. He married Marie Josephe "Gosetta" Ouimet, married February 6, 1792.
Children:
i. Antoine Rossignol (sometimes Nightingale), b. January 12, 1793, d. date unknown.
ii. Marie Josephe Rossignol, b. February 26, 1794, d. March 10, 1794.
3. iii. Francois Rusnell (Francis Rusnell) b. March 29, 1795.
iv. Francoise Rossignol, b. July 17, 1796, d. date unknown.
v. Joseph Rossignol (Rushnell), b. April 12, 1806, d. May 11, 1892 in Huntington Township, north of Belleville, Ontario, Canada, buried in Foxborough Cemetery. He married Allena Josetta Alcombrack, married date unknown.
vi. Pierre Rossignol, b. April 15, 1808, d. April 11, 1902. He married Mary Yake, married date unknown.

Generation Three

3. Francois Rusnell (Francis Rusnell), b. March 29, 1795 in St. Rose, Quebec, Lower Canada, d. July 26, 1871 in Utica, Reach Township, Ontario, Canada, buried in Kendall Cemetery. He married Harriet Odel (Odell), married date unknown.
Children:
4. i. Peter Rusnell b. 1830.

Generation Four

4. Peter Rusnell, b. 1830, d. 1912. He married Roseanne (Ann) Nesbitt, married November 13, 1855 in Reach Township, Ontario, Canada, b. 1835, d. 1907.
Children:
5. i. Roseanne Rusnell b. 1857.

Rusnell Descendants **P-2**

Generation Five

5. Roseanne Rusnell, b. 1857 in Canada West, d. June 24, 1927 in Uxbridge Township, Ontario, Canada. She married John Beach (formerly Beech), married 1873, b. May 23, 1851 in Uxbridge Township, Canada West, d. March, 1901 in Uxbridge Township, Ontario, Canada.

Children:

i. John (Jack) Beach, b. 1876 in Uxbridge Township, Ontario, Canada, d. 1929.
ii. Angus Beach, b. 1877 in Uxbridge Township, Ontario, Canada, d. 1900.
iii. Frank Beach, b. 1879 in Uxbridge Township, Ontario, Canada, d. 1945.
iv. Edlin Beach, b. 1880 in Uxbridge Township, Ontario, Canada, d. 1917.
v. William Beach, b. 1881 in Uxbridge Township, Ontario, Canada, d. 1949.
vi. Elizabeth (Lizzie) Beach, b. 1884 in Uxbridge Township, Ontario, Canada, d. 1935.
vii. Laura Beach, b. 1886 in Uxbridge Township, Ontario, Canada, d. 1930.
viii. Edith Beach, b. 1888 in Uxbridge Township, Ontario, Canada, d. 1892.
ix. Arletta (Lettie) Beach, b. 1889 in Uxbridge Township, Ontario, Canada, d. 1951.
x. Oliver Beach, b. 1892 in Uxbridge Township, Ontario, Canada, d. 1975.
xi. Warren Beach, b. 1896 in Uxbridge Township, Ontario, Canada, d. 1972.
6. xii. Walter Thomas Beach b. December 24, 1897.

Generation Six

6. Walter Thomas Beach, b. December 24,1897 in Uxbridge Township, Ontario, Canada, d. December 5, 1967 in Uxbridge Township, Ontario, Canada. He married Margaret Isabella Wallace, married September 22, 1926 in Thorah Township, Ontario, Canada, b. September 16, 1900 in Thorah Township, Ontario, Canada, d. January 9, 2000 in Orillia, Ontario, Canada.

Children:

i. Beverley Wallace Beach b. January 31, 1932.
ii. Catherine Rose Beach b. April 20, 1940.

NOTE: Information on Generations Seven, Eight and Nine in the John Thomas Beach and Roseanne (Rusnell) Beach family is listed in Appendix M, Beach Descendants.